D1031747

Finance Fundamentals for Nonprofits

Building Capacity and Sustainability

WOODS BOWMAN

WILEY

John Wiley & Sons, Inc.

Published by John Wiley & Sons, Inc., Hoboken, New Jersey.
Published simultaneously in Canada.

For general information on our other products and services or for technical support, please contact our Customer Care Department within the United States at (800) 762-2974, outside the United States at (317) 572-3993 or fax (317) 572-4002.

Wiley also publishes its books in a variety of electronic formats. Some content that appears in print may not be available in electronic books. For more information about Wiley products, visit our web site at www.wiley.com.

Library of Congress Cataloging-in-Publication Data:
Bowman, Woods, 1941–
  Finance fundamentals for nonprofits: building capacity and sustainability/
Woods Bowman.
      p. cm. — (Wiley nonprofit authority)
   Includes bibliographical references and index.
   ISBN 978-1-118-00451-7 (hardback); 978-1-118-11398-1 (ebk); 978-1-118-11400-1 (ebk); 978-1-118-11399-8 (ebk)
   1. Nonprofit organizations—Finance.   2. Nonprofit organizations—United States—Finance.   I. Title.
   HG4027.65.B69 2011
   658.15—dc22

                                                                2011014328

Printed in the United States of America

10 9 8 7 6 5 4 3 2 1

To Michèle

Contents

Preface

I am an economist, so when my university assigned me to teach nonprofit finance 15 years ago, I naturally wondered: What is the nonprofit analogue of profit? Should nonprofits try to maximize it, like businesses strive to maximize profit? If not, do they maximize anything in particular? Should they?

It took me a while to find satisfying answers. I concluded that profit (surplus) is a relevant concept for nonprofits, but there is more than one way to define it and each version is useful in the appropriate context.

Nonprofits should not try to maximize surplus, because they have a public service mandate to "spend" it to produce more, to increase quality, to lower their price, to grow to meet future demand, or all of these at once. By *minimizing* surplus, nonprofits can maximize spending on their mission-related objectives. But this realization raised another question: Is there an acceptable *lower* limit for surplus that is greater than zero? This line of inquiry led me to the sustainability principle that I describe in this book.

This book blends business and public service perspectives on nonprofit financial management, so I hope it will be useful to both practitioners and academics. There is much about nonprofit finance that is different—particularly in accounting, investing, and budgeting. Before the issue of sustainability can be addressed, these differences must be understood, so Chapters 2 through 5 lay this groundwork.

Chapters 6 through 10, which form the core of this book, provide several formulas for goal-setting and diagnostic measurement of sustainability, and the companion concept of capacity. I searched the literature for tried-and-true formulas familiar to practitioners, favoring formulas with the fewest variables so their interrelationships would be transparent. Nevertheless, I had to redefine a few variables in familiar formulas, and in some cases it was necessary to invent new formulas.

One contribution of this book is showing how a variety of financial concepts, as described by these formulas, are interrelated and work together to tell a coherent story. To aid practitioners, the publisher's web site has spreadsheets that automatically calculate all of the formulas using only data from an IRS Form 990 informational return.

To illustrate concepts, nearly every chapter begins with a vignette of a real problem, which I analyze after the chapter lays the necessary groundwork. Wherever my commentary seemed critical, I avoided using an organization's real name. Organizations featured in published accounts are usually identified. The opening vignette of Chapter 10 uses actual names but the financial data are publicly available and it focuses on an organization whose story is recounted by a book readily available in libraries. The analysis parses decisions made generations ago that left a permanent mark on the organization; it does not reflect on the current leadership.

Practitioners who are most likely to find this book useful are successful businesspersons on nonprofit boards trying, as I once did, to adapt what they know about business to a nonprofit organization. Executive directors who worked their way up through a series of service-delivery roles and who have learned finance on the job may find it useful as a way to fill in gaps in their knowledge about the business of being nonprofit.

I tried to translate business concepts into jargon-free language without sacrificing technical accuracy. I retain terms like *markup* that are common in business even if they sound strange in a nonprofit context. I define all terms upon first use and provide a Glossary to help readers quickly summon a definition when needed later. When not discussing my own research, I make copious use of citations to recognize landmark contributions and to support substantive statements with state-of-the-art research by experts. Any recommendations are based on the weight of the best available evidence.

Researchers may find this book's systematic treatment of certain topics helpful as a reference on matters where nonprofits and for-profits differ. It could also be used as a text in nonprofit financial management, but instructors might want to assign supplemental material on basic financial topics, such as cash flow analysis, that are common to both businesses and nonprofits. A particularly helpful feature for the classroom is how this book compares and contrasts different types of nonprofits: ordinary service providers, endowed service providers, membership associations (including cooperatives), and grantmakers.

I would like this book to be readable and interesting as well as useful, so I make extensive use of endnotes for technical details that are likely to be of interest only to specialists, and for color I scatter snippets of history here and there.

Woods Bowman
Chicago, Illinois
March 2011

Acknowledgments

I began this book in 2008 while lecturing at the Rotterdam School of Management of Erasmus University in the Netherlands. I thank my host Lucas Meijs and his faculty colleagues and staff of the Department of Business Society Management for the invitation and their support.

In 2009 I taught a special topics course in the Kellstadt School of Business of DePaul University using the new materials, and for this opportunity I thank Dean Ray Whittington of the School; Scott Young, chair of the Management Department; and Pat Murphy, director of the School of Public Service, where I am a member of the faculty.

I completed most of a first draft of the manuscript in 2010 while visiting at the Department of Public Management and Policy of the Andrew Young School of Policy Studies of Georgia State University in Atlanta. I thank my host Dennis Young and his faculty colleagues and staff for the invitation and their support.

Readers will share my gratitude to the many experts—academic and practitioner—who read portions of the manuscript, which improved the final product considerably: Grace Budrys, Chris Einolf, Bonnie Frankel, Michael Frigo, Deborah Gillespie, Andy Holman, Marc Jegers, Denise Nitterhouse, Michael O'Neill, George Rosen, Monroe Roth, Keith Skillman, Rob Taylor, and Dennis Young. I cannot thank them enough. I would like to acknowledge persons affiliated with various pseudonymous organizations used as illustrations, but it might compromise their organizations' anonymity. I am grateful for their help nevertheless.

I truly appreciate the work of my graduate assistants who labored over the manuscript in its final stages: Mary Kate Murray of Georgia State University and Liz Schering, Joan Pinnell, and José Rodriquez-Domingos of DePaul University deserve considerable thanks for tirelessly reading and correcting the manuscript.

I want to acknowledge my students at DePaul University, Erasmus University, and Georgia State University whose questions helped me refine my ideas. I also owe a debt to practitioner participants in the many forums where I presented my preliminary work, including the Program for Nonprofit Excellence in Memphis, the Helen Bader Institute Executive Workshop in Milwaukee, and the Executive Leadership Program for Nonprofit Organizations in Georgia.

I hope that constant sifting and testing of ideas removed all errors, but I know better. I bear full responsibility for the remaining ones. When the time came to publish, I sought advice from Peter Frumkin, Kirsten Grønbjerg, and Harvey Rosen, who were very helpful and they too have my thanks.

CHAPTER 1

Introduction

How Nonprofits Are (and Are Not) Like Businesses

It is not enough to do good. It must be done well.
—Vincent de Paul (1581–1660)

What are we to make of for-profit charities like Google.org or nonprofit corporations like the furniture purveyor IKEA[1] and (before 2006) that icon of American capitalism, the New York Stock Exchange? These crossover examples serve to remind us that nonprofits and for-profit businesses have much in common. However, their rarity also indicates fundamental differences.

Finance Fundamentals for Nonprofits sheds light on similarities and differences between nonprofits and for-profit businesses. It is intended to provide a foundation in nonprofit finance for graduate students, assist nonprofit managers, and instruct corporate executives on nonprofit boards. It does not delve into finance techniques that are the same in nonprofit and for-profit businesses.

The book's subtitle (*Building Capacity and Sustainability*) signals its emphasis on two concepts of particular importance to nonprofits. Whereas for-profit managers are concerned with maximizing their firm's market value, nonprofit managers may have many financial goals.[2] *Finance Fundamentals for Nonprofits* proposes that nonprofit managers should be primarily concerned with having the financial capacity their mission requires and sustaining it over time.

Financial capacity for a nonprofit consists of the resources necessary to seize opportunities and respond to threats.[3] The amount needed depends on its mission, service delivery method, operating environment, and risks of potential adverse economic events. Maintaining assets takes time, effort, and money, so managers choose a capacity level that balances the costs of maintaining capacity with its benefits.

Financial sustainability is simply the rate of net change in financial capacity. It is a clear-cut issue for most profit-maximizing businesses. By maximizing profit, assets grow as fast as possible and sustainability takes care of itself. However, sustainability is an issue for nonprofits that trade off surpluses (the profits of nonprofits) in favor of serving more people and serving them better. They must take care not to spend too much on such worthy objectives because over the long run they must be able to keep their assets in good shape *and* maintain their reserves at a level commensurate with anticipated economic risks. A *sustainability principle* requires consistency between the short run (as measured by annual surpluses) and the long run (as measured by asset growth). This is the subject of Chapters 6 through 9.

A major difference between nonprofit and for-profit financial management is that many nonprofits generate income from sources other than selling goods and services as for-profits do. Such *alternative income* includes gifts, grants, dues, and income from endowments. Even if a nonprofit has no sources of alternative income it can choose to develop them, which gives it strategic options foreclosed to a for-profit firm.

Financial models used by for-profit managers must be modified before applying them to nonprofits, because alternative income reverses financial logic. In for-profit firms production creates revenue through sales; but in nonprofits with alternative income the amount of income determines how much can be produced.

This chapter introduces the book's agenda, beginning with a discussion of alternative definitions of nonprofit—or *not-for-profit*, as accountants call them—attempting to discern the essential character of "nonprofitness." Then it describes the intrinsic similarities and differences between for-profit and nonprofit corporations, highlighting the advantages and disadvantages of the nonprofit type.

A few technical terms are necessary for this discussion. Later chapters on related topics will define them. In the meantime, readers may consult the Glossary at the end of the book to clarify unfamiliar terms.

What Are Nonprofits?

The simplest and most common definition of a nonprofit organization is one that is "barred from distributing its net earnings, if any, to individuals who exercise control over it, such as members, officers, directors, or trustees" (Hansmann 1980).[4] The prohibition on distributing net earnings to private parties is widely known as the *nondistribution constraint*. The principal shortcoming of this legalistic definition is that it makes no reference to non-economic values, which is the social justification for nonprofits. The United Nations (UN) uses a more robust definition, which defines nonprofits as:

> *organizations that do not exist primarily to generate profits, either directly or indirectly, and that are not primarily guided by commercial goals and considerations. [They] may accumulate surplus in a given year, but any such surplus must be plowed back into the basic mission of the agency and not distributed to the organizations' owners, members, founders or governing board.* (United Nations 2003, 18)

This definition is not explicit about the noneconomic values because it must apply in all countries despite their cultural differences. *Finance Fundamentals for Nonprofits* uses the UN definition because it implies the primacy of values. In the United States, tax exemption laws address nondistribution through intermediate sanctions and keep nonprofits mission-focused by specifying acceptable exempt purposes (see Chapter 5).

For-profit firms may espouse social values, but these values usually are secondary to maximizing a firm's economic value or they are instrumental toward that end. The Body Shop and Ben & Jerry's are well-known examples of values-centered for-profit firms, but it is significant that they earned their reputations *before* going public—meaning before selling stock on a public exchange—and acquiring investor-owners.

Social values are the *business* of nonprofits. As Rose-Ackerman says, nonprofit customers "are buying reified ideology" (1997, 128). Nonprofits practice *values-centered management*—a control regime in which social, cultural, and spiritual values join with economic necessity to define an organization's management objective.[5] The absence of owners seeking a handsome return on their investment enables nonprofits to practice values-centered management.

"Cooperatives, mutuals [mutual benefit organizations], and self-help groups share some, if not most, of the defining features of a nonprofit organization, and fall into a 'grey area' between the nonprofits and for-profit businesses. In some countries they are considered legally to be nonprofits; in others, not" (Anheier 2005, 52). The source of confusion is the fact that the purpose of a membership association, and especially cooperatives, is to confer benefits on its members and patrons.

Cooperatives strive to maximize economic benefits to their patrons, which may include an explicit distribution of annual surplus.[6] However, cooperatives are typically committed to social goals of common interest to the group. In Francophone regions these organizations form a very important cluster known as the Social Economy. The UN standard is sufficiently broad to include them, so *Finance Fundamentals for Nonprofits* treats membership associations, including cooperatives, as if they were nonprofits.[7]

Why Are There Nonprofits?

The standard economic paradigm explaining why nonprofits exist is based on a three-sector structure of society consisting of market, government, and nonprofits. Each sector serves to check excesses and compensate for the shortcomings of the other sectors.[8]

Weisbrod (1975) proposed that a bloc of people will always be dissatisfied with the amount of goods and services provided by government. Individuals who want more of a service will form a nonprofit organization to provide it with voluntary donations. This is known as the *government failure* model.

Hansmann (1980) argued that nonprofits are needed as a response to situations where consumers cannot easily compare products and prices, negotiate with a provider, or determine whether the provider complied with an agreement and obtain redress if it did not. In his view, a legal nondistribution constraint solves the problem neatly. This is known as the *market failure* or *contract failure* model. The antiexploitive nature of the nondistribution constraint is intrinsically attractive to stakeholders, preventing them from shirking (Valentinov 2008).

Salamon (1987) turned these explanations on their heads, arguing that it is more reasonable to suppose that people initially organize to provide a new service voluntarily and then turn to government to finance expansion, or even provide it directly, after the product was proven and demand established. History is on his side: Voluntary fire brigades date to Roman times, and libraries in the United States were initially organized as membership associations.

However, nonprofits have limitations that are more easily overcome by markets or government: Nonprofits may favor one particular group over others and some groups may go without service (particularism). The interests of donors, not the needs of the community, may determine choices nonprofits make about whom to serve and how to serve them (paternalism). Nonprofits attract well-meaning people, but either as employees or volunteers they are often in over their heads (amateurism). This is known as the *philanthropic failure* model (Salamon 1987).

Steinberg (2006) refers to this set of explanations as the Three Failures Theory of the nonprofit sector. Recent empirical research casts doubt on the underlying assumption of Hansmann's contract failure model. Although survey data confirm that consumers say they are more likely to trust nonprofits, the data reveal that a high proportion of consumers is unable to identify whether well-known organizations are in fact nonprofit. Even frontline staff working for those organizations often were unable to correctly identify them as nonprofit (Handy, Seto, Wakaruk, Mersey, Mejia, and Copeland 2010).

The Three Failures Theory is demand-driven. There is only one supply-side theory. Young (1983) posits that certain personality types are particularly inclined to be nonprofit founders. He shows how different types respond differently to the nature of a service, social priority, ethic of service, degree of professional control, income potential, bureaucratic structure, and ego. His supply-side model explains why there are no nonprofit automobile repair shops, despite being a clear case of contract failure, but fixing cars is not high on the list of priorities of people who are motivated to establish a nonprofit. (It should be noted that auto repair is not an exempt purpose in tax law.)

Nonprofits as Businesses

Although nonprofits are not in business to make money, they are nevertheless in business: They hire people, they produce goods and services, and they have bills to pay. This section explores how nonprofits are similar to, yet different from, for-profit businesses.[9]

"Whether an association will function satisfactorily in relation to third parties is to a very high degree a question of whether it becomes a [corporation], i.e., a body which is regarded in law as having a personality and existence distinct from that of its members." Corporate status greatly enhances the ability of an organization to own, manage, and defend property in all of its forms (Hemström, 2006, 27).

Eleemosynary organizations and membership associations pioneered the development of corporation law. The first corporations emerged in first-century Rome (Avi-Yonah, 2005, 772). Their principal use was for municipal governance, guilds, religious cults, and philanthropic foundations. Romans did not use corporations for business enterprises. Medieval companies of significant size were quasi-permanent partnerships involving multiple partners. Precisely when the first application of the corporation to for-profit business occurred is unknown; however, we do know that by the year 1283 family corporations had become "common" in Florence (Hunt 1994, 76). These business corporations were akin to modern cooperatives because their stock was not transferable.

In 1650 Massachusetts awarded the first corporate charter in America to Harvard College (O'Neill 1989, 54). The first commercial corporation was not chartered until Connecticut took the step in 1732 (Micklethwait and Wooldridge 2003, 43). Alexis de Tocqueville's *Democracy in America,* first published in 1835 and still in print, is considered one of the most insightful commentaries on American society. Some oft-quoted phrases are: "Americans of all ages, all conditions, and all dispositions constantly form associations. . . . Wherever at the head of some new undertaking you see government in France, or a man of rank in England, in the United States you will be sure to find an association" (Tocqueville 2007, 452).

His observations are often taken as "timeless truths about charity, philanthropy, and voluntarism in American life" (Gross 2003, 30) but it is tempting to speculate that he was merely observing the consequences of differences in the relative ease of forming corporations in the United States compared with Britain and France. At the time of de Tocqueville's visit, it required an act of Parliament to incorporate in Britain and incorporation did not become common in France until the late nineteenth century.

"By the end of the 18th century many states had general incorporation laws for religions, academies, and libraries, but *not business corporations*" (Roy 1997, 48, emphasis added). "General acts provided incorporation for a broad range of charitable, religious, and literary purposes in Pennsylvania in 1791 and for libraries in New York in 1796 and in New Jersey in 1799. Fire companies could be chartered under general acts of Virginia of 1788 and of Kentucky of 1798" (Hurst 1970, 134).

What are the advantages of corporate status? All corporations are legal persons possessing a minimal set of common attributes (Vikramaditya 2005): (1) they have an indefinite life (i.e., self-perpetuating self-government), (2) they are able to sue and be sued in their own name, (3) they are able to own property in their own name, (4) they have centralized management empowered to act in their name (subject to laws regarding fiduciary responsibility), and (5) liability for the organizations' debts is limited to the organizations' capital.[10] Without protection from personal liability for an organization's debts, potential transactions costs of doing business would be far higher and persons would understandably be reluctant to become actively involved.

Laws typically grant all corporations considerable flexibility to govern themselves through bylaws of their own devising. Business corporations can change their line of business and nonprofit corporations can change their mission, provided they follow whatever process their bylaws require.

As commonly perceived, the nonprofit sector consists of small organizations coexisting with a few wealthy research institutes, universities, and hospitals. This is true but small organizations are equally prevalent in the for-profit sector. According to Table 1.1, small organizations comprise approximately one-half of the 29 million for-profit businesses and the 1.7 million tax-exempt nonprofits (including religious congregations).

TABLE 1.1 Nonprofit Organizations and For-Profit Businesses in 2005

	Total*	Small Organizations[†]
Nonprofits		
Federally tax-exempt public charities	876,164	310,683
Including religious congregations (est.)	*1,176,164*	*610,683*
Federally tax-exempt nonprofits	1,401,454	528,023
Including religious congregations (est.)	*1,701,454*	*828,023*
Nonprofit corporations (est.)	3,503,635	Unknown
All voluntary nonprofits (est.)	9,000,000	Unknown
For-Profit Businesses		
Publicly traded corporations (est.)	18,000	18,000
For-profit business corporations	5,558,000	4,241,000
All for-profit businesses	28,696,000	12,090,000

*For nonprofits, this is the number registered with the Internal Revenue Service (IRS) in 2005. For businesses, this is the number filing tax returns with the IRS (with or without reportable net income) in 2004.

[†]This refers to nonprofits with less than $25,000 of revenue. For businesses, it is tax filings that report gross receipts of less than $25,000.

Sources: Bowman (2011b); Wing, Pollak, and Blackwood (2008), Tables 1.1 and 5.1 (estimates by author based on Grønbjerg and Smith 1999); *Statistical Abstract of the United States, 2008 edition*, Tables 721 and 722.

Although for-profit corporations are three times more numerous than nonprofit corporations, nonprofits are *more likely* to be incorporated. One-third of all 9 million nonprofits are incorporated compared to one-fifth of all 28.7 million for-profit businesses.

Why? A large number of small businesses consist of self-employed individuals whose personal finances are intertwined with their business, so incorporating offers no special advantages. However, nonprofit activity is inherently a group activity, so it is important for there to be a fire wall between the finances of the group and the individuals who govern and manage it, although there is little advantage to incorporating a nonprofit that owns no assets.

The most prominent advantages of incorporation to nonprofits are: immortality, collective ownership of assets, and limited liability. Immortality is especially important for philanthropic projects initiated by persons who intend their perpetual continuation. Because nonprofit corporations are immortal and controlled by multiperson boards, they are indispensable vehicles for protecting capital from misappropriation by custodians and for transmitting that capital to subsequent generations.[11]

There is only *one* difference between nonprofits and for-profit businesses—nonprofits are not investor-owned. It might be said that they own themselves. The implications of this sole difference are powerful. It gives nonprofits the flexibility to decide whose interests it will serve and for whom it will act as fiduciary. [A *fiduciary* is an entity "who obligates himself or herself to act on behalf of another . . . and assumes a duty to act in good faith and with care, candor, and loyalty in fulfilling the obligation" (Findlaw 2011).]

Every organization is a fiduciary in some sense. For-profits have a fiduciary duty to stockholders. Among nonprofits different types of nonprofit alternative income imply different fiduciary duties: Dues imply a duty to members, endowment income implies a duty to future generations, and donations imply a duty to the current generation.[12]

Advantages and Disadvantages of Being Nonprofit

An absence of investor-owners confers advantages on nonprofits: attractiveness to donors, insulated management, protected management, and endowment ownership.

- *Attractiveness to donors.* Individuals are more likely to donate to a nonprofit organization than to a for-profit one regardless of exemption or deductibility of donations, especially if they perceive nonprofits to be more trustworthy and/or public-spirited (Hansmann 1980; Valentinov 2008).[13] Deductibility of donations merely provides further incentives.
- *Insulated management.* Some nonprofits are sponsored by another nonprofit or by a unit of government because donors want assurance that their gifts will not disappear into the general treasury, and by controlling the board donors can exert a countervailing influence to political processes.[14]
- *Protected management.* If a for-profit publicly traded corporation performs poorly, a group of investors may buy it. Then, using their newly acquired power, they can replace the management team. Except for membership associations with elected leaders, only state attorneys general may sue to remove management, which occurs rarely (Fremont-Smith 2004).
- *Endowment ownership.* An endowment is a portfolio of investments managed so as to produce a perpetual source of income to subsidize goods and services below their cost of production indefinitely. If a for-profit firm produced a product that cost more to produce than it earned, the firm would drop it, not endow it. If it did attempt to endow it, a group of investors would surely emerge to take control of the organization and its endowment. Protected management enables nonprofits to own endowments.

The foregoing discussion focused on intrinsic differences between nonprofits and for-profits due to the absence of investor-owners. However, public policy also favors nonprofits. Heading the list of these advantages is tax exemption.

Despite popular perceptions, nonprofit status and tax exemption are not congruent. In Indiana, for example, the number of nonprofits recognized by the IRS approximately equals the number not recognized (Grønbjerg, Liu, and Pollak 2010). (Technically, the IRS does not confer exemption; it *recognizes* an organization as being exempt.) Charitable nonprofits further benefit from deductibility of contributions by donors.

Bankruptcy laws are more favorable: A nonprofit's creditors cannot force it to involuntarily liquidate, and when nonprofits choose to reorganize in Chapter 11 they remain debtors in possession.[15]

Unlike publicly traded companies, the law does not require nonprofits to have an annual meeting open to the public or to have their financial statements audited. The most recent federal law on corporate accountability (Sarbanes-Oxley) exempted nonprofits from all but two provisions. The U.S. Supreme Court has made it clear in a series of decisions that state and local laws cannot compel nonprofits to disclose their fund-raising and administrative costs to prospective donors.[16]

The only information available to the public about tax-exempt nonprofits is from an informational return they are required to file annually with the IRS (see Chapter 5); but one-quarter of nonprofits with at least $500,000 in donations reported no fund-raising expenses, and a significant number of Form 990 reports allegedly contain material omissions, misrepresentations, or falsifications (Hall 2000).

These advantages, taken together, enable nonprofits *to behave* differently. Their *business* is promoting values and even in industries with the greatest dependence on commercial income they act differently. To some observers, nonprofit hospitals are "large and highly commercial" enterprises that "do not look, feel, or act very much like the mental images that most of us have of nonprofit organizations" (Hodgkinson and Weitzman 2001, 5).

Schlesinger and Gray (2006, Table 16.1) reviewed all peer-reviewed research on the topic and found that in 114 comparative hospital studies, nonprofits performed better in terms of economic performance (21 studies), quality of care (14 studies), and accessibility for unprofitable patients (28 studies). Only 11 of these studies found that proprietary hospitals performed better on these same criteria. Furthermore, in 68 empirical studies of nursing homes, for-profit homes had better economic performance (19 compared to 5) but nonprofit nursing homes unambiguously performed better in terms of quality and accessibility (26 compared to 6). However, there are several disadvantages of being nonprofit.

- *Mission constraint.* State laws typically restrict the purposes that they allow nonprofits to undertake, and tax laws discourage others (see Chapter 5). However, arguably these limitations and disincentives do not affect the outcome much. To repeat an earlier example: Although auto repair may not be a permitted purpose for incorporation and is not an exempt purpose for relief from taxation, there are probably few people who want to do it anyway.
- *Capital constraint.* This may be the most important disadvantage. Although nonprofits receive gifts of capital, these are not free. Fundraising costs may be substantial. In addition, the pool of major donors is limited for nonprofits, whereas the pool of capital available to for-profits is virtually unlimited and truly global. When a for-profit has an initial public offering (IPO), its stock sells out in a day. Although the investment banker is well compensated, the amount of money raised relative to issuance expenses is small compared to fundraising (Bowman 2011a).
- *Mission drift and waste.* Although having no investor-owners provides space for amateurs to learn on the job and make mistakes, this advantage comes with an increased prospect of mission drift and wasteful management. (See the opening vignette of Chapter 11.) If a for-profit company is not doing a good job of looking out for its investor-owners' interests, one or more of them can make a tender offer to buy a controlling share and replace ineffectual management. There is no mechanism for replacing derelict directors and officers of nonprofits other than a state attorney general filing a lawsuit.
- *Risk.* In for-profit corporations stockholders share business risks. Individually they can mitigate their risk exposure by selling the company's stock (if they shun risk) or buying more (if they like risk). Because nonprofits have no stockholders, their clientele absorbs the entire risk alone and, unlike a for-profit's stockholders, clients of nonprofits have no way to mitigate risk. Nonprofit directors and officers must be more sensitive to the risk associated with various revenue sources and services offered, particularly new ones with unknown risk characteristics.

Table 1.2 summarizes the advantages and disadvantages of being nonprofit. For some activities, like producing microwave ovens, the disadvantages outweigh the advantages. For other activities, like disaster relief, the advantages outweigh the disadvantages.

From society's point of view, the advantages of a robust nonprofit sector outweigh the disadvantages. Nonprofits provide "a large variety of partially tested social innovations," which Smith (1973) calls "social

TABLE 1.2 Advantages and Disadvantages of Nonprofit Status and Tax Exemption

	Tax Exempt	Not Exempt

Nonprofit	Capital constrained*
	 Donations*
	 Protected and
	    insulated managers
	 Can be endowed*
	 Restricted to exempt
	    purposes
		Capital constrained
		 Donations
		 Protected and
		    insulated managers
		 Can be endowed
		 No purpose
		    restrictions

For-Profit	Null	Capital available
		 No donations
		 Managers neither
		    protected nor insulated
		 Never endowed
		 No purpose
		    restrictions

*Tax-exempt nonprofits are likely to be less capital constrained and receive more donations and endowment-building gifts than if they are taxable.

risk capital." They create intellectual space for "countervailing ideologies, perspectives, and worldviews"; searching for "novelty and beauty"; providing "fellowship, sociability, and mutual companionship"; preserving "values, ways of life, ideas, beliefs, artifacts"; representing the sense of "mystery, wonder, and the sacred"; and offering "unique opportunities for personal growth."

Nonprofits are custodians of society's values, and the most prominent values-driven organizations are affiliated with religious congregations. "Universally, religious groups are the major founders of nonprofit service institutions. We see this in the origins of many private schools and voluntary hospitals, in the U.S. and in England, Catholic schools in France and Austria, missionary activities in developing countries, services provided by Muslim wacfs [religious trusts], and so on" (James 1987, 404).

This Book's Agenda

Both for-profit businesses and nonprofits must pay their bills. When resources are chronically inadequate, liquidation is inevitable for both. As the saying goes, "no money, no mission." However, nonprofit accounting rules are different, which has consequences for budgeting. Endowed nonprofits have additional legal constraints that affect their financial operations.

The next four chapters take a fresh look at common financial tools—financial statements, investment portfolios, and budgets—and tax law relevant to different types of nonprofits.

Chapter 2 reviews accrual accounting, highlighting treatment of noncommercial (alternative) income.

Chapter 3 covers legal and management issues an endowment raises. It describes the Uniform Prudent Management of Institutional Funds Act, which nearly every state has adopted in some form.

Chapter 4 explains how to configure budgets to be consistent with nonprofit accounting rules and how to reconcile a budget with a financial statement and IRS Form 990.

Chapter 5 describes how federal tax law classifies tax-exempt institutions and how this is similar to, yet different from, the archetypical nonprofits that define the themes of the following chapters. This chapter introduces each archetype with a brief history of important events in its evolution in the United States.

Each of the next four chapters focuses on a specific *archetype*, which is defined by the group of persons to whom a nonprofit organization owes a fiduciary duty, because it is reasonable to suppose that different responsibilities influence the range of normal financial behavior.

All archetypes are analyzed within a similar tripartite temporal framework: (1) in the long run the objective is to maintain or expand services, (2) in the short run the objective is resilience to occasional economic shocks, and (3) in the current period the objective is to pay bills on time.

Chapter 6 focuses on *ordinary service providers*. These nonprofits have a fiduciary duty to act in the best interests of one or more indefinite groups of living persons (Bowman and Fremont-Smith 2006). *Indefinite* means that members of the relevant group cannot be identified by name—only by common characteristics such as income, age, culture, and interests. The modifier *ordinary* indicates that they do not have endowments. It may seem a mundane descriptor but it serves to indicate that they are the most common type.

Chapter 7 features *membership associations*. Membership associations have a duty to act in the best interests of a specific group of living persons, or other organizations, called members or patrons, who are usually able to participate in election of decision makers for the group. Dues are a financing source that is unavailable to providers of goods and services, and therefore these nonprofits need different benchmarks.[17] As indicated previously, cooperatives are difficult to classify. Chapter 7 treats them as membership organizations while indicating how they differ from noncooperative associations.

Chapter 8 is about *endowed service providers*. A growing body of literature calls attention to the importance of endowments and their unique management issues (Ehrenberg 2000; Gentry 2002; Fisman and Hubbard 2003; Bowman 2002b, 2007; Weisbrod, Ballou, and Asch 2008; Lerner, Schoar, and Wang 2008). These organizations, like ordinary service providers, have a duty to an indefinite group within the current generation but they *also* have a duty to future generations. The large investments of these organizations require modification of the diagnostic formulas for capacity and sustainability.

Chapter 9 highlights *grantmakers*. These organizations are agents of donors with a duty to act as the donors would under similar circumstances. There are three kinds of grantmakers: conduit, limited life, and endowed. Conduit grantmakers pass through current income from donors to service-providing nonprofits. Limited life grantmakers are established with the intention that they will spend themselves out of existence within a finite period of time. Endowed grantmakers serve future generations.

Table 1.3 summarizes the characteristics of these archetypes, showing how organizations are classified according to the nature of their fiduciary duty to present and future generations.

Chapter 10 explains how the types of goods and services produced affect the composition of revenues and describes how producers of goods and services can improve sustainability through revenue management.

Chapter 11 describes ethical duties of nonprofit organizations and applies the lessons of previous chapters to exploring the use and misuse of business principles by nonprofits.

TABLE 1.3 Nonprofit Archetypes

	Generation Served	
	Current	Future
Indefinite Group	Service providers and endowed grantmakers	Endowed service providers and endowed grantmakers
Definite Group	Membership associations and other grantmakers	Endowed membership associations (rare)

Note: Membership associations include cooperatives; other grantmakers include limited life and conduit grantmakers.

Concluding Thoughts

Returning to the questions that opened this chapter, what *are* we to make of the New York Stock Exchange operating as a nonprofit for nearly 200 years, for-profit charities like Google.org, and for-profit companies operating as nonprofits, like IKEA?

Until 2006 the New York Stock Exchange was a comfortable nonprofit membership association. Until recently it was competitive with other exchanges around the world. Then the market changed and it needed substantial fresh capital quickly to retool its operations and to combine with investor-owned exchanges. It had literally outgrown its nonprofit charter.

Google attempted to overcome the nonprofit capital constraint by using its ability to sell stock to finance an ancillary social mission. Its goal was nothing less than reinventing philanthropy, but it has yet to find a new workable model (Helft 2011). To an outside observer, DotOrg (as company insiders call the philanthropic division) appears to operate more like a venture capital firm with a social agenda. It is a novel and useful paradigm, even if it has not inspired other corporations to follow suit.

IKEA has enjoyed a near-monopoly in the do-it-yourself furniture market, so it has not needed external sources of capital to grow. The nonprofit arrangement has served its founder well by allowing him to remain firmly in control for decades. It remains to be seen how well the arrangement will serve the organization after he is no longer at its helm, especially if and when a rival company finally emerges to challenge its supremacy in its market niche.

It is interesting to note that IKEA has established what amounts to an endowment with retained earnings. However, its purpose is not to subsidize products below their cost of production as nonprofit endowments do but to be a pool of capital-in-waiting for establishing new stores. The definitive study of IKEA has yet to be written, but a probable consequence of self-financing is slower growth, which it accepted as the trade-off for tight control over all aspects of operations.

Each of these examples, odd as they seem at first sight, illustrates the advantages and disadvantages of being a nonprofit organization. Experimentation with hybrid organizations can be interpreted as efforts to combine the advantages of both pure types (nonprofit and for-profit), meanwhile diminishing their disadvantages.

CHAPTER 2

Accounting
Measuring Past Performance

A well-respected and apparently successful organization suddenly went out of business. The last board chair alleged that accounting rules had obscured what was happening, but it would be more accurate to say that the board did not understand the rules. This chapter develops the vocabulary and concepts necessary to discuss finance and to identify life-threatening problems like the one this hapless organization experienced. The concluding section explains how the organization imploded.

For-profit accounting is designed to monitor exchange transactions in which one party gives goods and services to another party in return for something of economic value. Not-for-profit accounting is more complicated because it must *also* be able to monitor transactions where one party gives something of value to another party, receiving nothing of economic value in return—in other words, voluntary contributions. Furthermore, not-for-profit accounting must also deal with the vexing problem of valuation of museum collections and historical sites.

Accounting professionals prefer the term *not-for-profit* to the more commonly used synonym *nonprofit*. This chapter employs the profession's favored term but elsewhere this book uses the common term.[1] It is organized into sections corresponding to different statements (tables) found in a complete set of financial statements, with a section showing how to reconcile financial statements with the IRS Form 990 informational return. Data from a pseudonymous university will illustrate the concepts.

The sections on statement of financial position, statement of activities, and statement of cash flows include background material for accounting novices. (Note to novices: A negative number is enclosed in parentheses.)

In these sections, readers who are already familiar with accounting can skip to subsections headed "The Not-for-Profit Difference." Following these sections is a discussion of what to look for when encountering a particular set of financial statements for the first time and an explanation of the relationship between information on financial statements and information on the IRS Form 990.

Basis of Accounting and Audits

There are two bases of accounting: cash and accrual. Cash accounting records transactions that increase or decrease an organization's cash balance. Roughly half of all 501(c)(3) public organizations use cash accounting.[2] However, cash accounting gives an incomplete picture of an organization's financial position. For example, it does not reveal when unpaid bills are piling up. Nevertheless, small not-for-profits like it because households use it and untrained bookkeepers are comfortable with it.

Accrual accounting *recognizes* (records) a transaction when an obligation to pay or be paid arises. It recognizes a purchase of services as an expense whether it is settled in cash or an invoice is left to languish on a desk unpaid. Generally accepted accounting principles (GAAP) require the accrual basis of accounting. In the absence of state law requiring audited financial statements, not-for-profits have the option to use cash or accrual accounting.[3] However, stakeholders (grantors, bankers, and major donors) may ask to see financial statements prepared according to GAAP.

GAAP for not-for-profits is promulgated by the Financial Accounting Standards Board (FASB) through Statements of Financial Accounting Standards (SFAS) and supplemented with published interpretations and opinions. The most significant statements pertaining to not-for-profits are SFAS 116, *Accounting for Contributions Received and Contributions Made* (FASB 1993a) and SFAS 117, *Financial Statements of Not-for-Profit Organizations* (FASB 1993b).[4]

There are five not-for-profit general-purpose financial statements plus notes prepared according to SFAS 117:

1. Statement of financial position (required for all).
2. Statement of activities (required for all).
3. Statement of cash flows (required for all).
4. Statement of functional expenses (required for voluntary health and welfare organizations only).
5. Statement of changes in net assets (optional).
6. Notes to the statements (required for all).

Audits also adhere to SFAS 117. Information in the notes is audited as well. Audits are conducted in accordance with auditing standards generally accepted in the United States (the Yellow Book), which require auditors to "obtain reasonable assurance about whether the financial statements are free of material misstatement."

Audited statements begin with a report of the independent auditor—sometimes called the audit letter or opinion letter. The date on this letter indicates the date the auditor completed fieldwork. A common misperception is that auditors prepare the statements. Opinion letters clearly state, "These financial statements are the responsibility of management. Our responsibility is to express an opinion on these financial statements based on our audit." The auditor's job is to opine on the quality of the information and not to analyze it.

An unqualified (clean) audit opinion will include the phrase: "In our opinion, the financial statements present fairly in all material respects. . . ." This implies that any remaining errors are likely to be "immaterial"—that is, they would not affect a considered judgment about the financial condition of the organization. If the auditors discover material weaknesses, their report will include the phrase "except for . . ." and identify the material weaknesses, followed by "the financial statements present fairly in all material respects. . . ."

In addition to their report, which is part of the audit document, auditors usually provide management with a list of reportable conditions, which are weaknesses in financial policies and procedures that do not rise to the level of a material weakness. This is called the "management letter," and it is not part of the audit document. It is a helpful road map for self-improvement.

Statement of Financial Position

A *statement of financial position* is an inventory of assets and liabilities taken at a particular moment, usually at the end of a fiscal year. It is commonly referred to as the *balance sheet*, as in a for-profit business. It is like a photograph of an organization's finances because it captures the situation at a single moment.

Assets are everything of value an organization owns, including obligations of other parties to pay the organization. Value in this context refers to market value and/or commercial (income-producing) value.

A statement of financial position is often presented in columnar format listing assets first, in decreasing order of the ease with which they can be converted into cash (liquidity). Current assets, which are likely to convert into cash within one year, head the list.

How an asset is valued depends on the type of asset. Marketable securities are valued at their market value. Property, plant, and equipment (PP&E) are valued at original cost minus accumulated depreciation. PP&E corresponds to land, buildings, and equipment (LB&E) on the IRS Form 990.[5]

Depreciation is "the cost of using up the future economic benefits or service potentials of long-lived tangible assets" in a given year (FASB 1987a, para. 3); it is a calculated, not measured, quantity. Accumulated depreciation of an asset is the sum of all depreciation from the date of acquisition to the present. (Note: Land does not depreciate.) The section on the statement of activities discusses depreciation further.

In a columnar format, liabilities follow assets. *Liabilities* are the value of all obligations an organization owes to other parties. *Current liabilities*, which are debts that will be coming due within a year, head the list. Noncurrent debt, such as mortgages, bonds, and postretirement employee benefits, are at the bottom of the liabilities list. Sometimes the current portion of a mortgage or bond issue is reported in a separate category under the heading *noncurrent liabilities*. This is the amount due with the next fiscal year. For analytical purposes, it should be added to current liabilities.

The last items on a statement of financial position are net assets, the not-for-profit analogue of net worth or owners' equity in a for-profit business. Net assets equal total assets minus total liabilities.

The Not-for-Profit Difference

If a donor makes a gift for a specific purpose or for use at a specific time, the asset is said to be *restricted.*[6] If a donor does not explicitly restrict a gift with a written gift agreement approved by the recipient, it is *unrestricted* and the recipient may use it for any purpose—even if the gift was made in response to a plea for a particular purpose. Property, plant, and equipment are unrestricted by definition.

Not-for-profits must classify their net assets by type of restriction.[7] Restrictions may be *permanent* or *temporary.*

- *Permanent restrictions* never expire and there is nothing an organization can do legally, short of getting court approval, to apply a permanently restricted gift to a different purpose.
- *Temporary restrictions* may expire after a donor-specified period of time (time-restricted) or after the donor-specified purpose has been achieved (purpose-restricted). Pledges without donor-imposed restrictions are nevertheless classified as temporarily restricted until they are fulfilled—that is, when the organization receives the promised gift.

If net assets are not classified, they are presumed unrestricted: Unrestricted net assets equals Assets minus Liabilities minus Restricted net

TABLE 2.1 Statement of Financial Position of Famous University, 2007 ($1,000s)

	2007	2006
Assets		
Cash and cash equivalents	$ 184,592	$ 177,588
Accounts receivable	232,939	224,474
Contributions receivable	105,343	96,305
Investments	6,496,665	5,272,712
Property, plant, and equipment*	1,250,093	1,191,254
Bond proceeds held by trustees	81,136	108,886
Other assets	118,389	90,446
Total assets	$8,469,157	$7,161,665
Liabilities		
Accounts payable and accrued expenses	$ 146,227	$ 113,455
Deferred revenue	244,689	236,524
Bonds and notes payable	610,883	588,111
Other liabilities	264,466	254,800
	$1,266,265	$1,192,890
Net Assets		
Unrestricted	$6,182,157	$5,017,368
Temporarily restricted	149,139	129,362
Permanently restricted	871,596	822,045
	$7,202,892	$5,968,775
Total liabilities and net assets	$8,469,157	$7,161,665

*Net of accumulated depreciation.

assets. The only way for restricted net assets to decrease is to satisfy donor restrictions. Spending restricted net assets for purposes not authorized by a donor causes a decrease in cash (or investments) and *unrestricted* net assets but not a decrease in restricted net assets.

A board may designate some or all unrestricted net assets for specific future purposes. In this case, the statement of financial position will show the amount designated by purpose. Unlike restrictions, which are binding, designations are not binding, because a board may reverse itself and eliminate a designated account at will.

Table 2.1 is a simplified version of a real, but pseudonymous, university's statement of financial position. This is a typical presentation.

Cash reflects currency and deposits or other accounts with financial institutions that may be deposited or withdrawn without restriction or penalty.

Cash equivalents represent short-term and highly liquid investments that convert readily to cash and carry little risk of change in value at maturity due to interest rate changes. (The next chapter on investing defines these terms.)

Accounts receivable and *accounts payable* refer respectively to obligations other parties have to pay the university within a year for services it rendered to them and obligations the university has to pay other parties within a year for services they rendered to it.

The next section explains deferred revenue.

A not-for-profit organization with custody of important artifacts, like a museum or historical site, may elect one of the following options: (1) not report the value of the collection, (2) report only the value of additions to the collection occurring after the adoption of SFAS 116, or (3) report the value of the collection on the financial statements (Ruppel 2007, 143). These assets may or may not be depreciated.[8]

The true value of a cultural asset, however, "is not determined through a net present value calculation of future cash flow it can generate; rather it is determined by the relevance of that asset to the broader cultural purposes and capacities of the institution to which it belongs" (Guthrie 1996, 153; see the Glossary for description of present value).

Statement of Activities

A *statement of activities* summarizes revenues and expenses occurring during a given time period—usually one year. Revenues increase net assets and expenses decrease them, so the former minus the latter is the change in net assets. Thus, a statement of activities reveals how net assets on a statement of financial position evolved from net assets on the previous one. If the statement of financial position is analogous to a photograph of an organization's finances, a statement of activities is analogous to a video showing how one photo relates to the previous one.

A statement of activities can be arranged in a single column or parallel columns, with one column for each type of restriction plus one for the total. Famous University uses a columnar format. It has a mixed revenue stream consisting of contributions, investment income, and program service revenue.[9]

Revenue is recognized (recorded) when it is *measurable* and *earned*.[10] GAAP recognizes some transactions as creating revenue because they increase net assets while providing no immediate cash for spending:

- When the market value of investments increase. The amount of increase is called *unrealized capital gains* (colloquially, *paper gains*) on investments.

TABLE 2.2 Statement of Activities, Famous University, 2007 ($1,000s)

Tuition and fees net of student aid	$ 429,053	
Auxiliary services	66,524	
Grants and contracts	367,338	
Private gifts	77,611	
Investment return designated for operations	258,111	
Other income	260,366	
Total operating revenue	$ 1,459,003	
Total operating expenses	$ 1,351,564	
Excess (deficiency) of operating revenues over operating expenses	**$ 107,439**	A
Private gifts and grants for buildings and equipment*	$ 14,277	
Investment gains reinvested	997,366	
Other nonoperating income (expenses)	(4,995)	
Net assets released from restrictions†	50,702	
Total nonoperating revenue (expense)	$ 1,057,350	
Change in unrestricted net assets	**$1,164,789**	B
Net assets released from restrictions†	$ (50,702)	
Change in temporarily restricted net assets	70,479	
Change in permanently restricted net assets	49,551	
Change in total net assets	**$1,234,117**	C

Note: Letters A, B, and C are labels referred to in the text.

*See Table 2.3.

†These items cancel. They are funds collected in a prior year but used this year in accordance with the donor's restrictions.

However, cash received is not always revenue, because it does not increase net assets:

- When an organization borrows (there is an offsetting liability).
- When cash is received in advance of its being earned (called an _advance_ or _deferred revenue_).

The last point requires explanation. When an organization receives payment _before_ performing a service, it is not revenue but it increases its cash assets. The organization records an equal liability called an _advance_ or _deferred revenue_, which cancels the impact of increased cash on net assets. As the service is rendered, the liability is removed and the revenue is recognized.

To illustrate: Assume that a not-for-profit theater sells season subscriptions for a series of five plays in a cash-only transaction. Before the season begins, none of the cash can be recognized as revenue because the theater has not yet earned it. Subscription sales go on the statement of financial position as cash, and the theater's accountants balance it by creating an equal amount of deferred revenue as an offsetting liability. Since net assets do not change, there is no revenue recognized at this time. It should be easy to see why cash received before being earned is a liability: If the theater cancels the season, it must refund the cash to its patrons. After each performance, deferred revenue is reduced by one-fifth, which increases net assets, causing recognition of one-fifth of the cash as revenue.

An *expense* is recognized when it is measurable and incurred, which implies an obligation to pay. Therefore, the following are not expenses:

- Spending to acquire property, plant, and equipment.
- Repayment of principal of borrowed funds (interest paid, however, is an expense).
- Payments to vendors in advance of receiving goods or services (*prepaid expenses*).

None of these examples are expenses because net assets do not change. In the first example, an asset replaces the cash used to buy it and the exchange cancels out on a statement of financial position. In the second example, repayment of debt reduces cash in the bank but also reduces liabilities (debt) by an equal amount. These changes cancel each other, leaving no impact on net assets, hence no expense is recognized. The last transaction is more complicated. This anticipatory transaction creates an equal prepaid expense asset on the organization's statement of financial position that replaces the cash, which is now in the vendor's hands. Upon receipt of goods and services, the organization removes the prepaid expense from its statement of financial position and records the amount as a real expense, which then decreases net assets.

Instead of recognizing the purchase of a building as an expense at the time of purchase, GAAP requires that the original cost be divided into pieces, with one piece being recognized as an expense in each year of its useful life. This is called *depreciating* an asset, and the annual decrement is called *depreciation*, which is classified as an expense. Most not-for-profits use the straight-line method of depreciation, which spreads the purchase price of a capital asset over its useful life in equal annual installments.[11]

The Not-for-Profit Difference

Not-for-profit revenue may include voluntary contributions. Contributions, also called *public support* on financial statements, are recognized when made.

A *contribution* is "an unconditional transfer of cash or other assets to an entity or a settlement or cancellation of its liabilities in a voluntary non-reciprocal transfer by another entity acting other than as an owner" (FASB 1993a, para. 5). On a statement of activities, contributions are sometimes called *public support.*

Tax-deductibility requires that a contribution be "an irrevocable transfer of property or cash from a qualified donor to a qualified donee [recipient] for less than full consideration" (Bryce 2000, 179). Furthermore, the donor must retain no rights in the property, exert no control over it, and receive no benefit from it. Pledges are usually reported net of an allowance for uncollectable amounts. Sometimes the balance sheet shows the allowance explicitly. Either way, an increase in the allowance is equivalent to an expense.

For simplicity, this book classifies contributions with revenue. GAAP recognizes some transactions as creating revenue because they increase net assets although they provide no immediate cash:

- Donated goods, known as noncash contributions, or gifts in kind.
- Promises to give (pledges), but only when a donor makes the pledge in writing and the recipient verifies acceptance (FASB 1993a, para. 6).

However, cash received is not always revenue, because it does not increase net assets:

- When a donor fulfills a pledge by writing a check because it had already been recognized when pledged.

Other not-for-profit revenue is classified as restricted or unrestricted subject to the following rules:

- The portion of a multiyear grant eligible to be spent in the first year is unrestricted provided it is used for its intended purpose. The portion earmarked for subsequent years is temporarily restricted. It will be reclassified to the unrestricted category in the year it is eligible to be spent. In the meantime, it is recognized at its present value. (See the Glossary for a description of present value.)
- Program service revenue is unrestricted by definition.
- Donated goods and services (known as noncash or in-kind) are unrestricted and recorded at current market value.

Expenses are unrestricted by definition.

GAAP allows reporting the value of volunteers' time only if: (1) the time is spent building an asset for the not-for-profit or the volunteer possesses a professional skill, such as an attorney or a certified public accountant (CPA), and (2) the not-for-profit would have paid for the service had it not been donated. Donated volunteer time is recorded twice—once as revenue and once as an equal expense, because the services would have been purchased if not provided by volunteers.

A not-for-profit need not recognize works of art, historical treasures, and similar assets if the donated items are added to collections that meet all of the following conditions:

> *(1) [They] are held for public exhibition, education, or research in furtherance of public service rather than financial gain; (2) [they] are protected, kept unencumbered, cared for, and preserved; or (3) [they] are subject to an organizational policy that requires the proceeds from sales of collection items to be used to acquire other items for collections.* (FASB 1993a, para. 11)

Net assets released from restrictions consist of prior-year gifts and grants that are legally available for spending in the current year.[12] The total of unrestricted revenue and net assets released from restrictions represents current resources available for spending. Reclassification of net assets does not increase the total; hence it is not revenue. Rather, it makes revenue that was recognized in an earlier period available for spending in the current period. Net assets released from restrictions are unrestricted by definition.

Statement of Cash Flows

"Cash is king," as the saying goes. Many transactions generate cash that is not revenue and many use cash that is not an expense. But all organizations need cash to operate. So it is important to keep track of which activities provide cash and which ones use it.

The *statement of cash flows* reconciles changes in cash and cash equivalents with changes cash between consecutive statements of financial position. If operating surpluses seem adequate but cash is short, a review of the statement of cash flows can help identify the problem.

GAAP permits a statement of cash flows to be presented according to one of two formats. The more common indirect method is described here. A statement of cash flows by the indirect method is arranged in a column. Changes in cash in Table 2.3 may be due to (1) financing, line F, (2) investing, line E, and (3) operations, line D, defined as follows:

> *Financing activities include . . . borrowing money and repaying amounts borrowed, or otherwise settling the obligation; and obtaining and paying for other resources obtained from creditors on long-term credit.* (FASB 1987b, para. 8)

TABLE 2.3 Cash Flow of Famous University 2007, Presented in Indirect Format ($1,000s)

Change in net assets (total)	$ 1,234,117	A
Adjustments to Reconcile Change in Net Assets		
to Net Cash Provided by Operations		
Depreciation	76,643	
Net gains (losses) on investments	(1,104,789)	
Private gifts and grants for buildings		
and equipment*	(14,277)	
Subtotal	$(1,042,423)	B
Changes in Assets and Liabilities		
Accounts receivable	$ (8,465)	
Contributions receivable	(9,038)	
Other assets	(27,943)	
Accounts payable and accrued expenses	32,772	
Deferred revenue	8,165	
Subtotal	$ (4,509)	C
Net cash provided by (used in) operations	$ 187,185	D = A + B + C
Purchase or sale of investments (net)	(119,164)	
Acquisition of land, buildings, and equipment	(135,482)	
Net cash used in investing	$ (254,646)	E
From bond proceeds held by trustees	$ 27,750	
From bonds and notes payable	22,772	
Private gifts and grants for buildings and		
equipment*	14,277	
Other liabilities	9,666	
Net cash provided by financing	$ 74,465	F
Change in cash and cash equivalents	$ 7,004	G = D + E + F

Note: Shaded area is change in working cash, which is discussed in the next chapter.
*See Table 2.2. This item is subtracted from operations and added to the financing section because it is long-term. Operations by definition are short-term.

> *Investing activities include making and collecting loans and acquiring and disposing of debt or equity instruments and property, plant, and equipment. . . .* (FASB 1987b, para. 7)

> *Operating activities fall into neither of these categories. They generally involve producing and delivering goods and providing services.* (FASB 1987b, para. 8)

In the following formula, Δ indicates a change in an item on a statement of financial position during the reporting period.[13] A positive change in net assets or liabilities, or a negative change in assets (other than cash), indicates that a change increased the organization's cash balance, *providing* it with cash. The reverse implies it *used* cash, and is indicated by parentheses.

> Δ Cash =
> Δ Net assets
> + Depreciation and other adjustments to changes in net assets that neither use nor provide cash
> − Δ Current assets other than cash
> + Δ Current liabilities
> − Δ Long-term assets (investing)
> + Δ Long-term liabilities (financing)

The boldface items are "net cash provided (used) by operations," a section of the statement of particular importance because it shows how an organization's working capital changed during the year. (The next chapter on investing discusses working capital.) The relevant items are shaded on Table 2.3. The statement of cash flows does not distinguish between restricted and unrestricted amounts. Line G in Table 2.3 equals the change in cash between 2006 and 2007 on Table 2.1.

Other Statements and Notes

Other GAAP statements are the statement of functional expenses and statement of changes in net assets. These statements are uniquely not-for-profit. GAAP requires a statement of functional expenses only for health and welfare organizations. A statement of changes in net assets is optional and rarely used.

Statement of Functional Expenses

The *statement of functional expenses*, required for health and welfare organizations, is a table showing the breakdown of expenses on a matrix: (1) functional expenses, which are classified on the IRS Form 990 form as administrative, fund-raising, and program expenses, and (2) natural categories, also known as budget *line items*.

When reading a 990 informational return, one must exercise caution. A national survey of 1,500 not-for-profits with at least $50,000 in contributions revealed that over one-third reported zero fund-raising expenses and 13 percent of not-for-profits report zero management and general expenses (Wing et al. 2006). Proper expense allocation requires maintaining records of staff time utilization, but only one-third of not-for-profits track staff time by functional expense category.

The same survey disclosed that only 25 percent of not-for-profits receiving foundation grants and 17 percent of not-for-profits receiving government grants properly classify proposal-writing costs. Foundation grants are equivalent to contributions, so proposal-writing costs should be treated as a fund-raising expense. When a grant involves an exchange transaction with a government agency, proposal-writing costs should be classified as administrative expenses.

Because budgets and accounting systems typically keep track of spending by natural categories, this breakdown is probably more reliable.

Statement of Changes in Net Assets

This statement shows balances in each category of net assets and shows reclassifications. It also shows board-designated funds and transfers into, out of, and between them. Although it provides backup for arguments in favor of having substantial net assets, few not-for-profits include this optional statement.

Notes to Financial Statements

On each page of tables is a phrase referring readers to accompanying notes. They are an integral part of the statement, and the information they contain is included in an audit.

Notes contain a wealth of information. The first note always describes the organization and significant accounting policies. Other notes to give details about investments, capital leases, and debt obligations, which are very helpful in assessing an organization's long-term financial prospects.

"Subsequent events" and "contingent liabilities," if any, are usually found at the end of the notes section. Subsequent events are events that occurred after the fieldwork was done.

What to Look For

Chapters 6 though 9 explain how to use financial statements to analyze an organization's financial capacity and financial sustainability, but it is helpful to know what to look for to get a quick first impression. Here is a short list, roughly in order of examination:

1. The auditor's opinion.
2. The first and last notes.
3. Unrestricted net assets.
4. Change in unrestricted net assets, or if the organization has considerable investments.

4b. Operating revenues minus operating expenses.
   5. Cash produced by (used in) operations.

It is obvious where to find the first two items. Item three is found on the statement of financial position, items four and five are on the statement of activities, and item six is on the statement of cash flows. All of the statements and notes are necessary for a complete picture, even a once-over-lightly first impression.

The first thing to discover is whether the information in the financial statements is reasonably free of material misstatement and, if not, what the weaknesses are. The first note describes the organization and its accounting policies. Combined with the opinion letter, this information tells a reader how to interpret the numbers.

The end of the notes section is information on subsequent events, if any, that might have a material impact on the organization's finances but occurred too late to be incorporated into the statements. Also at the end of the notes section is information on contingent liabilities, if any, such as pending lawsuits that could result in a major judgment against the organization.

Solvency

Solvency refers to the ability of an organization to remain in business (to be a *going concern*) while continuously satisfying all ongoing financial obligations in a timely manner. The complementary concept, *insolvency*, is predictive of an organization's demise at the hands of its creditors. There are three kinds of insolvency: (1) balance sheet insolvency, or insolvency in liquidation, (2) cash flow insolvency, or operational insolvency, and (3) capital inadequacy (Heaton 2007). This subsection discusses the first type of solvency; the next two subsections take up the others in turn.

A for-profit business is *balance sheet insolvent* if its net assets are less than zero. Upon liquidation, such an organization would be unable to discharge all existing obligations to creditors. A not-for-profit is balance-sheet insolvent if its *unrestricted* net assets is negative. It will be unable to fulfill commitments made to donors of restricted grants as well as its creditors. Famous University had over $6 billion in unrestricted net assets in 2007, so it is very solvent in this sense. This is typical of endowed not-for-profits.

The Bottom Line

The key summary figure of a statement of activities is the so-called bottom line. For a for-profit business it is profit (earnings), which is revenue minus expenses, but all revenue of a for-profit firm is unrestricted and investment revenue is usually a minor factor (except for financial institutions).

Because not-for-profits may have restricted revenue, GAAP requires reporting of two bottom lines, which differ as a consequence of donor restrictions:

1. Change in total net assets (*total surplus*) equals total revenue minus total expenses (line C, Table 2.1).
2. Change in unrestricted net assets (*unrestricted surplus*) equals unrestricted revenue minus total expenses (line B, Table 2.1).

If an organization has no investments and no restricted gifts, these variants of the bottom line are equal.

GAAP does not use the word *surplus*, but it is commonly used by not-for-profits and it simplifies exposition. A negative surplus is called a *deficit.* Some authorities refer to negative net assets as a deficit, but it is more accurate to say that negative net assets are an accumulated deficit.

Although deficits frequently produce cash shortages, surpluses do not necessarily result in larger cash balances. Repeated operating deficits on the statement of activities will eventually impair an organization's ability to pay its bills on time, although it could continue operating as long as it is able to sell off its assets to generate cash. If an organization is balance sheet solvent but it cannot pay its bills when due, it is *cash flow insolvent* (or *operationally insolvent*).

All endowed not-for-profits, such as Famous University, and some for-profit businesses focus on a third bottom line, operating surplus. GAAP gives organizations latitude to define it as it best describes their situation. Generically:

- *Operating surplus* equals operating revenue minus operating expenses (line A, Table 2.1).

Because GAAP does not define it, one may observe differences in definition and captioning between statements. If an organization has restricted revenue but no investments, then unrestricted surplus and operating surplus are equal. Further discussion of operating surplus is deferred until Chapter 3.

Capital Inadequacy

There is no precise definition of the third type of insolvency—capital inadequacy. However, it is worth mentioning because it has been implicated in some bankruptcy cases (Heaton 2007). It occurs when assets barely exceed liabilities and the organization has been paying its bills but almost always late.

Capital inadequacy comes into play when an organization is solvent on the first two criteria but everyone knows that it is struggling and some have given up on it. As a rule of thumb, when an organization's net assets are less than 10 percent of total assets, its statement of cash flows should be examined with special care.

If an organization has been using cash in operations over a period of years, then the conclusion follows that it has been able to stay solvent according to the first two criteria by selling its assets. If it has very little capital remaining, liquidation is inevitable. This is capital inadequacy insolvency.

The statement of cash flows shows exactly how an organization is raising cash. In Table 2.3 this appears on the line "Net cash provided by (used in) operations." Famous University's operations produced $187 million in 2007, so it is solvent by this test as well.

IRS Form 990

Audited financial statements is the preferable source of financial information on a not-for-profit organization. However, in some cases an analyst has access only to IRS Form 990 reports (GuideStar 2010).

At first glance, an IRS Form 990 informational return appears to provide the same financial data as an audited financial statement provides, but there are four important differences. (See Chapter 5 for a discussion of filing requirements.)

1. Revenue is not disaggregated by type of donor restriction.
2. Form 990 does not show the increase in market value of investments, which financial statements consider as revenue.
3. Form 990 shows cash (non-interest-bearing) and savings (interest-bearing) but there is no "savings" line on financial statements. Instead, financial statements divide interest-bearing investments between cash equivalents and investments. There are other differences, but fortunately the section of the IRS Form 990 immediately following the financial position section contains information on items that are included in one but excluded from the other.
4. There is nothing on an IRS Form 990 that corresponds to a statement of cash flows. For simple organizations without investments, it might be possible to construct one as described in this chapter but not for endowed organizations.

The bottom lines discussed in the previous section can be computed from information on IRS Form 990 as follows:

- Change in total net assets (total surplus) is line 73B minus line 73A of the pre-2008 IRS Form 990 and page 11, line 33B minus line 33A of the 2008 form.
- Change in unrestricted net assets (unrestricted surplus) is line 67B minus 67A of the pre-2008 IRS Form 990 and page 11, line 27B minus page 11, line 27A of the 2008 form.
- Operating revenue and expenses must be inferred using techniques explained in subsequent chapters.

In a comparison between the audited statements and IRS Form 990 informational returns of 350 not-for-profit organizations, investigators (Froelich, Knoepfle, and Pollak 2000, 251) concluded that the informational return is "a reliable source of information for basic income statement and balance sheets entries," namely total income, total expenses, total assets, and total liabilities.

"In general, small organizations demonstrate greater consistency in financial reporting than large organizations." Further, human services and health organizations show greater consistency than those in education or the arts (Froelich, Knoepfle, and Pollak 2000, 251).

The following groups show the reliability of informational return data relative to audited statements:

- *Reliable:* total assets, total liabilities, total income, and total expenses.
- *Somewhat reliable:* total contributions, program service revenue, program service expenses, and fund-raising expenses.
- *Use with caution:* net rental income, gross profit from sales, and to a lesser extent, management expenses. Table 3.4 in the next chapter elaborates further.

Concluding Thoughts

It is said that "what cannot be measured cannot be managed." Not-for-profit accounting rules promote values-centered management by enabling not-for-profits to be good stewards of gifts and grants entrusted to them for specific purposes, reflecting the common values of donor and recipient. If donors were unable to verify that their gifts are used in accordance with their wishes, they would understandably be less likely to give.

Leaders of the organization featured in the first paragraph of this chapter did not appreciate the distinction between total net assets and unrestricted net assets. They thought they were in great shape because changes in total net assets were consistently positive. Meanwhile they ignored repeated unrestricted deficits. The staff had been spending restricted gifts and grants for other purposes. This reduced the organization's net assets without discharging obligations to its donors, so net assets could not be released from restrictions, thereby causing unrestricted deficits. The organization remained viable as long as it continued to attract new gifts and grants to replace the misapplied funds. When new grants diminished, it still had unfulfilled obligations without the cash to meet them, and its house of cards fell.

CHAPTER 3

Investing
Looking to the Future

Many years ago a lucky nonprofit received a bequest allowing it to establish an endowment and to nearly balance its budget with endowment income alone. While the stock market boomed it was usually able to balance its budget by withdrawing no more than the annual return, including capital gains; but nearly 25 years later it was exceeding these limits. By then the endowment had ceased making more than a negligible contribution to the budget.

The next section builds a basic vocabulary needed for discussing endowment management. Persons knowledgeable about investing may proceed directly to the discussion of the law of institutional investing. The endowment section features alternative definitions and identifies the necessary conditions for sustaining an endowment. It also defines operating surplus of endowed organizations. The final section explains socially responsible investing (SRI) and program-related investing (PRI).

This chapter would be too long if it explored every issue related to endowments, so Chapter 8 covers the debate over whether endowments are socially desirable and Chapter 9 continues the discussion in the context of foundations. Chapter 8 also covers management issues related to building endowment.

Investing

Organizations with funds available for investing should have an investment committee, comprised of experts, to advise the board, and they should have a written investment policy that spells out a due diligence process, risk tolerance, and liquidity needs. BoardSource publishes sample investment policies. The American Association of Individual Investors (AAII 2011), a nonprofit organization, produces tutorials and other general materials on investing.

The most important money management concepts are liquidity, risk, and return. These will be taken up in turn after some preliminaries.

Due Diligence

Due diligence, a process of verifying the legitimacy of money managers, investment vehicles, and investment strategies, is of utmost importance for loss prevention. The process is commonsensical but stories abound of organizations failing to ask even the most obvious questions and coming to grief.

In 2009 thousands of investors, including many nonprofits that had entrusted their money to Bernie Madoff, lost billions when the largest Ponzi scheme in history collapsed.[1] A consistent theme of their stories was failure to do due diligence. Some, however, avoided tragedy by taking a pass on this amazing "investment opportunity." They walked away when they discovered that senior staff consisted mostly of his relatives, his multibillion-dollar firm employed a sole practitioner as independent auditor, and he had no credible explanation for achieving strangely stable returns year after year.

Do not invest with someone you haven't checked out.[2] Letters from satisfied clients are virtually useless because they are filtered by the money manager. In a bull (rising) market everyone can claim to be an investing genius, so be wary of money managers who have not experienced at least one bear (falling) market. Do credit and criminal background checks of the principals of start up and small money management firms. Be wary of investment firms staffed with relatives of the principals. The size and reputation of the audit firm are equally important.

Do not allow money managers to violate the investment policy. Do not let them utilize investment vehicles or strategies that you don't understand. If you are unsure, ask questions. Start with the person who is soliciting or conducting your business, but pursue the issue further with a knowledgeable but disinterested person.

Definitions

An investment *portfolio* is a collection of assets that are managed jointly. They may include (1) cash, which does not earn interest, and cash equivalents, (2) *stocks*, also called equities; and (3) *bonds*. A generic name for stocks and bonds is *securities*. Bonds are also called fixed-income securities because they provide a constant stream of interest payments.

Stocks are shares of ownership. The issuer of shares of stock may or may not pay stockholders a portion of its profit in a given year as a dividend. Nevertheless, stockholders in principle have a claim on a proportional share of profit.

Bonds represent money lent to issuers until some specified date (maturity) when they redeem the bond at face value from the bondholder (investor). Until maturity a bond usually pays interest periodically, but sometimes interest is paid in one lump sum at maturity.

Increasingly, large institutions are turning to *alternative investments*, which include private equity, real estate, venture capital, commodities, derivatives, and hedge funds, to name a few.[3]

Liquidity

The most important concept in investing is liquidity, which is an ability to get cash quickly when it is needed. The first point an organization's investment policy should address is cash needs.

If an organization's cash flow is negative during a few months each year, it needs an internal revolving loan fund called a *working cash fund*.[4] A working cash fund must be highly liquid, which necessitates investing it in money market funds or bonds of very high credit quality and very short maturity—such as U.S. Treasury bills (T-bills). The size of the fund should be sufficient to finance the largest expected negative cash flow and be backstopped with an external line of credit. Working cash funds are replenished within one budget cycle (typically one year).

Many organizations have one or more *operating reserve* funds to cover unexpected budget shortfalls, to provide seed money for projects that will eventually become self-supporting, to save for purchase of equipment, and so forth. There is no one-size-fits-all amount for an operating reserve. Factors deserving consideration when sizing an operating reserve are: type of organization, mission, long-term plans, corporate structure, size of physical plant, complexities of debt structure, funding sources, and self-insurance. Like working cash funds, these funds are internal revolving loan funds, but managers will repay loans from these funds with money budgeted for such purpose in future years. These funds should be fairly liquid but need not be as liquid as working cash funds.

Permanently restricted net assets should never be used for operating reserve (KPMG and Prager, McCarthy and Sealy LLC 1999, 3–4). Pledges (net of allowance for doubtful accounts) discounted to their present value, which GAAP classifies as temporarily restricted, may be included in an operating reserve provided the donors have imposed no restrictions on their pledge. (See the Glossary for a description of present value.)

Risk and Return

Other things being equal, higher return is better. But a higher return on a particular stock or bond (which is desirable) is usually associated with higher risk (which is undesirable). The nub of every investment problem is finding an optimal trade-off between risk and return. This trade-off varies from investor to investor and depends on their need for return and appetite for risk. The next few paragraphs define these concepts.

Total return is interest paid on bonds and dividends paid on stock plus *capital gains* (or minus *capital losses*), which are the increase (or decrease) in market value of securities during a given period of time. Capital gains (or losses) on an asset can be realized or unrealized. They are realized—converted into cash—upon sale of the asset. They are unrealized as long as the asset remains unsold (colloquially, *paper* gains and losses).

There are many ways to quantify *risk*, but all of them relate to variability in total return, where greater variability corresponds to higher risk and greater likelihood of losses. A common definition equates risk with the standard deviation of total returns in excess of a so-called risk-free investment, such as T-bills.[5] In Table 3.1 risk is defined more simply as total return in the worst year during a given period of time.

When we speak of appetite for risk we are using a continuous scale that measures attitudes toward risk with strongly risk preferring at one end and strongly risk avoiding at the other. A *risk-preferring* (aggressive) investor is one who prefers a risky investment to a risk-free investment earning the same average return. A *risk-avoiding* (conservative) investor has the opposite preference. He or she prefers a risk-free investment to a risky one earning the same average return. A *risk-neutral* investor is one who would be willing to flip a fair coin to decide between the two options.

TABLE 3.1 Effect of Asset Allocation on Portfolio Return and Risk, 1970–2006

Investing Style	Stocks Large Cap	Stocks Small Cap	Stocks Int'l	Bonds	Cash	Return per Year	Worst Year
Conservative	15%	0%	5%	50%	30%	8.6%	0.1%
Moderately conservative	25	5	10	50	10	9.8	−6.6
Moderate	35	10	15	35	5	10.6	−12.9
Moderately aggressive	45	15	20	15	5	11.1	−19.1
Aggressive	50	20	25	0	5	11.4	−23.6

Large cap = companies worth over $5 billion; small cap = companies worth $250 million to $1 billion; int'l = international. Rows add to 100 percent.
Source: Charles Schwab (2011).

The probability of failing to meet a given rate of return is a function of the time period selected for purposes of analysis—the *planning horizon*. One study found the probability of failure to meet or exceed the target return in one year to be double the probability over a 10-year period (DeMarche 1999, 36). The exact relationship between these extremes depends on the risk and return characteristics of assets in the portfolio, but this example is sufficient to demonstrate that the length of the planning horizon can have a substantial impact on investment decisions. No planning horizon is intrinsically better than another. In general, managers should take a long view of returns, pick a planning horizon, and stick with it.

Standard practice is for investors (1) to define risk and choose a planning horizon appropriate to their situation, (2) to assess their tolerance for risk within their planning horizon, (3) to choose a maximum tolerable risk level, and (4) to find the *efficient portfolio*—the combination of investments that maximizes return without exceeding this maximum risk level.

Total risk of a portfolio is the sum of systematic and unsystematic risk. Systematic risk, also known as market risk, is common to a large class of assets and liabilities. Unsystematic risk equals total risk minus systematic risk, and it is determined by factors unique to each asset.

Financial planners say the single most important decision an investor makes is the mix of asset types to include in his or her portfolio—a decision known as *asset allocation*. Although imperfect, this is the best available strategy for dealing with systematic risk. "Governing boards have a responsibility to consider their asset mix decisions carefully together with the implications these decisions have on spending policy" (DeMarche 1999, 40).

Table 3.1 shows total annual return and risk (measured by the worst year in the entire period) for five alternative portfolios. Cash and cash equivalents are the most conservative investments, so the portfolio with the highest proportion of these investments (30 percent) is the most conservative. Bonds (fixed income securities) are moderate risk and moderate return investments. Stocks (equities) have the highest returns but also the highest risks. Going from a conservative investment style to an aggressive style increases risk more rapidly than return, which implies that even small changes in a portfolio can have large impact on risk.

Most organizations with large portfolios hire one or more professional managers with specialization in various classes of assets. The average university has approximately 11 professional managers; those with less than $10 million use an average of two managers (Commonfund 2003, 27).

External investment managers often collect their fees directly from the assets they control, so organizations must exercise diligence to monitor them. Historically, Cornell University's money management expenses have consumed 0.7 percent of its endowment value annually (Ehrenberg 2000). The average commercially available domestic stock mutual fund charges 1.43 percent of invested assets annually.[6] These numbers may seem small, but they should be compared to expected return. Assuming expected return is 10 percent, Cornell would realize 93 percent of that amount and the average mutual fund investor would realize just 86 percent.

Law of Institutional Investing

Historically, states restricted nonprofit institutions from investing in various assets that their legislatures considered risky.[7] Since the 1960s these restrictions have fallen away and been replaced by a Prudent Investor Rule, which requires nonprofits to manage the totality of their assets in the same manner a prudent person would manage his or her assets under similar circumstances.[8] Prudent investors focus on the risk-return trade-off of a portfolio as a whole.

The Prudent Investor Rule is statutory in the states that have adopted some form of the Uniform Prudent Management of Institutional Funds Act (UPMIFA), as nearly all have (Uniform Law Commission 2010).[9] The law gives fiduciaries great latitude in determining what kinds of investment instruments are appropriate to achieve their risk-return objectives, and they may delegate investment and management functions, subject to safeguards. Key provisions include these five points:

1. Portfolio managers are not limited in the kinds of assets sought for the portfolio.
2. Costs must be managed prudently in relation to the assets, the purposes of the institution, and the skills available to the charitable institution.
3. Total return expenditure is expressly authorized under comprehensive prudent standards relating to the whole economic situation of the charitable institution.
4. UPMIFA abolished an earlier rule, which absolutely protected the historic dollar value of restricted assets.
5. States may adopt an optional rule that presumes expenditure exceeding 7 percent of total return is imprudent.

> *A charity can spend the amount [it] deems prudent after considering the donor's intent that the endowment fund continue permanently, the purposes of the fund (and not just of the charity), and "general economic conditions."* (Gary 2007)[10]

In effect, UPMIFA allows a charity to borrow from itself. The new law came none too soon. The market collapse in the fall of 2008 left many endowments underwater—the term describing an endowment with a current value less than the original gifts that established it. Thomas Pollak and Katie Uttke, researchers at the Urban Institute, estimated that 12,000 of 20,000 endowments were *underwater.*

The primary aim of UPMIFA is to protect donor intent and maintain an endowment fund as defined by gift instruments. Its emphasis is on *prudence.* If an organization withdraws an unsustainable amount from its investments to cope with an economic emergency, that organization incurs an obligation to rebuild its portfolio as soon as feasible.

A disciplined response is essential to preventing overspending before conditions return to normal and the endowment is restored. In the end, an organization that liquidates investments to pay current bills may find that it only postponed the pain. Delayed budget cuts are deeper budget cuts, and, once an endowment runs out, current revenue must support the entire budget. Building an endowment from scratch is extremely difficult.

As a rule of thumb, an organization should spend no more than 10 percentage points above its normal spending formula in any given 50-year period (equivalent to 2 percent for five years) and subsequently adjust the formula to allow restoration of pre-emergency real spending levels. Once an investment portfolio is able to support this level of spending, the spending formula can return to normal.

Finally, most states prohibit related-party transactions, such as personal loans, use of organizational assets by board members, or sale or lease of land or other key assets to a board member without valuations and/or court approval (Bowman, Keating, and Hagar 2007).[11]

Endowment

The obvious question is: What is endowment? However, the answer is far from obvious. This section explores alternative definitions and explains how to calculate them for endowed organizations.

Definitions

Lawyers define endowment as a "gift of money or property to an institution (such as a university) for a specific purpose, esp. one in which the principal is kept intact and only the interest income from the principal is used" (Garner 2009). At the other extreme, economists define endowment as all of an organization's net assets (e.g., Core, Guay, and Verdi 2004; Fisman and Hubbard 2003). The legal definition, sometimes called *true endowment,* is too narrow because it overlooks unrestricted funds functioning as endowment. The economic definition is too broad because it implies that *every* solvent organization is endowed.

The American Institute of Certified Public Accountants (AICPA) takes a pragmatic middle road: *Endowment* is "an established fund of cash, securities, or other assets to provide income for the maintenance of a not-for-profit organization. . . . Endowment funds are generally established by donor-restricted gifts and bequests to provide a permanent endowment, which is to provide a permanent source of income, or a term endowment, which is to provide income for a specified period." When an organization's governing board earmarks a portion of its unrestricted net assets to provide income for a long but unspecified period, the funds are called *quasi-endowment* or *funds functioning as endowment* (AICPA 1996, para. 366).

Given the lack of agreement among professions on the definition of endowment, *Finance Fundamentals for Nonprofits* invents what might be called a managerial definition, which is a simplified version of the accountants' concept: *An endowment is a portfolio of investments that provides an organization with a perpetual source of income.* The point of having an endowment is to permanently self-subsidize goods and services below their cost of production.

The existence of a perpetual source of income to support chronic money-losing activities alters an organization's financial capacity and raises new issues regarding sustainability, so this book develops formulas to measure capacity and sustainability specifically for endowed organizations. To standardize the decision about which formula should be used in any given case, *Finance Fundamentals for Nonprofits* treats an organization as *presumptively endowed* when the value of securities and other investments is larger than total expenses.[12] The next section explains the reason.

Endowments are not to be confused with working cash funds or operating reserves. A working cash fund provides liquidity to smooth fluctuations in cash flow. Operating reserves are for responding to emergencies of various kinds, including unexpected budget shortfalls. Hence the former tends to invest in money market funds. The latter consists of investments of slightly longer terms but comparably shorter than those in an endowment. Endowments emphasize long-term assets like bonds of long maturities, stocks, and alternative investments. A budget determines the sizes of a working cash fund and an operating reserve fund, whereas an endowment determines the size of a budget.

Sustaining Endowments

Sustaining an endowment *in perpetuity* requires achieving an acceptable trade-off in the portfolio between risk and return and adopting a spending formula such that the spending rate plus the expected long-run rate of inflation is less than, or equal to, the average expected rate of return. Higher spending rates are sustainable only with greater risk exposure due to the typically positive correlation between risk and return.

Simulations conducted for the Council on Foundations that assumed a 4 percent rate of inflation showed that the upper limit for annual indefinitely sustainable spending from an endowment averages 5.5 percent of investments over successive three-year rolling periods (DeMarche 1990).

A Goldman Sachs study concluded that a portfolio of 50 percent stocks and 50 percent bonds combined with a 5 percent spending rate "would face a greater than 40 percent probability that, over a decade, the real, or inflation-adjusted, value of its corpus, or principal, would decline by more than 10 percent" (Kogelman and Dobler 1999). This argues for a moderately aggressive style (according to Table 3.1) or a lower spending rate.

More recent simulations assume a 3 percent rate of inflation and show that a 5 percent spending rate is "perhaps slightly too high to maintain purchasing power in perpetuity" (Cambridge Associates 2008, 1). The similarity of these results is remarkable given the substantially different underlying assumptions.

These numbers are consistent with the 1969 Tax Reform Act, which mandates a 5 percent payout rate for foundations. (*Payout rate* is the term for foundation spending rate.) Although educational institutions are exempt from the 1969 Act, the average endowment spending formula for educational institutions is 4.9 percent of investments (Commonfund 2003).

The simplest spending formula applies a constant spending rate to a moving (or rolling) average of the market value of the endowment over several prior years. Some formulas are more complicated but provide better response to inflation. Yale University's formula has two components that are sensitive to inflation in opposing ways, allowing greater preservation of capital on the downside and more spending on the upside (Ramsden 2003).

Allowable spending (in dollars) under the Yale formula is a weighted average: 70 percent of the allowable spending in the prior fiscal year, increased by the rate of inflation, *plus* 30 percent of the long-term spending rate multiplied by the most recent four-quarter market average of the endowment's value. In the short term, considerable weight is given to last year's spending rate, which depends on the previous year's spending rate, and so on, but market return dominates in the long run.

Now it should be clear why an organization is presumptively endowed if its securities and other investments exceed its annual operating expenses. If the value of securities and other investments is larger than total expenses, then investments are sufficient to finance at least 5 percent of a budget in perpetuity.[13] The 5 percent threshold is near the largest perpetually sustainable spending rate. Besides, an income source that provides less than 5 percent of a budget is not likely to be critical for long-term success. This rule probably overstates the support that investments give to budgets, because some investments are for operating reserves. For example, the investments of Famous University that are *not* in its endowment are 25 percent of the total (see Table 3.2).

In a specific situation, if information is available on the size of an endowment and the spending rule, then it is preferred to the aforementioned rule defining a presumptive endowment. Notes to financial statements supply important information on endowment, including size and spending formula. The IRS Form 990 had no information prior to 2008. It now captures information on endowment, but not on the spending formula, so analysts must use a pro forma rate, such as 5 percent.

Operating Surplus

The operating surplus of an endowed organization *excludes* capital gifts, capital grants, and total return on investments, but it *includes* the maximum withdrawals from the endowment allowed by a spending formula (not actual withdrawals). An organization's financial statements will contain this information. Table 2.2 in Chapter 2 revealed that Famous University had a robust operating surplus of $107 million in 2007.

Operating surplus = Unrestricted operating revenue + Net assets released from restrictions for operations − Total return on investments + Allowed spending from endowment pursuant to formula − Total expenses. In terms of pre-2008 IRS Form 990 line numbers:[14] Operating surplus = 1e + 2 + 3 + 6c + 9c + 10c + 11 + 0.05 (54aA + 54bA) − (68B − 68A) − (69B − 69A) − 17.

Financial analysts should exercise caution when calculating operating surpluses of large endowed organizations, especially hospitals and universities. A comparison of operating surplus from Famous University's financial statements with a calculated value from its 990 report shows discrepancies. Expenses on Table 3.3 are $200 million higher on the 990 report than on the financial statements, whereas operating revenue is $200 million *lower*.

These differences are due to conflicting requirements between GAAP and IRS rules. Institutional aid (scholarships) is reported on a net basis on financial statements but on a gross basis on 990 reports.[14]

Values-Centered Investing

Unlike most for-profit corporations, a nonprofit organization espouses social values and has a public mission. These considerations may affect its investment decisions. This section addresses two principal responses: socially responsible investing and program-related investing.

TABLE 3.2 Investments of Famous University, 2007 ($1,000s)

Purpose	Operations and Plant	Annuity and Life Income*	Quasi-Endowment	Permanent Endowment	Total
Long-term balanced pool	$ 739,655	$37,882	$1,951,227	$2,864,212	$5,592,976
Medium-term bond fund†	671,542	0	35,702	0	707,244
Separately invested	543	57,888	57,917	7,300	123,648
Working cash	72,797	0	0	0	72,797
Total investments	$1,484,537	$95,770	$2,044,846	$2,871,512	$6,496,665

*Annuities and life income funds managed by the university for the benefit of living donors, which transfer to the university upon a donor's demise.
†Medium-term bonds in operations and plant are essentially an operating reserve.

TABLE 3.3 Comparison of Famous University's Financial Statements with IRS Form 990 Data ($1,000s)

	Financial Statements	990 Report	Difference
Assets			
Cash and cash equivalents (and savings)	$ 184	$ 187	($ 3)
Accounts receivable	233	229	4
Other current assets	105	159	(54)
Investments	6,496	6,374	122
Total assets	$8,469	$8,818	($349)
Liabilities			
Accounts payable	$ 146	$ 36	$110
Deferred revenue	244	244	—
Total liabilities	$1,736	$1,626	$110
Net assets	$7,202	$7,190	12
Expenses, Revenues, and Surpluses			
Operating revenue	$1,459	$1,521	(62)
including investment return to operations	258	319	(61)
Operating expenses	1,351	1,546	(195)
including depreciation	82	81	1
Operating surplus	107	(25)	132
Investment gains reinvested	997	?	?
Total surplus	$1,234	$1,216	18

Note: Only selected items are shown. Detail below level of totals is partial.

Socially Responsible Investing[15]

The Social Investment Forum (2003, 3) defines socially responsible investing (SRI) as "an investment process that considers the social and environmental consequences, both positive and negative, within the context of rigorous financial analysis." A complete arsenal of institutional SRI strategies includes screening investments purchased for the institution's portfolio, taking advantage of the institution's position as a shareholder to advocate for changes at shareholder meetings and investing in communities underserved by traditional financial services.

SRI screens can be exclusionary, qualitative, or inclusionary. *Exclusionary* screens proscribe so-called sin stocks in certain industries (e.g., alcohol, gambling, and tobacco) or in companies with a record in conflict with the investor's values regarding the environment, human rights, animal rights, or corporate governance. *Qualitative* screens identify companies with socially desirable products or services, or companies with good records on particular issues (e.g., diversity, executive compensation). *Inclusionary* screens identify companies that pledge themselves to specific conduct. Ceres (pronounced "series"), a national network of investors, environmental organizations, and other public interest groups, has developed a popular set of 10 principles (Ceres 2007).

Fiduciaries are reasonably concerned about a possible adverse effect that an SRI screen might have on a portfolio's return. Reasoning that social screens restrict investing decisions, could preclude fiduciaries from owning securities that could improve a portfolio's performance. *Could,* however, is not same as *would.* A 2003 analysis conducted by Morningstar, the mutual fund research company, provides evidence that SRI screens are not necessarily detrimental to financial performance (Israelsen 2010). The Prudent Investor Rule is sufficiently flexible to permit using all SRI strategies.

However, the average domestic stock SRI mutual fund tends to charge fees that are 0.21 percentage points (21 basis points) above the average non-SRI domestic stock fund, so socially responsible investors will need to shop around with care.

Program-Related Investing

Program-related investing (PRI) is a way to provide capital to tax-exempt nonprofits while allowing the owners of the capital to "make money." The Internal Revenue Code (IRC) defines program-related investing in the section applicable to foundations, but it offers guidance to any endowed nonprofit organization seeking investment opportunities:

> *The primary purpose is to accomplish one or more of the foundation's exempt purposes, production of income or appreciation of property is not a significant purpose, and influencing legislation or taking part in political campaigns on behalf of candidates is not a purpose. In determining whether a significant purpose of an investment is the production of income or the appreciation of property, it is relevant whether investors who engage in investments only for profit would be likely to make the investment on the same terms.* (U.S. Department of the Treasury 2010b)

PRI may be either at or below market rate. "If an investment incidentally produces significant income or capital appreciation, this is not, in the absence of other factors, conclusive evidence that a significant purpose is the production of income or the appreciation of property" (U.S. Department of the Treasury 2010b).

In the case of market-rate investments, PRI risks are probably disproportionate compared to market investments with similar returns. If the risks were not disproportionate, the borrower would find it equally advantageous to borrow from a commercial lender and would have no reason to obtain PRI. An implicit subsidy arises when an investor assumes above-normal risk. On the other hand, PRI below market rates provides an explicit subsidy and may or may not be riskier than other market-rate investments in a portfolio.

Just because PRI may expose an organization to higher risks on a few investments does not imply that the entire portfolio is riskier. If PRI returns are negatively correlated with returns on the other investments, overall risk could actually be lower for a given overall return. In practice a slight positive correlation is likely.

PRI is growing rapidly: 16.2 percent per year between 2002 and 2007, compared to 2.9 percent per year during the preceding 32 years (Cooch and Kramer 2007, 2).[16] Used judiciously, PRI reduces investment returns by a fraction of 1 percent—something on the order of the additional cost associated with management fees of an SRI fund.

Concluding Thoughts

Had the organization in the opening vignette adhered to a spending discipline spelled out in this chapter, the endowment might have been seven times larger and would have funded half of the budget and quite possibly much more (author's estimates).

Though a substantial portfolio of investments is a rich resource, it takes organization management to a new level of complexity. Endowed organizations face new and different risks, bodies of law to comprehend, and novel policy decisions, such as socially responsible investing. It is an important tool of values-centered management: "There has been a fundamental continuity in values among the [wealthy donors], even as there has been a shift in their composition and prominence" (Ostrower 1995, 139–140).

Endowment is a powerful tool for values-centered management because it permanently subsidizes goods and services below their cost of production, thereby severing production from profit. The management issues of financial capacity and sustainability do not disappear but are instead transformed. The formulas in Chapter 6 apply to organizations that are *not* presumptively endowed; the formulas of Chapter 8 apply to presumptively endowed organizations. Chapter 9 focuses on endowed grantmakers.

Appendix

Table 3.4 shows that the rule of thumb that separates endowed from ordinary organizations discriminates fairly well and produces plausible results. It introduces no size bias; in fact, endowed nonprofits at the 25th, 50th (median), and 75th percentiles actually spend slightly less on operations. Ordinary nonprofits at each of these percentiles have an insubstantial 10 percent of their assets in the form of securities and other investments. Endowed nonprofits, however, have total assets that are roughly five times larger at the 25th, 50th (median), and 75th percentiles. This gap is large but not surprising given that total assets include endowments.

TABLE 3.4 Comparison of Ordinary and Presumptively Endowed Nonprofits ($1,000s)

	25th Percentile	Median	75th Percentile
Ordinary (N = 86,567)			
Total assets	$ 201.30	$ 756.10	$ 2,855.50
Long-term financial assets*	$ 12.30	$ 49.50	$ 218.00
Productive assets†	$ 189.00	$ 706.60	$ 2,637.50
Spending on operations	$ 234.20	$ 688.00	$ 2,442.30
Endowed (N = 10,891)			
Total assets	$1,374.10	$4,198.90	$15,941.10
Long-term financial assets*	$1,096.40	$3,007.60	$10,517.10
Productive assets†	$ 277.70	$1,191.30	$ 5,424.00
Spending on operations	$ 171.20	$ 590.20	$ 2,340.60

*Long-term financial assets = Securities + Other investments.

†Productive assets = Total assets – (Securities + Other investments).

CHAPTER 4

Budgeting
Taking Control of the Present

When Helping Hand (not its real name) found itself chronically short of cash, it considered seeking bankruptcy protection in federal court. However, a review of its finances revealed it was an exceedingly successful fundraiser. In little more than six years, its unrestricted net assets had increased by $1.3 million, helped by a half-million-dollar bequest. Such success is rare in nonprofit bankruptcy cases, but the organization's cash balance was indeed shrinking. The board's inattention to proper budgeting was the reason, which the final section of this chapter explains.

Restricted gifts and income from endowment create budget issues not found in for-profit budgeting. There are no budgeting standards analogous to GAAP. This chapter discusses common principles and practices and, using these concepts, reconciles budgets to financial statements for organizations with and without endowments; property, plant, and equipment (PP&E); and donations. Reconciliation with IRS Form 990 is also explained. The final section analyzes Helping Hand's problem.

Budgeting Practices

Financial statements are retrospective reports of actual revenue and expenses. A budget, in contrast, is a prospective document that shows how an organization *plans* to pay for its spending in the coming year. (Note: *Spending*, as used here, refers to one of the following: cash expenditure, accrual expense, or encumbrances, which are to be explained later.) A budget also facilitates spending *control*. Therefore, a budget promotes accountability in stewardship of resources. The following principles are generally the same in for-profit businesses but they are worthwhile reviewing before examining templates for nonprofit budgets.

Statements and Budgets Should Reconcile

Because a budget is an instrument of financial control, sources of income and objects of spending should correspond to the accounting system's chart of accounts. A *chart of accounts* is a codebook that classifies transactions by type and (in large organizations) by administrative unit. An organization's finance director or (in large organizations) comptroller assigns an identification number from the chart of accounts to every transaction. For the sake of recording consistency, similar transactions have the same account number.

The following example is for illustration only. Codes in an actual chart may have more or fewer than four digits.

1000–1999: asset accounts
2000–2999: liability accounts
3000–3999: equity accounts
4000–4999: revenue accounts
5000–5999: expense accounts

Each category is divided into as many subcategories as an organization finds necessary and useful. Though a small number simplifies bookkeeping, it may impede tight budget control. While a large number facilitates control, it may bewilder all but skilled professionals. As an organization grows, it should consider occasionally revising its chart of accounts and upgrading the professionalism of finance staff.[1]

Each digit or group of digits in an account code has a specific meaning. In this example, the first digit indicates the accounting category of a transaction. The following digits identify the revenue source or object of spending. To hold managers of departments accountable for spending in their area of jurisdiction, codes must include department-specific numbers or the accounting system will be unable to report the amounts spent by each department and how much program service revenue it generated. It is pointless for budgets to show greater detail or different categories of spending than a chart of accounts allows.

Budgets and accounting systems often follow different rules. Chapter 2 discussed cash and accrual systems that are used in accounting. However, organizations that require prior authorization for all purchases manage their budgets according to a third set of rules that recognizes *encumbrances.* At the moment the comptroller authorizes an employee to place an order for goods (by issuing a purchase order), this officer deducts the entire authorized amount from the balance in the proper budgetary account. This is called encumbering the funds. This practice ensures that budget accounts will not be overdrawn accidentally due to the time lag between ordering goods and receiving a bill for them.[2]

At the end of the year, a statement of *activities* will recognize as expenses only obligations actually incurred through drawing down the balance on a purchase order. Balances remaining on purchase orders representing unspent authorization (*open* balances) are not reported on a statement of financial *position*. Some open balances will never be spent, so periodically it will be necessary to cancel them.

Finally, it is advisable that software that supports fund-raising be compatible with accounting and budgeting systems. Otherwise, reports on the same topic—for example, the amount of pledges that were paid in a given period—that are produced by incompatible systems may yield different numbers, requiring manual reconciliation.

Operations and Capital Budgets Should Be Separate

An operating budget is a plan for spending on goods and services with a useful life of one year or less and financing it with current income. Therefore, an *operating budget* using the chart of accounts just given would be primarily concerned with revenue and expense accounts.

Generally, *capital budgets* feature spending on property, plant, and equipment, but they may include spending on services such as remodeling of facilities or the services of investment bankers on bond transactions. An organization's capital budget is primarily concerned with asset and liability accounts and those revenue accounts pertaining to gifts and grants for capital purposes. A capital budget provides for purchases that: (1) are expensive, (2) have long useful lives, and therefore (3) are purchased less frequently than annually.

Capital budgets typically *exclude* physical assets that cost less than a given amount (the *capitalization threshold*) regardless of their useful life—for example, a stapler or a desk lamp. The capitalization threshold is determined by organization policy and typically is in the range $500 to $5,000, depending on the size of organization. The operating budget provides for spending on physical assets below the capitalization threshold.[3]

Operating Budgets Should Be Balanced

Deficits are dangerous, so operating revenue should usually equal or exceed operating expenses net of depreciation. Constructing a budget that includes a surplus is an insurance policy against a deficit and allows the organization to remain nimble and responsive to constituents. Unexpected adverse circumstances will create a smaller surplus than anticipated, but this unhappy situation is better than an actual deficit.

An annual surplus allows a nonprofit to accumulate resources needed to pay cash to acquire property, plant, or equipment, or to service a debt. The amount of planned surplus should depend on the long-term reliability of an organization's operating revenue. Higher risks require higher surpluses.

As stated at the beginning of the chapter, budgeting does not have standard rules like GAAP for accrual accounting, but the following patterns are common:

- Only operating revenues and operating expenses belong in a budget. Proceeds from borrowing and use of designated funds on a statement of financial position are not operating revenue; they are means of financing an annual deficit.
- One-time revenues, like bequests or proceeds from asset sales, should be used for capital or other spending that does not repeat annually. Small amounts in an operating budget are not harmful, so organizations should establish a policy that limits the amount of one-time income that will be included in an operating budget. If a bequest exceeds this amount, the organization should parcel it out to its operating budget over several years.
- Small amounts of capital spending may be incorporated directly into the operating budget, but large amounts should be programmed in a capital budget. The operating budget would then show transfers to the capital budget as a spending item.
- Pledges are revenue but obviously do not belong in an operating budget. When donors fulfill a pledge by writing a check, cash received is not classified as revenue; it is classified as net assets released from restrictions.
- A presumptively endowed organization should not include in its operating budget interest, dividends, capital gains, or new contributions to the endowment, but it should include withdrawals from the endowment pursuant to a spending formula.
- Interest expenses should be included in an operating budget and long-term borrowing should not be undertaken unless the asset it acquires increases an organization's cash flow or the preacquisition cash flow is sufficiently robust to absorb the interest cost.

Because operating budgets are prospective, actual income and spending may vary from their budgeted amounts. Management's responsibility is to keep total actual spending within total actual income despite any and all unexpected reductions in income or unavoidable increases in one or more spending accounts. This duty requires managers to have some flexibility to transfer spending authority between accounts.

Boards should adopt a policy authorizing transfers up to a fixed dollar limit (for small accounts) or percentage limit (for large accounts). Managers would have to return to their board and request a budget amendment if they needed additional transfer authority in specific situations. This safety valve ensures that boards are fully informed about major financial disruptions synchronously.

However, transfers undermine the utility of a budget for planning, control, and accountability. Large, pervasive, and routine transfers render a budget meaningless. Therefore, estimates of prospective revenues and spending in a budget proposal should be as accurate as possible.

After the fact, when an organization has a budget surplus, the board should explicitly consider whether to transfer it to an operating reserve or designate it for some other purpose. The default option is to build up the organization's bank balance.

Capital Budgets May Be Financed with Debt

Operating revenue is the only sustainable means of financing an operating budget. This source of funding is also available for capital projects (pay-as-you-go), but there are other options available, such as savings and borrowing. Borrowing is legitimate for capital assets because they have long productive lives, but the term of a debt should not exceed the useful life of the asset. Thus, a 30-year mortgage for real estate is appropriate. A 30-year loan for a motor vehicle is not. The depreciation schedule for different kinds of assets is an appropriate guideline.

Budget Structure

First and foremost, a budget is a control document. To facilitate accountability, every person with operating duties who reports directly to the chief executive should be responsible for a *portion* of the budget. Of course, the chart of accounts must reflect the organizational structure. These subbudgets should add to the total for the organization, assuming the line items representing internal transfers are adjusted to count revenue and spending in only one location. A complete budget document has supporting subbudgets in addition to the organization-wide budget.

Second, a budget is a tool for analysis and planning. Therefore, each program within an administrative unit's budget should have its own budget. At this level, the issue is whether programs cover their direct costs—costs attributable to that and only that program.

TABLE 4.1 Outline of Program-Level Budgets

Direct costs of Program A
minus: Program service revenue of A
minus: Contributions restricted to A
minus: Net assets released from restrictions for A
Equals: Gross margin (deficit) of Program A

minus: Program A's share of indirect cost at administrative unit level
minus: Program A's share of indirect cost at organization level
Equals: Net margin (deficit) of Program A

Table 4.1 shows how to calculate the difference between direct costs of a program and the revenue specific to that program, called *gross program margin*. Costs incurred in support of more than one program, including the organization as a whole, are indirect costs. Each program's share of indirect costs is based on a formula.

The simplest method for allocating indirect costs is to assign each program a proportionate share based on a single item of cost that all programs use, such as full-time equivalent (FTE) employees.[4]

The difference between all costs of a program (direct and indirect) and the revenue specific to that program is called *net program margin*. The suggestion to use FTEs to allocate indirect costs is based on the fact that significant cost reduction usually involves layoffs.[5] When a program's FTEs shrink, indirect costs allocated to that program will automatically shrink, as they should.

Programs having a positive net margin contribute an organization's budget surplus. They are a source of subsidy in the same manner as unrestricted contributions or endowment income. When it becomes necessary to balance a budget by cutting costs, cutting programs with positive net margins will worsen a budget deficit.

Programs with a negative net margin but a positive gross margin make a partial contribution to indirect costs. To reduce an organization's deficit by $1, it is necessary to cut more than $1 from such programs.

The only programs where cutting $1 reduces an organization's deficit by $1 are those with negative gross margins. Conversely, expanding programs with negative gross margins increases an organization's deficit or, if it has a surplus, expansion will reduce the surplus.

When an organization needs to cut spending, it will be at a disadvantage if its budget does not have the level of detail this section describes. During periods of surplus this structure allows organizations to compare programs based on the amount of general unrestricted income they absorb.

To illustrate: If Program A requires 45 cents for every dollar of direct expense and Program B requires 20 cents for every dollar of direct expense, we can say A is 2.25 times more expensive than B *to the organization.*

Part of a nonprofit board's fiduciary duty is to evaluate the social value of each program. If the board determines the programs to be equally valuable socially, then it is best to cut A and simultaneously to expand B until their claims on general unrestricted income are equal. However, to use the same example, if management believes that A is more or less 2.25 times more socially valuable than B, it should not re-allocate resources between the two programs.

Reconciling Budgets and Financial Statements

Financial statements are essential tools enabling boards and managers to pe-riodically review their organization's financial capacity and sustainability. They are external stakeholders' windows into an organization's finances. Budgets, however, are the primary tool for managing organization finances on a daily basis. Boards and managers must anticipate how budget decisions affect financial statements.

Conversely, boards and managers should understand how to design budget policy to achieve their goals for financial capacity and sustainability, which are defined in terms of quantities extracted from financial statements.

The next section explains how to reconcile budgets and financial state-ments, beginning with a review of various definitions regarding nonprofits' bottom line. The section continues with reconciliation in the simplest case, gradually increasing the level of complexity. A subsection on reconciling both documents to IRS Form 990 concludes the discussion.

Defining the Bottom Line

Although GAAP does not use the word *surplus*, it is commonly used by non-profits and simplifies exposition, so *Finance Fundamentals for Nonprofits* uses it throughout. GAAP requires nonprofits to report two bottom lines: (1) change in net assets, known as total surplus, and (2) change in unrestricted net assets, also known as unrestricted surplus. For nonprofits without an endowment, unrestricted surplus minus depreciation is close to a cash-basis budget surplus.

A third bottom line, operating surplus, is closer to cash-basis budgetary surplus for endowed organizations like Famous University. GAAP gives or-ganizations latitude to define operating surplus as relative to their specific situation. Generically, operating surplus is operating income minus operat-ing expenses.

Operating income of for-profits is defined as revenue from operations, but nonprofit operating revenue is income produced *for* operations: Nonprofit operating revenue = Unrestricted operating revenue + Net assets released from restrictions for operations – Total return on investments + Allowed spending from endowment pursuant to formula. If the calculated amount differs from the actual amount withdrawn, the calculated amount should be used in this formula.

Operating surplus appears as line A of Table 2.2, "Excess (deficiency) of operating revenues over operating expenses." Because GAAP does not define it, one may observe differences in definition and captioning between statements. *Finance Fundamentals for Nonprofits* defines operating surplus so that it is equivalent to unrestricted surplus for organizations without investments.

Encumbrance budgeting recognizes encumbrances as spending and unrestricted cash receipts as current income (unless the restrictions can be fulfilled within the year received). There is no encumbrance for depreciation, because it does not involve using cash. Thus, encumbrance budget rules correspond to neither cash nor accrual. For analytical purposes of this book, an encumbrance surplus is deemed to be closer to an operating cash surplus than to an operating accrual surplus.

The remaining portion of this section introduces a series of templates for increasingly complicated organizations: first, the simplest organizations, which own no investments or physical property (PP&E) and receive no gifts or grants; second, organizations that own physical property, but have no other complications; third, organizations having PP&E and receiving gifts and grants; and fourth, endowed organizations with all of the other complicating factors, too. As the discussion moves from one budget template to the next, italicized words indicate new elements.

The Simplest Organizations

The simplest budget shows only unrestricted current revenue (no gifts or grants), no endowment income, and no depreciation (because it does not own securities or property, plant, and equipment). Table 4.2 is a template for an operating budget of this type.

The only feature of Table 4.2 that distinguishes this budget from a for-profit business is special events, which are budgeted on a gross basis, meaning that they will have at least one revenue line and at least one expense line in a budget.[6] This is a GAAP requirement on financial statements: "To help explain the relationships of a nonprofit organization's ongoing major or central operations and activities, a statement of activities shall report the gross amounts of revenues and expenses" (SFAS 117; FASB 1993b, para. 24).

TABLE 4.2 Budget Template for Organizations without Gifts, Grants, or PP&E

OPERATING REVENUE Gross receipts from special events Program service revenue
Operating Revenue (Unrestricted Revenue for Operations) **OPERATING EXPENSES** Spending on special events Other expenses for operations
Operating Expenses
OPERATING SURPLUS = Operating revenue – Operating expenses
BUDGETARY SURPLUS (DEFICIT), Accrual Basis

	Subtract transfers to capital budget
CHANGE IN UNRESTRICTED NET ASSETS	**BUDGETARY SURPLUS (DEFICIT), Cash Basis**

Deficit financing: Transfers from board-designated funds

In this example, operating surplus equals budgetary surplus on an accrual basis and it also equals change in unrestricted net assets. An accrual-basis budget surplus (or a deficit) increases (or reduces) *unrestricted* net assets on a statement of financial position, whereas a cash-basis budget surplus (or a deficit) increases (or reduces) cash balances. For the hypothetical organization in this simple example, all of these definitions of surplus give the same result.

When a board identifies a portion of unrestricted net assets for particular purposes, these resources appear on a statement of financial position as "board-designated" net assets. Spending from these accounts is placed below the budgetary surplus because the resources were not received during the budget year. Resources that accumulated in past years and are now residing on a balance sheet finance a deficit, but do not eliminate it. This rule applies to both change in unrestricted net assets and budgetary surplus on a cash basis. Every board-designated fund that finances a budget should have its own line.

Organizations Having PP&E and Minimal Investments

Property ownership complicates surplus calculations, causing results to depend on a precise definition of surplus. Table 4.3 shows the effect of owning both financial and physical assets. Although the financial investments are small, the organization is not presumptively endowed.

Physical assets are a source of depreciation expense, which, other things being equal, reduces accrual-basis budget surpluses. Depreciation, however, does not use cash, so it must be added back when calculating budgetary surplus on a cash basis.

Interest and dividend income play an ambiguous role. Organizations with few bonds and stocks may consider interest and dividends as revenues for operations and include them in the operating budget. In such cases, interest and dividends would appear at the top of the table as operating revenue. Table 4.3 assumes they are not applied toward the operating budget.

TABLE 4.3 Budget Template—No Gifts and Grants, No Endowment, but Owning PP&E and Minimal Investments

OPERATING REVENUE Gross receipts from special events Program service revenue	
Operating Revenue (Unrestricted Revenue for Operations) **OPERATING EXPENSES** Spending on special events Interest on debt *Depreciation* Other expenses for operations	
Operating Expenses	
OPERATING SURPLUS = Operating Revenue − Operating Expenses	
Add interest and dividends	
BUDGETARY SURPLUS (DEFICIT), Accrual Basis	

Add capital gains and losses on financial investments	Add depreciation Subtract transfers to capital budget
CHANGE IN UNRESTRICTED NET ASSETS	**BUDGETARY SURPLUS (DEFICIT), Cash Basis**

Deficit financing: Transfers from board-designated funds

Note: New feature compared to Table 4.2 is in italics.

Therefore interest and dividends in this illustration are shown as part of an accrual-basis budgetary surplus but not part of the operating surplus.

Budgets should be balanced with recurring revenue. Proceeds from asset sales are one-time resources and should be used to finance capital spending, not operations. However, if an organization sells assets to support an operating budget, the full amount realized from the sale should be counted, not just the capital gains or losses as shown in IRS Form 990. Unrealized capital gains or losses obviously do not belong in a budget, because they cannot be spent.

An organization's cash position will change by accrual-basis budgetary surplus (deficit) plus depreciation minus transfers to the capital budget assuming that all funds appropriated to the capital budget will be spent.

Organizations Having Gifts and Grants

Gifts and grants introduce two issues into nonprofit budgeting: donor restrictions and noncash (in-kind) resources.

Noncash resources are negligible for many nonprofits, though there are notable exceptions such as resale stores and food pantries. GAAP requires reporting on the value of noncash gifts. "Quoted market prices, if available, are the best evidence of the fair value of monetary and nonmonetary assets, including services. If quoted market prices are unavailable, fair value may be estimated based on quoted market prices for similar assets, independent appraisals or valuation techniques such as the present value of estimated future cash flows" (FASB 1993a, para. 19). (See the Glossary for description of present value.)

There is no convention describing inclusion of noncash resources in an operating budget or whether to include them at all. There are several reasons *for* inclusion. The first is consistency with financial statements. Not reporting them makes it more difficult for managers to anticipate the impact a budget will have on financial statements. Second, including them shows how noncash and cash resources are changing relative to one another, allowing insight into service quality and productivity.

For example, additional personnel in a food pantry's budget could be the result of either additional food distributions or growing inefficiencies within the distribution system. There is no way to infer the cause without information on anticipated amounts of collected and distributed food. (See note 14 in Chapter 3.)

There are two ways to include noncash items. One is to treat them as any other revenue and expense items and include the value of donated items in the same section of a budget as other revenues and include the portion used in the expense section of the budget. Noncash capital gifts

TABLE 4.4 Budget Template—Owning PP&E and Receiving Gifts and Grants

	OPERATING REVENUE *Net assets released from restrictions for operations* *Unrestricted gifts and grants* Gross receipts from special events Program service revenue
A	Operating Revenue (Unrestricted Revenue for Operations)
	OPERATING EXPENSES Spending on special events Interest on debt Depreciation Other expenses for operations
B	Operating Expenses
	NONCASH OPERATING REVENUES AND EXPENSES *Dollar value of noncash donations for current use* *Dollar value of currently used noncash donations*
C	*Net Accumulation (Depletion) of Noncash Operating Resources*
	OPERATING SURPLUS = A − B + C
	Add interest and dividends
	BUDGETARY SURPLUS (DEFICIT), Accrual Basis

Add net assets released from
   restrictions for capital
Add capital gifts used in this period
Add capital gains and losses
	Add depreciation
	Subtract net accumulation
	   of noncash resources
	Subtract change in pledges
	Subtract transfers to capital budget

CHANGE IN UNRESTRICTED **NET ASSETS**	**BUDGETARY SURPLUS** **(DEFICIT), Cash Basis**

Deficit financing: Transfers from board-designated funds and asset sales

New features compared to Table 4.3 are in italics.

should not bypass the operating budget, because they are technically unrestricted and are needed to reconcile the operating budget surplus with
change in unrestricted net assets on financial statements.

However, noncash items are not easily fungible, so separating them
from the objects of spending in a budget is generally preferable. Table 4.4
shows how this might be done. Noncash gifts such as food are unrestricted,

so the budget should show noncash capital gifts as being simultaneously transferred to the capital budget (lower right of Table 4.4).

If managers choose to exclude noncash donations from a budget, they must add the net accumulation (total value of noncash items received minus total value of noncash items used) to accrual-basis budgetary surplus to reconcile with the change in unrestricted net assets reported on financial statements.

The second major budget issue regarding donations is donor restrictions. As Chapter 2 indicated, GAAP requires reporting all pledges as being temporarily restricted.

When a pledge is fulfilled (paid) and an organization complies with donor restrictions, the assets (net of associated liabilities) are reclassified as unrestricted and appear on financial statements as "net assets released from restrictions" (first line on Table 4.4). It is reasonable that these funds be considered as operating revenue when they are used, not when they are given.

To illustrate, assume an organization receives an unrestricted multiyear grant in one payment. The first year is reported as unrestricted revenue, but the portion of the grant applicable to subsequent years is classified as temporarily restricted revenue. In each year of the grant an additional amount will be reclassified as unrestricted.

If a restricted gift is for a capital project, it should bypass the operating budget and go directly into the capital budget. If gifts are raised for a capital project but they are not accompanied by a gift agreement, they are technically unrestricted. In the interest of consistency between the budget and financial statements, the budget should show all unrestricted gifts as revenue (second line, Table 4.4) and simultaneously show how much is being transferred to the capital budget (lower right-hand corner, Table 4.4).

Organizations Having Endowments

Endowed organizations often own property and receive public support, so they are among the most financially complex nonprofits. Table 4.5 is a template for a budget that draws on an endowment.

The amount reported as operating revenue is that amount the spending formula permits to be withdrawn for operations, not the actual amount withdrawn. Faced with a budget shortfall based on the nominal withdrawal from the endowment, a board might approve spending from the endowment in excess of the nominal amount. Subsequent actual end-of-year data would show spending equal to unrestricted revenue for the year plus actual withdrawal from the endowment, and the organization would appear to have had a balanced budget. However, exceeding a nominal spending rate is unsustainable because it causes the purchasing power of the endowment to

TABLE 4.5 Budget Template—Endowed Organizations

	OPERATING REVENUE *Withdrawal from endowment pursuant to a spending formula* Net assets released from restrictions for operations Unrestricted gifts and grants Gross receipts from special events Program service revenue
A	Total Operating Revenue (Unrestricted Revenue for Operations)
	OPERATING EXPENSES Spending on special events Interest on debt Depreciation Other expenses for operations
B	Total Operating Expenses
	NONCASH OPERATING REVENUES AND EXPENSES Dollar value of noncash donations for current use Dollar value of currently used noncash donations
C	Net Accumulation (Depletion) of Noncash Operating Resources
	OPERATING SURPLUS = Operating Revenue – Operating Expenses
	BUDGETARY SURPLUS (DEFICIT), Accrual Basis

Subtract withdrawal from endowment
   pursuant to a spending formula
 	
Add total return on investments
	Add depreciation
	Subtract net accumulation
	   of noncash resources
	Subtract new pledges
	Subtract transfers to capital budget

CHANGE IN UNRESTRICTED NET ASSETS	**BUDGETARY SURPLUS (DEFICIT), Cash Basis**

Deficit financing: Transfers from board-designated funds, asset sales, and withdrawals from endowment in excess of a spending formula

New features compared to Table 4.4 are in italics.

diminish over time. So, it is better to acknowledge a deficit in the operating budget financed by withdrawals from the endowment.

For accounting and budgeting purposes, total return (current income plus capital gains or losses) is divided into two parts. One part is the amount the spending formula permits to be withdrawn for operations. This part is included in operating revenue. (In Table 2.2 it is "Investment return designated for operations.") The second part is total return minus the first part, and this is included in change in unrestricted net assets. (In Table 2.2 it is "Investment gains reinvested.") When total return is less than permitted spending, the second part is negative. Thus, there would be nothing to reinvest in Table 2.2.

Reconciling Budgets and IRS Form 990

The financial sections of Form 990 (old form parts I, II, and IV; new form parts VIII, IX, and X) provide much of the same information found in general-purpose financial statements. The line numbers given in this section refer to the old (pre-2008) form because they were consecutive page to page. Translation to lines on the new form is straightforward.

Total surplus using IRS 990 data equals end-of-year net assets (line 73B old form) minus beginning-of-year net assets (line 73A old form). For organizations with neither investments nor restricted gifts, total surplus is the difference between total revenues and total expenses on Form 990.

Unrestricted surplus equals end-of-year unrestricted net assets (line 67B old form) minus beginning-of-year unrestricted net assets (line 67A old form).

The revenue sections of both old and new forms do not report unrealized capital gains or losses and make no distinction between restricted and unrestricted income. The difference between total revenues and total expenses (part I, line 18, old form) is neither wholly accrual nor wholly cash and can be misleading.

Table 4.6 illustrates the relationships between change in unrestricted net assets and (1) total assets and (2) surplus per Form 990 as defined previously. They are straightforward.

TABLE 4.6 Reconciliation to Surplus per IRS Form 990

Change in Unrestricted Net Assets
Add change in temporarily restricted gifts and grants
Add change in permanently restricted gifts and grants
Change in Total Net Assets
Subtract unrealized capital gains and losses on investments
Subtract net increase in noncash gifts
Surplus on IRS Form 990

Concluding Thoughts

Despite appearing fairly strong by most objective measures, Helping Hand, the organization featured at the beginning of this chapter, was financially distressed by problems of its own making: Unplanned capital spending depleted the organization's cash while leaving unrestricted net assets unaffected. Helping Hand also used proceeds from two capital campaigns to pay debt service—including interest—on a substantial debt.

The organization should have used gifts for capital to prepay debt instead of merely paying debt service. This may seem like a technical matter of no consequence, but, as any homeowner knows, the first few years of mortgage payments largely pay interest. If this organization had used proceeds from capital campaigns to reduce mortgage principal, it would have reduced monthly payments as well—eventually to a point where the operating budget could support the interest portion of debt service.

Proper budgeting promotes values-centered management, enabling nonprofits to be good stewards of gifts and grants entrusted to them for specific purposes. Helping Hand raised money for capital, but spent it on interest instead. The group assumed interest was part of a capital program, but they were mistaken. After two successful capital campaigns, Helping Hand is still saddled with substantial debt.

CHAPTER 5

Nonprofits in History and Tax Law
Why Nonprofits Do What They Do

The Sierra Club is one of the largest, best known, and most politically active nonprofit organizations in the United States, but it is actually *three* separate organizations: a membership association, a supporting foundation, and a political action committee.[1]

As the Sierra Club expanded its advocacy activity in the 1950s, it became concerned over a possible threat to its tax deductibility, so in 1960 it created a separate educational foundation. Six years later, after a major fight to block construction of two dams on the Colorado River, the Internal Revenue Service (IRS) withdrew recognition of the Club's 501(c)(3) tax status and its foundation became the fiscal sponsor of the Club's educational activities.

As a result of its restructuring, contributions for educational activities remained deductible whereas contributions for political activities did not. If this new arrangement has had an adverse impact on the Sierra Club, it is not obvious.

As this example shows, legal structure is the key to pursuing a full and complete agenda. It pays to know the law. Conversely, failure to follow the law can result in fines and, in some cases, loss of tax-exemption.

The federal tax system performs several functions:

1. *Support* through tax exemption.
2. *Equity* through exemption and deductibility of charitable contributions.
3. *Regulatory* through various rules of conduct.

4. The so-called *border patrol* between sectors through prohibitions on private gain (inurement) and political activity (Simon, Dale, and Chisolm 2006, 267).[2]

This chapter covers all four functions, describing major categories of tax-exempt nonprofits and how the Internal Revenue Code (IRC) circumscribes their operations. Each section begins with a brief history of important events in the evolution of the associated archetype. The law is complex, and one chapter cannot contain it all. Chapter 3 covers the law of institutional investing and Chapter 11 covers corporate transparency law applicable to nonprofits (Sarbanes-Oxley). Regrettably, this chapter does not have the space to treat estate and gift taxes.

Classification

Table 5.1 shows 31 categories of exempt organizations. The column labeled "Reporting" refers to the number of organizations filing an informational return with the IRS (Form 990). Religious congregations and certain other religious organizations, and state and local governments and other public bodies are exempt from filing. Beginning with the 2010 tax year, tax-exempt nonprofits with less than $200,000 of income and $500,000 of assets may file a shorter 990-EZ. Public organizations with less than $50,000 of income may file a postcard notice of operation 990-N. All private foundations must file a 990-PF, regardless of income or assets (GuideStar 2010).

If a category has fewer than 100 entities nationwide, Table 5.1 does not indicate the number to improve readability of the table overall.

Membership Associations

Membership associations have been part of the fabric of civilization for millennia but had no permanent legal status until the first century when Roman law provided for corporations (Fremont-Smith 1965). In the medieval period merchant and craft guilds regulated local economies and confraternities were popular. Many of the latter provided burial services for their members and were sources of public charity (Black 2001). Confraternities were prototypes for modern fraternal benefit societies.

Political authorities have often been suspicious of membership associations. The Roman Emperor Trajan, fearing that membership associations were nuclei for sedition, outlawed all of them, including volunteer fire brigades (Cotter 1996, 82). George Washington warned the country in his farewell address that they were breeding grounds for ambitious men.

TABLE 5.1 Federal Tax Exempt Entities, 2005

Code	Section		Recognized	Reporting	Reported Expenses (Bn $)
501(c)	(1)	Corporations organized by act of Congress	—	—	—
501(c)	(2)	Title-holding corporations for exempt organizations	5,850	2,783	1,220
501(c)	(3)	Religious, charitable, and similar organizations	984,386	400,709	1,099,799
		Including education		*78,074*	*165,339*
		Including health		*26,904*	*637,067*
		Including philanthropic and grantmaking foundations		*72,825*	*54,842*
501(c)	(4)	Civic leagues and social welfare organizations	116,890	24,327	44,067
501(c)	(5)	Labor, agricultural, and horticultural organizations	56,819	20,591	18,844
501(c)	(6)	Business leagues, chambers of commerce, and so on	71,878	30,798	29,872
501(c)	(7)	Social and recreational clubs	56,369	16,567	10,466
501(c)	(8)	Fraternal beneficiary societies and associations	63,318	7,077	12,919
501(c)	(9)	Voluntary employee-beneficiary associations	10,088	6,887	126,975
501(c)	(10)	Domestic fraternal societies and associations	20,944	2,822	541
501(c)	(11)	Teachers' retirement fund associations	—	—	—
501(c)	(12)	Benevolent life insurance associations, and so on	5,901	3,540	34,807
501(c)	(13)	Cemetery companies	9,808	2,221	790
501(c)	(14)	State-chartered credit unions and mutual reserve funds	3,565	1,304	14,366
501(c)	(15)	Mutual insurance companies and associations	1,646	558	2
501(c)	(16)	Cooperative organizations to finance crop operations	—	—	—
501(c)	(17)	Supplemental unemployment benefit trusts	300	115	325

(*continued*)

TABLE 5.1 (*Continued*)

Code	Section		Recognized	Reporting	Reported Expenses (Bn $)
501(c)	(18)	Employee-funded pension trusts (before 6/25/59)	—	—	146
501(c)	(19)	War veterans organizations	35,113	6,576	1,103
501(c)	(20)	Legal service organizations	—	—	—
501(c)	(21)	Black lung benefits trusts	—	—	—
501(c)	(22)	Withdrawal liability payment funds	—	—	—
501(c)	(23)	Veterans organizations created before 1880	—	—	—
501(c)	(24)	Trusts per Employment Retirement Security Act of 1974	—	—	—
501(c)	(25)	Title-holding corporations or trusts with multiple parents	1,133	931	913
501(c)	(26)	Organizations providing health coverage for high-risk persons	—	—	—
501(c)	(27)	Workers' compensation reinsurance organizations	—	—	—
501(d)		Religious and apostolic organizations	—	—	—
501(e)		Cooperative hospital service organizations	—	—	—
501(f)		Cooperative service organizations of operating education organizations	—	—	—
Other		Organizations NEC, including charitable risk pools	4,105	163	424
		Total	1,448,485	528,023	1,401,454

*State-sponsored; — indicates number reporting is < 100; omitted data in total.

Source: Wing, Pollak, and Blackwood (2008), Table 1.1; copyright by the Urban Institute and used with permission.

Until the industrial revolution, membership associations were local (Smith 2000). In the United States, the period from 1820 through 1850 was particularly important for formation of national membership associations, and growth continued after the Civil War. Since the 1960s the number of national membership associations in the United States has more than doubled to about 26,000 today.

Membership in associations has been stable from the early 1980s to the early 2000s, although membership of large federated (chapter-based) membership associations has been in decline (Skocpol 2003). Meanwhile, at the local level the number of (local and national combined) per 1,000 of population peaked at 5.4 in 1900 and then slowly declined to 4 in 1940 (Gamm and Putnam 1999).[3]

The IRC classifies membership organizations by their exempt purpose as follows (except cooperatives), where the subpart of Section 501 is given in parentheses:

Public organizations and private foundations (c)(3)
Civic leagues and social welfare organizations (c)(4)
Labor, agricultural, and horticultural organizations (c)(5)
Business leagues and professional associations (c)(6)
Social and recreational clubs (c)(7)
Fraternal beneficiary societies (c)(8)
Voluntary employee-beneficiary societies (c)(9)
Domestic fraternal societies (c)(10)
War veterans associations (c)(19)
War veterans associations created before 1880 (c)(23)
Religious and apostolic associations (d)

The IRC requires tax-exempt membership associations to be organized for purposes other than profit and prohibits them from distributing net earnings to members or shareholders. Nevertheless, they may be critical to profit making by their members. The New York Stock Exchange prior to 2006 was a membership association of traders. Professional football leagues, which are coordinating bodies for profit-making businesses, are 501(c)(6) organizations.

The IRS recognizes over 358,000 tax-exempt membership associations. We may safely assume that many more are too small to bother seeking recognition of their exempt status. Therefore, only 101,000 report annually to the IRS. Their expenses total $105 billion.[4]

Cooperatives

"A cooperative is an enterprise in which individuals voluntarily organize to provide themselves and others with goods and services via democratic control and for mutually shared benefit. Members generally contribute to, and control via a democratic process, the cooperative's capital" (Reference for Business 2011).

The earliest cooperative probably emerged in the Middle Ages in Italian city-states. "Members of the [Peruzzi] lineage united to form the property acquisition corporation of 1282 . . . but company shareholdings were strictly individual and mainly owned by those prepared to work for it" (Hunt 1994, 37).

The Peruzzi family's business corporation was similar to a modern cooperative because it was owned in part by unrelated persons, some ownership shares were based on work performed, and shares could not be transferred to nonworkers at the shareholder's sole discretion.

Modern cooperatives can be traced to a food cooperative founded in 1844 in Rochdale, England (ICA 2007). Today, cooperatives are prominent in France and Quebec. The largest cooperative grouping in the world is the Israeli Kibbutzim, founded in 1910 (Altman 2009). The Mondragon Cooperative Association, a Spanish workers' cooperative consisting of over 160 companies in manufacturing, distribution, and finance, is another exemplar of a national cooperative movement.

In a large sample of organizations incorporated as cooperatives, 37 percent are recognized as tax-exempt and file a 990 return, 43 percent are taxable cooperatives and file a 990c or 1120c return, 13 percent are taxable corporations and file a corporate 1120 return, and the remainder file as government entities or partnerships (Deller et al. 2009, 7).

"Cooperatives calculate taxable income and use tax rates like other corporations"; however, they may deduct dividends paid on capital stock and amounts paid or allocated to patrons on a basis other than patronage (Frederick 2005, 28). Patrons are taxed on their full patronage refund, including noncash items.[5] Earnings from noncooperative ventures are taxed as ordinary corporate income.

The following types of cooperatives may be recognized as nonprofit by special provisions of the IRC (the subpart of Section 501 is given in parentheses):

Benevolent life insurance associations (c)(12)
State-chartered credit unions and other mutual financial organizations (c)(14)
Mutual insurance companies (c)(15)
Cooperative organizations to finance crop operations (c)(16)
Cooperative hospital service organizations (e)
Cooperative service organizations of operating education organizations (f)
Farmers' cooperatives (Section 521)

Foundations

Although *foundations* are commonly perceived as grantmaking institutions, tax law identifies them based on how they raise funds, not how they spend them. Many of the oldest and most famous foundations were established by bequest.

It seems strange today, but for centuries the law in Europe and the United States raised barriers to bequests of property to institutions. (The word *nonprofit* did not exist in this period.) Finally, in 1844 the U.S. Supreme Court (*Vidal et al. v. The Mayor, Aldermen, and Citizens of Philadelphia*) secured for donors a right to establish charitable trusts.[6] Most states updated their laws to conform to federal law, but several states continued restrictions on testamentary gifts to charity into the twentieth century (Fisch 1964, 307).

Arguably the first modern foundation of national importance, the Peabody Education Fund, was organized in 1867 to help rebuild devastated Southern states. The Russell Sage Foundation, which Hall (2006) calls the "first modern grant making foundation," was established in 1907 "for the improvement of social and living conditions in the United States of America." In 1914 the first Community Foundation began in Cleveland, and the concept quickly spread throughout the Midwest and Northeast (Hammack 1998, 335).

The IRC divides 501(c)(3) organizations into public organizations and private foundations. The default category is private foundation. An applicant for 501(c)(3) recognition must pass a series of tests. Failure on any one is sufficient to recognize the organization as a private foundation.

First an organization must fulfill the requirements for recognition as a 501(c)(3)-exempt organization. An applicant must pass one organization test and several operations tests.

The organization test is simple: "An organization's organizing documents (articles of incorporation, trust documents, articles of association) must: limit its purposes to those described in section 501(c)(3) of the IRC; not expressly permit activities that do not further its exempt purpose(s), i.e., unrelated activities; and permanently dedicate its assets to exempt purposes." Exempt purposes are:

> *Charitable, religious, educational, scientific, literary, testing for public safety, fostering national or international amateur sports competition, and preventing cruelty to children or animals. The term* charitable *is used in its generally accepted legal sense and includes relief of the poor, the distressed, or the underprivileged; advancement of religion; advancement of education or science; erecting or maintaining public buildings, monuments, or works; lessening the burdens of government; lessening neighborhood tensions; eliminating prejudice and discrimination; defending human and civil rights secured by law; and combating community deterioration and juvenile delinquency.* (U.S. Department of the Treasury 2010a)

The operations tests require that a 501(c)(3) organization

1. *must ensure that its earnings do not inure to the benefit of any private shareholder or individual;*
2. *must not operate for the benefit of private interests such as those of its founder, the founder's family, its shareholders or persons controlled by such interests;*
3. *must not operate for the primary purpose of conducting a trade or business that is not related to its exempt purpose, such as a school's operation of a factory;*
4. *must not engage in political activity;*
5. *may not have purposes or activities that are illegal or violate fundamental public policy; and*
6. *must restrict its lobbying activities to an insubstantial part of its total activities.* (U.S. Department of the Treasury 2009, 3; numbering not in the original)

Organizations that pass these tests[7] are subjected to a series of other tests to determine whether they qualify as a public organization. To be classified as a public organization, a 501(c)(3) applicant must pass one of three tests described in the next section. Organizations that fail all three of these tests are then classified as private foundations.[8]

It is more advantageous to be a public organization. First, donors to public organizations may deduct gifts up to 50 percent of their adjusted gross income, whereas donors to private foundations may deduct no more than 30 percent (Bryce 2000, 197). Second, private nonoperating foundations must distribute at least 5 percent of the value of their assets in the preceding year.[9] Also, private foundations

1. must pay an excise tax on their net investment income,
2. have restrictions on self-dealing with their substantial contributors and certain other persons,
3. have limits on their holdings in private businesses, and
4. may not make investments that interfere with fulfilling their exempt purposes (U.S. Department of the Treasury 2009).[10]

The Tax Reform Act of 1969 limited self-dealing and donor control, regulated investment practices and foundation payout, and required filing financial reports (Hall 2006, 54). Note: The term analogous to *spending formula* for grantmakers is *payout rate.*

Donor-advised funds have been around since the 1930s (Jones 2004), but in the 1990s they blossomed as charitable affiliates of for-profit mutual funds, allowing small donors to effectively set up their own limited life grantmaking organizations cheaply.[11]

What we know about foundation finances comes from the annual report an organization files with the IRS: 990-PF. In 2003 public organizations numbered over 300,000, whereas foundations numbered 59,637.[12]

An important subset of foundations is *operating foundations*, which "conduct their own research programs or provide a direct service" (Bryce 2000, 94). They are *not* primarily grantmakers. In the same year, there were 4,159 operating foundations owning assets of $27.9 billion and making $1.7 billion in grants. A private foundation that is not an operating foundation is, by default, a *nonoperating* foundation.

Public Organizations

The first recognizable nonprofit in colonial America was Harvard University, which was incorporated by the Massachusetts colony (O'Neill 1989, 54) nearly a century before the first commercial trading corporation (Micklethwait and Wooldridge 2003, 43).[13]

In 1751 Benjamin Franklin helped his friend, Dr. Thomas Bond, to raise money for the first private hospital in colonial America, the Pennsylvania Hospital for the Sick Poor. Franklin persuaded the governing body of the Pennsylvania colony to appropriate 50 percent of the amount needed, with public expenditure contingent upon private philanthropy raising the first 50 percent. The tactic quickly raised the needed money (McCarthy 2003, 19).

Did Franklin invent the contingent matching grant? Certainty is elusive, but without question he was an unparalleled social innovator. He is credited with organizing the first subscription library (1731), the first volunteer fire company (1736), and possibly the first learned society (American Philosophical Society, 1743). His last will and testament created a surprisingly modern microfinance program to help apprentices become established in business (McCarthy 2003, 79).

Finally, "General acts provided incorporation for a broad range of charitable, religious, and literary purposes in Pennsylvania in 1791 and for libraries in New York in 1796 and in New Jersey in 1799. Fire companies could be chartered under general acts of Virginia of 1788 and of Kentucky of 1798" (Hurst 1970, 134).[14]

The distinction between for-profit activity and activity of other types was not fully appreciated until the late nineteenth century. The concept of "nonprofit" did not achieve permanent salience until the Income Tax Act of 1913. The term *nonprofit organization* did not appear in newspapers until 1953. However, academics and policy makers did not view nonprofit organizations as a coherent sector of the economy until the 1970s

(Hall 2006). Only contributions to 501(c)(3) organizations are categorically tax deductible to the donor.[15]

As the previous section pointed out, an organization applying for 501(c)(3) recognition will be subjected to three tests to determine if it qualifies as a public organization, which is the more favorable category.[16] The tests are as follows:

1. Section 509(a)(1). These organizations must either (1) receive at least 30 percent of their income from a governmental unit or from the general public or (2) receive at least 10 percent from these sources and meet a "facts and circumstances" test (Bryce 2000, 70–71). Public support includes net income from unrelated businesses and, of course, gifts, contributions, gross investment income, and the value of facilities furnished by government if such facilities are usually rented or owned.
2. Section 509(a)(2). These organizations must both receive at least 30 percent of their income from a governmental unit or from the general public and *not* normally receive more than 33 percent of their income from investments and unrelated business income combined. Public support for these organizations includes receipts from the sale of mission-related goods and services. "This latter test has the effect of forcing the search for public financial support even for organizations that could be self-supporting. As price is the measure of value in a commercial setting, public welfare is a measure of value with these types of nonprofits" (Bryce 2000, 74). Evidently the dollar volume of gifts from numerous sources is an indicator of public welfare.
3. Section 509(a)(3). These organizations exist specifically to benefit one or more public organizations. Such organizations, called *supporting organizations,* must be "operated, supervised, or controlled by"; "supervised and controlled in connection with"; or "operated in connection with" a public organization (U.S. Department of the Treasury 2010d).[17] Other 509(a)(3) organizations may be merely "operated in connection with" public organizations working "in tandem with them but are formed by them and are not their subordinates" (Bryce 2000, 80). Section 509(a)(3) is a flexible tool for managing joint ventures and for owning and managing real estate or investment portfolios.

Not every grantmaker is a foundation, and some foundations distribute very little money: 20 percent of private foundations do not give grants, but 50 percent of operating foundations and 95 percent of nonoperating foundations do give them.[18]

Tax-exempt organizations, other than private foundations, must file using Form 990 or the shorter Form 990-EZ, which is designed for use by midsize tax-exempt organizations and nonexempt charitable trusts. (The threshold for midsize is income $1 million or lower and assets of $2.5 million or less.) A supporting organization must generally file, regardless of income or asset size.

Unrelated Business Income Tax

The tax on unrelated business income (UBI) dates to 1948 when New York University's law school received a bequest in the form of a pasta factory. When it decided to keep the factory and use the profits to finance scholarships, taxpaying pasta manufacturers cried foul and persuaded Congress to adopt a tax on the net income of all businesses unrelated to exempt purposes. The fairness question is deferred until Chapter 10. This section examines the resulting tax.[19]

Although the IRC does not provide a specific threshold (a so-called *bright line* test), empirically it seems that unrelated income greater than 25 percent of gross revenue poses a serious threat to retention of tax exemption (Yetman and Yetman 2008). One-third of nonprofits with assets over $100 million conduct taxable business activity through taxable subsidiaries, which is 15 percent of the largest 15,000 nonprofits (676). Taxable subsidiaries are further discussed in Chapter 10.

An exempt organization is not taxed on income related to its exempt purpose (i.e., mission), even if it is derived from a "trade or business." However, exempt nonprofits that deviate from their exempt mission are liable for a tax on unrelated business income.

Unrelated business income is the income from a

1. *trade or business*
2. *regularly carried on by an exempt organization and*
3. *not substantially related to the performance by the organization of its exempt purpose or function, except that the organization use the profits derived from this activity.* (U.S. Department of the Treasury 2010e, 3; numbering added)[20]

A *trade or business* "generally includes any activity carried on for the production of income from selling goods or performing services. . . . Business activities of an exempt organization are considered *regularly carried on* if they show a frequency and continuity, and are pursued in a manner similar to comparable commercial activity of nonexempt organizations. A business activity is *not substantially related* to an organization's exempt purpose if it does not contribute importantly to accomplishing that purpose (other than through the production of funds)" (U.S. Department of the Treasury 2010e, 3).

Unrelated business income tax (UBIT) is a legal minefield. It is impossible to rely on intuition to determining what will or will not expose a tax-exempt organization to tax liability. A few examples illustrate this point.

- A tax-exempt organization can put its logo on a credit card, but promoting the card renders the income taxable. It can own a parking lot, but leasing it to a parking lot operator may result in taxation of the rental income. Tours must be related to the exempt purpose of the organization, must be educational, and must be unlike commercial packages.
- When leasing its mailing lists, an exempt organization may not be involved in controlling how the mailing list is used, may not participate in profits from use of the list, and may not promote a product of the lessee. Leasing to one's own subsidiary doesn't change the tax consequences.
- Corporate sponsorships require extra caution to avoid the appearance of an endorsement of the sponsor's product or an exhortation to buy the product. Income is taxable if it is pegged to the size of the audience or if sponsorship is exclusive.
- Some issues are particularly relevant to membership associations: different classes of dues-paying members and advertising revenue where circulation income exceeds production costs.
- Games of chance cannot be the primary mission of a tax-exempt organization. Income from games of chance is exempt only if state law allows nonprofits (and only nonprofits) to conduct such games.
- However, a trade or business where "substantially all of the work is performed for the organization without compensation [i.e., volunteers] is not an unrelated trade or business." (U.S. Department of the Treasury 2010e, 7)

If an organization's unrelated business and its exempt activities are completely separate, one can argue that UBIT promotes efficient resource allocation (Sansing 1998, 295). However, it is common for these different activities to share overhead costs and, in such cases, cost shifting from the taxable activity to the exempt activity is frequently observed (Yetman 2001a, 2001b). Cost shifting encourages inefficient investments (Sansing 1998, 301).

Intermediate Sanctions

The requirements regarding compensation and sanctions for paying excessively as described in this section apply only to 501(c)(3) and 501(c)(4) nonprofits.[21]

Since 1884 the Bishop Trust's mission has been to provide free elementary and secondary education to indigenous Hawaiians and their descendants. As the largest landowner in Hawaii, its total assets in 1997 were larger than those of Harvard and Yale combined. At the time, its trustees were receiving annual compensation of $800,000 to $900,000. Objections were muted until the Trust announced major budget cuts affecting the schools.[22]

The IRS threatened to withdraw recognition from the Trust unless the trustees resigned or were removed from office. By the end of 1999 all but one trustee (a recent appointee) had resigned or been removed by court order. In 2001 the IRS issued regulations pursuant to new law defining excess benefits and providing for restitution and taxes on the excess benefits (called *intermediate sanctions*).[23] The following description is sketchy. Interested persons and organizations should seek professional legal advice.

The law targets persons who exercise "substantial control" over an organization (*disqualified persons*). Officers and directors, their families, any organization owned 35 percent or more directly or indirectly by such persons, and anyone with responsibility for managing the organization's financial assets are always covered.

Depending on facts and circumstances, founders, substantial contributors, consultants, and even vendors may be included depending on how their compensation is calculated. Not covered are other 501(c)(3) organizations, employees paid less than $80,000 per year (a figure the IRS adjusts annually), and persons acting *solely* as an attorney, accountant, investment manager, or investment adviser.

Compensation beyond that which is reasonable for services rendered constitutes *excess benefits*. Compensation is not merely wages and salaries. It also includes the value of property above fair market value, deferred salary, retirement annuities, severance packages, and organization-provided perquisites such as homes, cars, cell phones, personal computers, and whole-life insurance policies naming family members as beneficiaries. Furthermore, compensation includes all benefits provided by entities controlled by an exempt organization.

Not included are economic benefits provided to a volunteer, a member, or a donor solely on account of a contribution, not targeted to specific individuals.

Reasonable compensation is the amount a similar organization pays for similar services in similar circumstances. Compensation is *presumed* to be reasonable if:

1. The compensation arrangement is approved in advance by the board or a committee composed entirely of individuals without a conflict of interest (the decision entity).
2. The decision entity obtained and relied on appropriate data as to comparability in making its determination.
3. The decision entity adequately and *contemporaneously* documented the basis for determination of reasonableness. Such compensation comparisons may include compensation paid by taxable organizations (TaxAlmanac 2005).

Upon final determination of excess benefit, the disqualified person must repay the amount of the excess with interest plus a 25 percent penalty tax. If restitution is not made within the taxable period, an additional excise tax equal to 200 percent of the excess benefit is imposed. Organization managers who knowingly, willfully, and without reasonable cause participate in the transactions resulting in the 25 percent penalty tax on a disqualified person are liable for a tax equal to 10 percent of the excess benefit. Moreover, the exempt organization may not reimburse.

Between 2004 and 2006 the IRS sampled 1,800 charities, found 600 cases of flaws in reporting executive compensation, and asked 40 individuals to pay $20 million (Strom 2007).

Lobbying and Political Action

The requirements regarding lobbying and political action as described in this section apply only to 501(c)(3) *public organizations.*[24]

Lobbying and advocacy activities are restrained by the IRC one of two ways: (1) the default option requires "no substantial part" of an organization's activities to involve influencing legislation, or (2) an organization may elect to be regulated by Section 501(h) of the IRC, which provides "bright line" guidance on what is impermissible activity and how much can be spent.

An organization that devotes a "substantial part" of its activities to lobbying and advocacy (the default option) may lose its tax exemption, but if an organization elects to be covered by Section 501(h) and fails to abide by its requirements it is merely fined, unless the errant behavior persists. (Only the default option is available to private foundations.) If either option is unacceptable to a 501(c)(3) organization, create a 501(c)(4) organization to lobby, which can lobby without restrictions other than a requirement to pursue a social welfare agenda.

For an organization to be tax-exempt under section 501(c)(3), it cannot "participate in, or intervene in (including the publishing or distributing of statements) any political campaign on behalf of (or in opposition to) any candidate for public office" (U.S. Department of the Treasury 2011b).

However, a 501(c)(3) organization may establish a PAC, which may give $5,000 to a candidate committee per election, or up to $15,000 annually to any national party committee, and $5,000 annually to any other PAC. The PAC may receive up to $5,000 from any one individual.

There are two kinds of PACs: separate segregated funds (SSFs) and nonconnected committees (NCs). SSFs are established and administered by corporations, labor unions, membership organizations, or trade associations, which may solicit contributions only from individuals connected to the sponsor. NCs may solicit contributions from the general public.

An SSF need not report fund-raising and administrative expenses paid by a sponsor, whereas an NC must report all operating and solicitation expenses. SSFs must inform persons they solicit of the political purpose of the SSF and of the individual's right to refuse to contribute without reprisal, whereas NCs are not subject to these solicitation restrictions. An SSF must register within 10 days of establishment by its sponsor. An NC, however, must register as a political committee within 10 days after it has received contributions or made expenditures aggregating in excess of $1,000.

State Law

The constitutions of 19 states explicitly require private owners of one or more classes of exempt property to be "nonprofit" or a similar requirement (Bowman 2002a, Bowman and Fremont-Smith 2002). The most popular constitutionally recognized categorical exemptions are (with the number of states indicated in parentheses): religious (35), charitable or benevolent (33), educational (33), and cemeteries (27); 19 states exempt all four categories. Other categories appearing in the constitutions of at least two states are: libraries (12), literary and scientific organizations (8), cultural organizations and museums (4), agricultural and horticultural organizations (3), patriotic and veterans' organizations (3). Only four state constitutions exempt hospitals per se; all other states exempt them only as charitable institutions.

However, in nearly every state property tax exemption is not awarded solely because the owner is nonprofit, even a federally exempt 501(c)(3). Every state has its own eligibility rules. The most common feature is that eligibility requires that the property actually be *used* for an exempt purpose. Property tax exemption is a political issue in some communities, and 9 percent of a recent poll of nonprofit executives indicated that they make payments in lieu of taxes to their host communities (abbreviated PILOTS; Salamon, Geller, and Sokolowski 2011).[25]

The state general sales tax exemption is worth approximately $2 billion to nonprofits in 25 states with a general sales tax, and the local exemption is worth an additional $0.4 billion. Insofar as sales *by* charities, seven states exempt 501(c)(3) organizations and eight others exempt sales by "charitable" organizations. Common law is the basis for defining *charitable* in the latter group of states. The savings from sales tax exemption on sales *by* nonprofits are only $0.1 billion (Bowman and Fremont-Smith 2006).

Nonprofits generally are not exempt from lesser taxes, user charges, and fees, such as those related to utilities, ticket sales, sewer fees, and garbage collection. In the same poll just mentioned, 17 percent of survey respondents reported paying these other taxes and 42 percent reported paying user fees (Salamon, Geller, and Sokolowski 2011).

Finally, most states regulate charitable solicitation. Although related to finance, it is unrelated to taxation, which it is the subject of this chapter. We take note because it is one of the few state regulatory efforts. Differences in these laws are so varied that a short summary is impossible. For an overview, see Fremont-Smith (2004) and U.S. Department of the Treasury, Internal Revenue Service (2001).

Concluding Thoughts

Tax law has many functions, and nonprofit organizations often have conflicting fiduciary duties because they may blend service to the public, service to members, and service to other organizations. Consequently, it is difficult to pigeonhole an organization into a single operational category. Table 5.2 shows how categories of tax exemption compare to the categories on which Chapters 6 through 9 are based.

The way the IRS collects and makes information available to the public in searchable data sets provides insufficient information to decompose the "other tax-exempt" category into direct service providers, grantmakers, and membership associations. However, the names of the exempt categories in Table 5.2 imply that most of the organizations in the "other" category are membership associations. A large number of organizations did not file annual reports; most of these are small (under $25,000 in annual revenue in 2005) or are religious institutions.

TABLE 5.2 Federal Tax-Exempt Entities by Type, 2005*

| | 501(c)(3) Organizations | | | |
Type	Public Charities	Private Foundations	Other Tax-Exempt	Total
Service providers	211,740	53,409	?	265,149
Grantmakers	23,284	31,654	?	54,938
Membership associations	16,004	1,592	70,727	88,323
Total reporting to the IRS	251,028	86,655	127,314	464,997
Not reporting	583,637		336,785	920,422

*Tax-exempt category includes all 501(c)(6), (7), (8), (9), (10), and (19).

Source: Author calculations using NCCS Business Master File and Wing, Pollak, and Blackwood (2008), Table 1.1.

CHAPTER 6

Ordinary Service Providers
Serving the Public Today

Youth Haven, a pseudonymous social service agency serving wards of the state and troubled youths, has financed 87 percent of its assets with debt.[1] Traditional financial analysis identifies excessive debt as an indicator of financial vulnerability (Tuckman and Chang 1991; Chang and Tuckman 1991), but Youth Haven has survived 40 years and continues to grow.[2] By contrast, many organizations that meet all goals of their capacity-building grants fail to achieve financial stability (Blumenthal 2003). How is it possible that an organization in such circumstances prospers while others that seemingly have more advantages fail to achieve financial stability? This chapter answers the question in terms of two key financial concepts: capacity and sustainability.

Financial capacity for a nonprofit consists of the resources (net assets) necessary to seize opportunities and respond to threats. The amount needed depends on its mission, service delivery method, operating environment, and risks of potential adverse economic events. *Financial sustainability* is simply the rate of net change in financial capacity.

A *sustainability principle* is introduced ensuring consistency between the short run (as measured by annual surpluses) and the long run (as measured by asset growth). The next section applies these diagnostic tools to the sector as a whole and develops benchmarks for putatively normal financial operations. Most material in this chapter first appeared in *Nonprofit Management and Leadership* (Bowman 2011c); used with permission of the publisher, John Wiley & Sons, Inc. This chapter applies only to nonprofit service providers not presumptively endowed. Organizations with securities and other investments exceeding total expenses should use the formulas of

Chapter 8. The companion web site to this book, www.wiley.com/go/
bowmanfinance, has spreadsheets that perform all calculations automatically.

Long-Term Objective: Maintaining Services

The model assumes that management's long-run objective is maintaining or
expanding services. Over the long run organizations must be able to keep
their assets in good shape *and* maintain their reserves at a level commensurate with anticipated economic risks.

On a long-run time scale—say, five years or more—donor restrictions
on net assets are not critical for diagnostic purposes, because temporarily
restricted net assets are eventually reclassified to unrestricted and organizations will not accept permanently restricted net assets unless they will
contribute to long-run capacity.

Physical assets are carried on a statement of financial position at original
cost minus accumulated depreciation, and financial assets are carried at current
market value. Both types must grow at a rate at least as fast as the long-run rate
of inflation in order that physical assets can be replaced at prevailing prices
whenever necessary and financial assets do not lose their purchasing power.

Financial Capacity

Debt destroys an organization's financial capacity because creditors possess
a claim on the organization that takes precedence over all other claims. If
assets are used as collateral, they become forfeit in case of nonpayment.
Because borrowing takes less effort than fund-raising, nonprofits must guard
against becoming overextended.

The equity ratio (ER) monitors the fraction of an organization's assets it
owns free and clear. (Equity equals Assets minus Liabilities.) Information on
its component parts is found on a balance sheet, and "[s]ince the balance
sheet is the result of all the organization's historical financial activities
viewed at a given point in time, it provides what might be thought of as the
'long term' view of an organization's asset acquisition and financing decisions" (Anthony and Young 2005, 501).[3]

$$ER = (Total\ assets - Total\ liabilities)/Total\ assets$$

or equivalently, in terms of line numbers on the pre-2008 IRS Form 990:

$$ER = Net\ assets/Total\ assets = Line\ 73B/Line\ 59A[4]$$

An ER of 1.0 implies that an organization has no debts, and it is up-
to-date on paying its bills. An ER of zero means that it is operating entirely
with borrowed assets. ER can even be negative if an organization's financial
obligations are greater than the value of its assets—a condition that Chapter 2
identifies as balance sheet insolvency.

Some authorities believe that an ER should be greater than 0.5 (Konrad and Novak 2000, 113). The origin of this recommendation is obscure but it likely represents a standard of creditworthiness originating with lenders seeking to minimize default risk.

From Tables 6.1a and 6.1b it is evident that Youth Haven's ER in 2007 was an astonishingly low 0.13, implying it has virtually no ability to invest for the future, to fend off threats to its market niche, or to act opportunistically. However, it has survived for decades in this vulnerable state.

TABLE 6.1A Balance Sheet for Youth Haven ($1,000s)

	2007	2006
Assets		
Cash and cash equivalents	$ 1,508	$ 567
Other current assets	8,006	7,983
Investments	748	5,708
Property, plant, and equipment (PP&E)*	9,650	5,586
Other assets	1,081	0
Total assets	$20,993	$ 9,844
Liabilities		
Current liabilities	$ 3,272	$ 3,348
Mortgages, bonds, and notes[†]	9,417	9,047
Other liabilities	4,481	5,325
Total liabilities	$18,204	$17,720
Net assets (unrestricted)	$ 2,790	$ 2,123
Total liabilities and net assets	$20,994	$19,843

*Net of accumulated depreciation.
[†]Excludes unsecured notes for working capital; information found in schedules.

TABLE 6.1B Statement of Activities for Youth Haven ($1,000s)

	2007	2006
Government contracts	$47,119	$36,442
Other income	7,380	4,845
Operating revenues	$54,499	$41,287
Expenses before interest and depreciation	$52,391	$40,330
Interest	707	616
Depreciation	744	480
Operating expenses	$53,842	$41,426
Operating surplus (deficit)	$ 657	$ (139)

A Note on Owning Buildings: Rented assets do not appear on a balance sheet, so they do not create financial capacity. Why should the act of acquiring ownership cause capacity to increase? The benefits of owning as a source of financial capacity derive from the following four operational reasons for accepting the responsibilities (and costs) of ownership.

1. If annual costs of maintaining and operating property are likely to be less than rental payments, then ownership is clearly beneficial.
2. Rental property tends to be standardized, and office space is the most readily available. If more specialized space is required for libraries, laboratories, theatrical productions, or museums, a nonprofit is faced with a decision to make leasehold improvements or build to own. If the cost of improvements exceeds build-to-own cost, ownership may be more cost-effective.
3. When the scale of a nonprofit's operations reaches a certain point, which varies from city to city and neighborhood to neighborhood, it will be unable to rent sufficient space at a single location. If it is important that staff or consumers have face-to-face communication with all departments, then it becomes necessary to create a campus.
4. Renters are vulnerable to losing their leases or being forced out when landlords raise rents to unaffordable levels. If doing business at a particular location is important, buying is preferable to renting.

As beneficial as it may seem to own instead of renting, an organization must be able to service the debt and cover new operating and maintenance expenses. Either the current surplus must be sufficient, ownership must reduce costs, or it must increase productivity.

Financial Sustainability

Given the definition of ER, it is natural to measure long-term sustainability by the change in the numerator divided by total assets. Revenue increases net assets, and expenses decrease net assets; so revenue minus expenses equals a change in net assets. This ratio for sustainability is known in the business literature as *return on assets* (ROA; Finkler 2005, 535; Anthony and Young 2005, 509).[5]

$$\text{ROA} = 100\% \cdot (\text{Total revenue} - \text{Total expenses}) / \text{Total assets}$$

or equivalently,

$$\text{ROA} = 100\% \cdot \text{Change in total net assets} / \text{Total assets}$$
$$= 100\% \cdot (\text{Line 73B} - \text{Line 73A}) / \text{Line 59B}$$

The long-term rate of inflation establishes a floor under long-term sustainability consistent with the choices an organization makes when it selects a target capacity level.

According to the author's calculations, the status quo ROA is 3.4 percent.[6] An actual return on assets above this rate will increase long-term capacity; an actual return on assets below this rate will decrease it. Despite its abysmally low long-term capacity, Youth Haven had an ROA of 3.2 percent, which is very close to the long-term rate of inflation of 3.4. With careful management, Youth Haven is sustainable indefinitely over the long term.

A Note on Return on Investment: For-profit businesses tend to focus on return on investment (ROI; change in net assets divided by net assets) instead of ROA. However, ROI favors riskier financial activity. To see how, assume a nonprofit owns $100,000 in assets, it has no liabilities, and its annual surplus is $5,000 per year. Therefore, ROA and ROI are both 5 percent. Now, assume it borrowed $50,000 to buy half of its assets. Its total assets are still $100,000 and its annual surplus is still $5,000 (before debt service) but its liabilities are $50,000. Its ROA is still 5 percent because it is calculated on the basis of total assets, but its ROI is 10 percent because it is calculated on the basis of equity. The ROI is higher, but it is also the riskier alternative because the organization may not be able to service the debt for the life of the loan.

Increased debt relative to equity (*leverage*) increases bankruptcy risk. In for-profit businesses this risk is borne by shareholders, who can manage it individually. They buy more shares if they like the risk-return trade-off, or sell their shares if they don't. However, nonprofits have no investor-owners, so the risks of a nonprofit are borne by the people it serves (its clients), who have neither a voice in selecting the organization's leadership nor ability to manage the risks. Nonprofit board members and managers do not experience the negative consequences of bad decisions as their clients do. Ethics dictates they adhere to a higher standard of stewardship. (See Chapter 11.)

Short-Term Objective: Resilience

An organization may have adequate long-term capacity but donor restrictions and limited financing options are constraining in a short term of, say, one to five years. An operating budget is an organization's primary tool of financial control, but it is a short-term instrument. This section explains how to use the annual budget to achieve the status quo long-term ROA.

This section introduces a *sustainability principle* that requires consistency between the short run (as measured by annual surpluses) and the long run (as measured by asset growth).

In the discussion that follows, Spending on operations equals Total expenses minus Depreciation, which approximates budgetary spending on a cash basis (see Chapter 2). It is the scale factor (denominator) of the short-term formulas.

Financial Capacity

Some authorities recommend that nonprofits maintain at least three months of spending on operations as a reserve (Konrad and Novak 2000, 113). The origin of this norm is unclear, but recently it received the endorsement of the Nonprofit Operating Reserves Initiative Workgroup (NORI) sponsored by the National Center for Charitable Statistics, Center on Nonprofits and Philanthropy at the Urban Institute, and United Way Worldwide (NORI 2008, 2).

If an organization lost all current income and tried to maintain its spending on operations at a constant level while searching for new sources, it must succeed within the calculated *months of spending* (*MS*) before running out of expendable resources. *MS* should not to be construed literally, as it is unlikely that any organization's income will drop to zero overnight. Expressing reserves in this way makes it easier to interpret intuitively.

$$MS = 12 \text{ months} \cdot (\text{Unrestricted financial assets}$$
$$-\text{Unsecured debt})/\text{Spending on operations}$$

or equivalently,[7]

$$MS = 12 \text{ months} \cdot (\text{Unrestricted net assets} - \text{Equity in PP\&E})/$$
$$\text{Spending on operations} = 12 \text{ months} \cdot [\text{Line 67B} - (\text{Line 55cB} +$$
$$\text{Line 57cB} - \text{Line 64aB} - \text{Line 64bB})]/(\text{Line 44A} - \text{Line 42A})$$

After 2008, escrowed liabilities should be subtracted in the numerator as well.

Equity in PP&E equals PP&E minus mortgages and bonds. This model classifies acquisition, divestiture, and financing of PP&E as long-term decisions—not to be undertaken for short-term gain; hence the numerator of this ratio is functionally equivalent to an operating reserve that an organization can tap in an emergency (NORI 2008).

Youth Haven also had minimal short-term capacity. Its MS in 2007 was slightly over two weeks (0.6 of a month). A sudden and significant drop in revenue would probably require budget cuts.[8] Perhaps Youth Haven has been lucky, but more plausibly it tolerates meager short-term capacity because it is confident in its ability to manage its government relations. (It must, because 86 percent of its revenue is from government sources.)

Financial Sustainability

Sustainability of short-term capacity is measured by the change in the numerator of months of spending (MS) divided by spending on operations, which is analogous to markup (MU) in the business literature.[9]

MU = 100% · (Unrestricted revenue including gifts and grants +
Net assets released from restrictions − Total expenses + Depreciation)/
(Total expenses − Depreciation)

Net assets released from restrictions are restricted gifts (including pledges) and grants received in an earlier accounting period but reclassified to unrestricted upon fulfillment of restrictions and payment of pledges in the current period.[10] *Total expenses* are always unrestricted by GAAP convention. *Depreciation* is the rate of change in the value of existing PP&E.[11] Adding it in the numerator is to cancel it from expenses. The numerator therefore consists of resources available for spending. Given that this chapter assumes no endowments, the MU equation can be rewritten in a form that easily derives from the second MS equation, thus:

$$MU = 100\% \cdot (\text{Change in unrestricted net assets} +$$
$$\text{Depreciation})/\text{Spending on operations}$$
$$= 100\% \cdot (\text{Line 67B} - \text{Line 67A} + \text{Line 42A})/$$
$$(\text{Line 44A} - \text{Line 42A})$$

This formula is similar to operating margin found in nonprofit finance texts (Finkler 2005, 534; McLaughlin 2002, 64) but depreciation is not added back to operating margin and its denominator is revenue instead of spending. Dividing by revenue is problematic because nonprofits have inaccessible revenues such as restricted gifts and endowment returns. Expenses, being unrestricted by definition, raise none of these problems, so MU uses expenses instead. ("Markup" may sound strange in the nonprofit sector, but in the business literature "margin" denotes division by revenue whereas "markup" denotes division by cost, or expenses.)

The MU that achieves long-term ROA of 3.4 percent is called the *status quo markup* (*SQ-MU*). The amount of cash that should be set aside every year for capital preservation is 3.4 percent times total assets. The operating surplus that is sufficient to maintain the status quo over the long term is SQ-MU times spending on operation*s*. Equating these two dollar amounts and solving for SQ-MU gives:

$$SQ\text{-}MU = 3.4\% \cdot \text{Total assets}/\text{Spending on operations} = 3.4\%$$
$$\cdot \text{Line 59B}/(\text{Line 44A} - \text{Line 42A})$$

This is a sufficient condition because the right-hand side includes restricted assets but the left-hand side does not. Unlike SQ-ROA, which is the same for all organizations, SQ-MU differs from one organization to the next because it depends on the ratio of each organization's assets to expenses.

TABLE 6.2 Shortfall from Status Quo Surplus

Years	33%	66%	90%
10	8	15	22
20	13	24	33
30	16	29	38

Organizations without assets need no surplus, whereas those with substantial assets relative to their expenses need large surpluses. In addition, nonprofits may plan surpluses for precautionary reasons or to build their asset base.

This is arguably the most important equation of the chapter because it establishes a relationship between annual budget surplus (the principal objective of financial control) and long-run sustainability (a principal object of financial planning).

Occasional failure to meet the status quo minimum can be tolerated, provided that surpluses in other years compensate. Consistent failure to meet the status quo minimum should put managers on notice that they will need to plan a capital campaign to upgrade their facilities. The formula enables calculation of the size of the capital campaign that will be necessary. The data in Table 6.2 are the present values (in millions of dollars) of the capital campaign needed to support a new $100 million investment in physical plant under different assumptions about the size of the shortfall and how long an organization waits to conduct one. (See the Glossary for a description of present value.)

Despite negligible short-term capacity, Youth Haven had an MU of 1.2 percent, which is very close to its status quo rate of 1.4 percent. With careful management, it can be sustainable indefinitely in both short *and* long terms without a capital campaign.

A Note on Museums and Libraries: Certain assets, like museum artifacts and library volumes, are one-of-a-kind assets and can never be replaced. These assets may or may not be recognized on financial statements. If the statements assign a value, this number should be subtracted from total assets and net assets before applying the diagnostic tests for long-term capacity and sustainability.

Unique artifacts are expensive to maintain. Guthrie (1996, 152) says, "Incumbent with ownership of those collections is an unremitting obligation to catalogue, conserve, protect, and make accessible millions of items." Such organizations must take extra care to be sustainable.

"Owning nonprofit assets results in a long-term financial cost, not a benefit[;] maintaining collections that are not directly related to an institution's mission diverts resources from the care and maintenance of the assets the institution values most" (Guthrie 1996, 154).

Current Objective: Paying Bills

The model assumes the current period objective is maintaining or increasing immediate access to cash to pay current bills. *Liquidity* refers to an ability to raise cash quickly and easily for meeting current obligations. Zietlow, Hankin, and Seidner (2007, 31) argue that "liquidity management is the single most important financial function of the donative [i.e., gift-supported] nonprofit." It is certainly the most immediate and persistent.

Financial Capacity

The concept of liquidity can be measured in several ways. A common variant originating in the business sector is working capital, defined as current assets minus current liabilities, not to be confused with working cash (see Glossary).

This definition has marketable securities on the list of current assets. However, nonprofits have compelling reasons for owning securities that do not include paying current bills (operating reserve, endowment, etc.), so securities and other investments are excluded from the definition of nonprofit current assets. Excluded too are receivables from (loans to) current and former officers, directors, trustees, and key employees because they are probably not liquid.

Donor-restricted assets should be invested short-term until needed for their intended purpose. GAAP does not partition current assets into temporarily restricted and unrestricted assets. Some liquid assets may actually be temporarily restricted, and they would appear on IRS 990 form as savings or pledges receivable, both current assets. Therefore, temporarily restricted net assets should be excluded from the definition of *nonprofit current assets.*

Nonprofit working capital, expressed as the number of months of spending, measures nonprofit liquidity.[12]

Liquidity $= 12\,\text{months} \cdot$ (Nonprofit current assets

$-$ Current liabilities $-$ Temporarily restricted net assets)/

Spending on operations

or

Liquidity $= 12\,\text{months} \cdot$ (Sum of lines 45B, 46B, 47cB, 48cB, 49B, 52B, and 53B $-$ Sum of lines 60B, 61B, and 68B)/(Line 44A $-$ Line 42A)

After 2008, escrowed liabilities should be subtracted from the numerator. Given that the standard payment cycle is 30 days, a reasonable target for

TABLE 6.3 Capacity and Sustainability Percentiles for Ordinary Nonprofits, Averages of 2001–2003

Ordinary: $N = 46,492$	Percentiles				
	25th	50th (Median)	75th	% > 0	% > SQ
Equity ratio	0.40	0.72	0.90	90	n.a.
Return on assets (%)	−4.3	1.0	7.0	55	38
Months of spending	0.7	2.7	6.5	84	n.a.
Markup (%)	0.0	4.2	11.3	75	56
Liquidity (months)	0.8	2.4	5.5	88	n.a.
Change in liquidity (months)	−0.3	0.1	0.6	56	56

n.a. = Not applicable.

this ratio is one to two months of spending. A negative number indicates that nonprofit current assets are insufficient to pay current bills. From Tables 6.1a and 6.1b it is evident that Youth Haven appreciates the importance of liquidity, because it has nearly three times the minimum recommended nonprofit working capital. Its capacity in the current period is robust—in stark contrast to its meager capacity in the long and short terms.

Financial Sustainability

For sustainability an organization's liquidity must be constant or increasing. The preceding sections on long- and short-term sustainability made use of an approximation that assumed the change in the numerator is small compared to the change in the denominator, which does not apply here because nonprofit working capital must grow in proportion to a change in spending on operations. Therefore current liquidity is sustainable when liquidity increases from the previous year.

$$\text{Change in liquidity} = \text{Liquidity (year } t) - \text{Liquidity(year } t - 1)$$

In the business literature this difference does not have a special name. Table 6.3 calls it simply "change in liquidity" expressed in number of months. Youth Haven's passion for liquidity caused it to add the equivalent of 10 days of spending on operations to its nonprofit working capital, which was already robust.

Application

Throughout this chapter Youth Haven has provided an illustration for each formula. This section pulls everything together in a complete financial diagnosis in a way that facilitates telling a coherent story about its financial condition.

Youth Haven's investments were insubstantial in 2007, indicating it is not endowed. It had $5.7 million of securities at the end of 2006 but liquidated most of them in 2007, apparently investing a large portion of the proceeds in land, buildings, and equipment.

Youth Haven's ER in 2007 was 13 percent, which is very low, implying that it has virtually no ability to invest for the future, to fend off threats to its market niche, or to act opportunistically. But it had an ROA of 3.2 percent, which is very close to the long-term rate of inflation of 3.4 percent, so it is probably sustainable. (The calculation is the return on assets only for 2007 to allow readers to easily reproduce it from Table 6.1a, but, in practice, a three-year moving average is recommended.)

Months of spending (MS) in 2007 was 0.6 of a month, or slightly over two weeks. Given its dependency on government contracts, it is extremely vulnerable to changes in public policy. Faced with a sudden reduction in contract income, Youth Haven would be unable to maintain service levels without borrowing. With negative short-term capacity, it is unlikely to be able to increase its credit limits. It would have no alternative but to implement immediate and painful budget cuts. It is no wonder that Youth Haven employs two lobbyists in the state capital. Despite having negligible short-term capacity, Youth Haven had an MU of 1.2 percent, which is below but very close to the status quo rate. However, Youth Haven is very liquid; it had nearly three times the minimum recommended working capital and its liquidity improved somewhat.

Youth Haven lives life on the edge. It has among the lowest positive values to be seen in the sector. (See the next section on benchmarks.) It takes to extremes the notion that a nonprofit should utilize its resources to their limits. The preceding calculations from one year of data offer a glimpse into its secret: sustainability. It intuitively understands that so long as it maintains its asset values at replacement cost and keeps a positive cash flow it can endure even abysmally low levels of capacity. That it has a sympathetic banker willing to extend credit despite these numbers is a tribute to the excellent job it does for its community.

Benchmarking

Tables 6.3 and 6.4 give an overview of the nonprofit sector, showing median and interquartile ranges for capacity and sustainability in every time frame. The most recent data file that contains all of the variables needed for analyses in this book is the digitized data set of the National Center for Charitable Statistics (NCCS). This analysis extracts a balanced panel consisting of

TABLE 6.4 Capacity Percentiles for Ordinary Nonprofits by Field of Activity, Averages of 2001–2003 (Interquartile Range in *Italics*)

Field of Activity (NTEE)[*]	N	Solvent %[†]	ER	MS	Liquidity
Arts and culture (A)	3,546	93	0.82	2.2	3.0
			0.38	*6.4*	*6.2*
Education (B)	4,734	95	0.71	2.6	2.3
			0.42	*6.1*	*5.1*
Environment (C)	727	97	0.87	3.3	4.5
			0.28	*7.1*	*7.1*
Health care (E)	6,648	89	0.60	3.1	1.9
			0.49	*5.7*	*3.3*
Mental health and crisis intervention (F)	2,642	94	0.66	2.0	2.0
			0.46	*3.5*	*2.8*
Disease-related (G)	1,262	96	0.80	3.5	2.9
			0.33	*5.9*	*4.8*
Crime prevention and legal (I)	1,184	96	0.76	2.3	2.7
			0.36	*4.3*	*4.0*
Employment (J)	1,219	94	0.72	2.5	2.1
			0.43	*4.7*	*3.5*
Housing (L)	4,062	61	0.20	4.4	2.3
			0.95	*9.4*	*6.4*
Recreation (N)	977	95	0.86	3.6	3.1
			0.34	*6.8*	*5.1*
Youth (O)	1,427	97	0.90	3.3	3.3
			0.21	*6.3*	*4.9*
Human services (P)	10,375	93	0.71	2.0	1.9
			0.48	*4.1*	*3.3*
International and foreign affairs (Q)	623	95	0.80	2.1	2.4
			0.46	*5.0*	*5.5*
Community improvement (S)	2,069	93	0.71	3.4	3.9
			0.48	*9.8*	*8.0*
Philanthropy and volunteerism (T)	1,287	96	0.78	4.2	7.2
			0.47	*7.0*	*10.2*
Religious (X)	1,033	91	0.83	2.3	2.2
			0.43	*5.9*	*4.3*
	43,815				

Note: The interquartile range is the difference between the 75th and 25th percentiles.

[*]NTEE: National Taxonomy of Exempt Entities. NTEE group excluded where $N < 500$.

[†]Solvent% = Percent of organizations where total assets > total liabilities.

Source: Bowman (2011c).

public charities that reported to the IRS on Form 990 every year from 1998 through 2003.

There is wide dispersion by field of activity (Table 6.4). The highest median equity ratio is between two and four times the smallest median for any given capacity metric—ER, MS, and liquidity. The equity ratio varies from a low of 0.20 for housing organizations to a high of 0.90 for youth-serving organizations. The low figure stands out because the next smallest is 0.60 (health care), but a low number is reasonable for housing organizations because they frequently borrow to build and they can rely on a fairly stable revenue stream from rents.

The return on assets of the median organization is 1.0 percent (Table 6.3). Long-term sustainability requires growth of total assets faster than the long-term rate of inflation of 3.4 percent. More than half (62 percent) are unsustainable in the long term, and 45 percent actually have negative returns. A large number of organizations probably reboot with a capital campaign now and then. This much is certain: managers should regard inferior returns seriously and begin planning a capital campaign when return on assets falls appreciably below 3.4 percent for a three-year moving average. If they ignore the danger sign, their organization will gradually sacrifice its ability to maintain service quality, output levels, or both.

Months of spending measures the assets a nonprofit can call upon in a protracted emergency. The median nonprofit has 2.7 months of spending, which is very close to the recommended level, but one-quarter has only 20 days or less and 16 percent have negative short-term capacity. Negative capacity is reason for concern. The number of months of spending across different fields of activity varies from 2.0 months to 4.4.

The higher figure is for the housing subsector. It is reasonable that heavily indebted organizations should strive to maintain a fair level of expendable assets because the consequences of being unable to service their debt during an economic downturn would be catastrophic. Although 75 percent of nonprofits have positive markups, only 56 percent are sustainable in the sense that they are accumulating enough cash to continue to guarantee a return on assets of 3.4 percent in the long term. Nonprofit managers should be wary of repeated poor performance of this indicator.

The median nonprofit is very liquid, having working capital equal to 2.4 months of spending on operations. Although 88 percent have positive working capital, 12 percent are technically *illiquid*; that is, their current liabilities plus temporarily restricted net assets exceed their nonprofit current assets. The change in nonprofit working capital is fairly symmetric and the median is slightly positive, suggesting that nonprofits aim for a slight increase in working capital every year and are as likely as not to hit their objective. The least liquid subsectors are health and human services, each with the equivalent of 1.9 months of spending in nonprofit working capital. The most liquid is philanthropy and volunteerism, with the equivalent of 7.2 months.

The data tell a familiar story: ordinary nonprofits stretching their resources to the limit and exposing themselves to long- and short-term risks to serve their clients. They get by from one day to the next by maintaining liquidity, as Zietlow, Hankin, and Seidner (2007) counsel. The financial model presented in this study raises a warning.

Just to stay even, an unsustainable nonprofit must plan for capital campaigns now and then to refresh its capital stock. Although the results are not shocking, this model gives nonprofits a framework for quantifying their financial condition, setting financial goals, and monitoring their progress.

Concluding Thoughts

Financial capacity is a management choice reflecting mission, values, service delivery method, external threats, and opportunities. The formulas enable a nonprofit manager to establish precise capacity targets and to calculate whether any given level of capacity is sustainable. A sustainable organization can continue to produce indefinitely the same volume of goods and services of the same quality with the same service delivery model.

An organization that is sustainable in the long term but unsustainable in the short term will be chronically short of cash. Conversely, an organization that is sustainable in the short term but not in the long term may have adequate cash but inflation will cause the value of its assets to erode over time. This, in turn, will cause the quantity and/or quality of services to diminish unless capital campaigns periodically bring infusions of new assets.

Appendix

Because the model applies only to ordinary nonprofits, the data were screened to exclude membership associations (dues > 1/3 of total revenue), grantmakers (grants > 1/3 of program expenses), and endowed organizations (investments > expenses). The data were further cleaned according to the method discussed in Bowman, Tuckman, and Young (forthcoming). This resulted in excluding organizations that (1) were inactive, (2) did not use accrual accounting, (3) did not follow SFAS 117,[13] (4) filed a group return, or (5) filed the 990-EZ form.

All data screens combined to reduce the sample from 254,000 reporting public charities to 97,500. Most filters had a negligible effect on sample size, but those for accrual accounting and SFAS 117 cut it in half. This is regrettable, but it would be misleading to mingle organizations that use different accounting rules.

To make the point with two examples: (1) pledges are not revenue for organizations that use cash accounting but they are accrual revenue, and (2) organizations using cash accounting record a capital purchase as an expenditure but organizations using accrual accounting do not recognize it as an expense. Although reliable interpretation of statistical results depends on all data on a given variable being measured according to the same rules, the large sample shrinkage from using these filters probably disproportionately eliminates small organizations.

Median values are better than averages for measuring the central tendency of financial variables, because they are not skewed by a few extreme cases (*outliers*). In benchmarking, an important issue is how to define "normal" practice. It seems reasonable to define a normal value of a capacity statistic as lying between the 25th and 75th percentiles (interquartile range), which embraces half of all nonprofits. Any given organization may have good reasons to operate outside of this range, but extreme capacity targets need extra justification.

Table 6.3 on page 90 shows the key financial indicators for the sector. The median equity ratio is 0.72. Although 90 percent have a positive equity ratio, 1 in 10 is *balance sheet insolvent*. This seems high and it is risky, but insolvent organizations might function provided they stay liquid and have adequate annual surpluses.

CHAPTER 7

Membership Associations
Serving People with a Common Purpose

Over 30 years ago, several deaf professionals and 12 clubs for the deaf collaborated to start the Membership Association for the Deaf (MAD) (*Nonprofit Quarterly* 2005).[1] For many years it thrived, but recently it has seen membership dwindle and deficits increase because external changes have challenged the assumptions of its founders: persons with disabilities were mainstreamed in the classroom and workplace, new technologies made hearing possible for some persons, and sign language began to assume equal status with lip reading as the preferred form of communication. Not everyone in the deaf community embraced the changes, and MAD struggled with finding a new focus. This chapter shows what financial analysis can bring to the discussion.

The focus of this chapter is on membership associations. It begins with the economic theory of clubs (the economists' term for membership associations). It then discusses membership associations that are not cooperatives, followed by a section featuring cooperatives. Another section presents metrics and benchmarks for evaluating the financial capacity and sustainability of membership associations. Data for the analysis are from ASAE/Center for Association Leadership (ASAE/CAL, formerly the American Society of Association Executives). Finally, the chapter returns to the MAD vignette and introduces another case study to illustrate the concepts of membership association finance.

Membership Associations

Membership associations are a diverse lot (Tschirhart 2006), which may be classified several ways: (1) by type of member, namely natural persons, organizations, or a combination (Smith 2000), or (2) by function. The standard functional classification is due to Mason (1996): *Expressive* clubs exist to promote values, such as humanitarianism, environmental quality, and animal rights; *affiliative* clubs exist to promote social intercourse; and *instrumental* clubs provide useful services in the form of shared member benefits.[2] These types are not mutually exclusive. For example, trade associations may promote values within society at large and social as well as material benefits to their members.

Theory

The word *club*, as it is commonly used, has connotations of a social character possibly tinged with elitism. To economists, it is a neutral label applicable to all membership associations, including informal, loosely organized groups.[3] "A club is a voluntary group deriving mutual benefit from members sharing one or more of the following: production costs, the members' characteristics, or a good characterized by excludable benefits" (Cornes and Sandler 1986, 159). The key characteristics of a club are its (1) voluntary nature, (2) member sharing, (3) excludable benefits, and (4) governance.

1. VOLUNTARY Membership is not compulsory,[4] but this is not to say that clubs must accept everyone who applies.

2. SHARING "The utility *jointly* derived from membership and the consumption of other goods must exceed the utility associated with non-membership status. . . . Sharing [benefits of membership] often leads to rivalry as larger membership crowd one another, causing a detraction in the quality of services received" (Cornes and Sandler 1986, 159; emphasis in the original). As clubs expand their membership, the incremental reduction in attractiveness to newcomers eventually balances the incremental decrease in the average cost per member. At that point, it is neither in the best interest of incumbent members to accept new members nor in the best interest of outsiders to join, and the club reaches stasis.

3. EXCLUDABLE BENEFITS This issue is primarily relevant to clubs that provide goods and services to their members. Managers of such clubs must monitor members' utilization and bar nonmembers from participation (free riding). Incumbent members decide admission requirements. U.S. tax law requires *economic* benefits to be available to members and non-members alike, but an organization has no obligation to promote such benefits to nonmembers and may charge nonmembers for them, earning program service revenue.

4. GOVERNANCE   Some authors add a fourth key characteristic: a member entitlement to share in the governance of the organization (Bowman 2010; Tschirhart 2006; Steinberg 2007; Hansmann 1996). But, others, like Robinson (2003, 4) use the term *member* to include donors, volunteers, and support-ers, who argue that "this kind of legal voting power is not necessary when creating a loyal cadre of members."[5]

Membership associations are financed by a combination of dues, charges (sales to members), unrelated business income (sales to the public), and perhaps donations. Dues are the price of membership—flat-rate payments made for the privilege of membership, regardless of utilization of specific services.[6] As already mentioned, payment of dues ordinarily determines eligibility to participate in a member-ship association's governance. Dues comprise only 35 percent of revenues of the median member organization of ASAE/CAL (ASAE/ CAL 2008, 30).

"The literature has not yet developed rigorous guidelines for optimizing rates and structures, but certain factors must clearly be involved. Organiza-tions should tailor their plans to their own particular mission, maintain solvency, embody shared notions of fairness, adjust for member character-istics, and consider the competition" (Steinberg 2007, 132). Dues-setting is very complex. A few of Steinberg's practical suggestions are:

- Public-serving organizations with instrumental missions should choose a dues structure that maximizes net revenues.
- Member-serving organizations emphasizing shared goods and services should strive to maximize net revenue from charges for services and devote that surplus to the provision of shared services.
- When maximizing membership enhances the organizational mission, dues should be set below cost, cross-subsidizing member benefits with revenues from other sources. Of course, some membership associations limit the size of their membership by policy—musical ensembles, for example.
- Raising the price of membership or cutting costs as budget-balancing tactics is likely to affect the number of members, so "Mechanical rules [for setting dues and cost-cutting] are too simple. The organization should think strategically" (Steinberg 2007, 137).

Taxonomy

"The essential [societal] function of an association is to be educational and informational, for its members and for others, particularly others in the line of business involved" (Hopkins 2006, 3).

The categories specified in Section 501(c) of the Internal Revenue Code (IRC) having more than 100 entities (see Table 5.1) are briefly described here together with the tax treatment of dues (U.S. Department of the Treasury 2011a; quotations are from the IRS):

> *Literary, scientific, and professional societies*, 501(c)(3). These are a subgroup of public charities. The IRC specifically includes literary and scientific societies in the (c)(3) category. Dues are tax deductible.
>
> *Civic leagues and social welfare organizations*, 501(c)(4). These organizations must be operated only to promote social welfare to benefit the community. Examples: civic associations and volunteer fire companies. "Donations to volunteer fire companies are deductible on the donor's federal income tax return, but only if made for exclusively public purposes."
>
> *Labor, agricultural, and horticultural organizations*, 501(c)(5). Payments to such organizations may be deductible as business expenses if they are "ordinary and necessary in the conduct of the taxpayer's trade or business."
>
> *Business leagues and non-(c)(3) professional societies*, 501(c)(6). "A business league, in general, is an association of persons having some common business interest, the purpose of which is to promote that common interest and not to engage in a regular business of a kind ordinarily carried on for profit. . . . [Contributions] may be deductible as trade or business expenses if ordinary and necessary in the conduct of the taxpayer's business."
>
> *Social and recreational clubs*, 501(c)(7). These clubs must be organized for "pleasure, recreation, and other similar nonprofitable [sic] purposes and substantially all of its activities are for these purposes. . . . The membership in a social club must be limited." Clubs should be supported solely by membership fees, dues, and assessments. If an organization otherwise qualifies to be recognized as exempt, it may raise revenue "from members through the use of club facilities or in connection with club activities." Donations are deductible as charitable contributions "only if used exclusively for religious, charitable, scientific, literary, or educational purposes or for the prevention of cruelty to children or animals."
>
> *Fraternal beneficiary societies and domestic fraternal societies*, 501(c) (8) and (10). The (c)(8) organizations must be fraternal and operate under a lodge system (local branches, chartered by a parent

organization and largely self-governing). They must provide for the payment of life, sick, accident, or other benefits to their members or their dependents and only to members and dependents. In lieu of member benefits just described, (c)(10) organizations must devote net earnings exclusively to "religious, charitable, scientific, literary, educational, and fraternal purposes."

Voluntary employee-beneficiary societies, 501(c)(9) and (17). These groups are organized "to pay life, sick, accident, and similar benefits to members or their dependents, or designated beneficiaries." They may also be a "supplemental unemployment benefit trust whose primary purpose is providing for payment of supplemental unemployment benefits."

Cemetery companies, 501(c)(13). A cemetery company must be "owned and operated exclusively for the benefit of its lot owners who hold lots for bona fide burial purposes and not for purposes of resale." Donations are deductible provided they are in excess of charges for perpetual care of specific plots.

War veterans associations, 501(c)(19). At least 75 percent of the members must be past or present members of the U.S. armed forces.

Cooperatives

"A cooperative is an enterprise in which individuals voluntarily organize to provide themselves and others with goods and services via democratic control and for mutually shared benefit. Members generally contribute to, and control via a democratic process, the cooperative's capital" (Reference for Business 2011).

Cooperatives are considered a special case of membership association but their operative focus is on *patrons*, not members. The different term signifies that dividends are paid to individuals based on patronage, not membership alone. In many cases, however, the concepts are interchangeable.[7]

Theory

Cooperatives tend to occur in situations where key markets are underdeveloped. Standard economic theory defines a market as the region where a given product trades at the same price. Under perfectly competitive conditions, neither buyers nor sellers can influence the price. In regions of chronic scarcity, sellers can influence price, whereas the advantage shifts to buyers in regions of chronic surplus. In theory, markets should automatically eliminate surpluses and shortages, but in regions where markets are not well developed they may not.

Market imperfections creating chronic shortages and surpluses are fertile ground for cooperatives, which enable the disadvantaged party to exercise countervailing market power. We observe the Inuit, who have a surplus of arts and crafts in their remote region, organize producers' cooperatives to find and cultivate consumers many miles away who are willing to pay top prices for the best work. We observe urban residents organize food cooperatives to get better prices and special types of scarce foodstuffs. There are also babysitting cooperatives consisting of parents who take turns caring for each other's children because reliable babysitters are hard to find.

Proponents of cooperatives argue that production in cooperatives is more efficient and point to the "overall psychological and social influence" arising from member control (Reference for Business 2011). If cooperative production is more efficient, one would expect cooperatives to dominate national economies, but as the New York Stock Exchange example of Chapter 1 suggests, there may be diseconomies associated with nonhierarchical control.

Banks are reluctant to lend to organizations in which a large group is in control of business decisions (Reference for Business 2011). Of course, cooperatives cannot raise equity capital outside their own membership. Further, members are tempted to opt out when they find they can accomplish the same ends on better terms from competing sources.

Taxonomy

Nearly 30,000 cooperatives operate at 73,000 places of business throughout the United States. Americans hold 350 million memberships in cooperatives, which generate nearly $79 billion in patronage refunds and dividends (Deller et al. 2009, 2).

Table 7.1 shows the number of cooperatives by type and size. Consumer cooperatives account for 92 percent of entities, 76 percent of

TABLE 7.1 Number and Size of Cooperatives by Type ($ in 1,000s)

	Assets	Wages	Firms
Worker	$ 128	$ 55	$ 223
Producer	23,632	2,970	1,494
Shared service	1,126,848	2,902	724
Consumer	1,975,805	19,085	26,844
Total	$3,126,413	$25,012	$29,285

Source: Deller et al. (2009, 11).

wages paid, and 63 percent of assets. "Consumer co-ops may be formed by individuals or businesses, and in the latter case are often referred to as 'purchasing' or 'shared service' co-ops. Producer co-ops include both those formed by businesses—often called 'marketing' co-ops and 'worker' co-ops whose members are individuals. Some co-ops are hybrids, combining elements of more than one type of co-op" (NCBA 2011). Consumer cooperatives may be eligible for federal tax exemption—Section 501(c)(6) of the IRC.

Like nonprofits with a nondistribution constraint, cooperatives are custodians and promoters of noneconomic values. Modern cooperatives subscribe to the following principles (ICA 2007):

- Voluntary and open membership
- Democratic member control
- Member economic participation
- Autonomy and independence
- Education, training, and information
- Cooperation among cooperatives
- Concern for community

Capacity and Sustainability

Section 501(c)(6) membership associations exist primarily to provide service to their members. Thus their finances can be analyzed using the same metrics as those used for typical service providers in the previous chapter. However, because they are governed by those receiving service, it is possible that normal values (benchmarks) for these metrics will be different.

To foster management improvement, the ASAE/Center for Association Leadership (ASAE/CAL)[8] gathers financial information periodically on the organizations represented by its members and publishes benchmarks for various operating ratios (ASAE/CAL 2008). Several formulas are slightly different from the ones in this book, but they are motivated by concepts similar to capacity and sustainability, and simple algebraic manipulation transforms them into the ratios presented in Chapter 6. The following analysis is based on these transformed ratios (see Appendix to this chapter).

Remarkably, the capacity for the median membership association and the median service provider is very close in the long term (67 percent and 71 percent respectively) and in the current period (4.0 and 4.1 respectively), although it differs substantially in the short term (9.4 and 2.6 respectively). The difference is probably attributable to membership associations having virtually no restricted assets and very little property, plant, and equipment, whereas the figure is much lower for typical service providers. This enables

membership associations to spend virtually all of their assets during a protracted economic slump, thus giving them a higher value on the months of
spending metric.

The median membership association is more sustainable than the median service provider in the long term, but they are similar in the short term.
In the long term the disparity is 6.0 percent for membership associations
compared to 1.7 percent for service providers. In the short term, it is 5.1 percent compared to 6.4 percent, respectively. There is hardly any disparity in
the difference between the status quo markup and the actual markup: it is
2.8 percent for membership associations and 2.1 percent for service providers. Thus, controlling for the different ratios of expenses to assets (or revenues to assets in the ASAE system), the median organization in both groups
equally sustainable. The larger asset base of service providers lowers their
return on assets for a given markup.

One might think that the median membership association should have a
lower return on assets and lower markup because its members want to keep
dues as low as possible. Instead, it seems that differences in financial performance can be attributed to a tendency for service providers to be more
asset-rich, especially in the form of land, buildings, and equipment. Perhaps
this is because many service providers require specialized physical facilities
(clinics, laboratories, classrooms, performance venues) whereas membership associations are content with generic office facilities. Ownership may
confer advantages in the former case but none in the latter.

Two Applications

The organization in the opening vignette, MAD, had an astonishingly small
amount of membership revenue—just $7,615, or $38 per member. Nearly all
of its revenue was from program services, averaging $1,712 per member.
MAD was selling services to nonmembers, which is not uncommon,
but most membership associations do not generate most of their revenue
from external sales. MAD should rethink its mission as a membership
organization.

Without anyone noticing, MAD had become a membership association
in name only. It faces two alternative futures: remain a membership association and operate with a volunteer staff or become a 501(c)(3) public charity,
solicit donations, and sell services. If it remains a membership association, it
must develop clear positions on the issues that are dividing the deaf community and stop trying to be all things to everyone.

The story of the Venerable Sports Club (VSC, also pseudonymous) is
similar to MAD's, except that the sports club ultimately liquidated. VSC was

founded more than a century ago to promote amateur sport and recreational activity in general. In the waning days of the twentieth century, club-based sports teams dwindled, and private fitness centers cut deeply into VSC's market.

As its facilities aged, its membership shrank. It responded to the changing environment by keeping dues low. A pricing strategy required increasing program service revenue, which meant charging members for things that similar clubs financed with member dues. As program service revenue grew relative to dues, VSC began to resemble a for-profit organization. The cost of maintaining a clubhouse was high, preventing it from lowering dues to a point where it could compete despite inferior facilities.

Unfortunately, the footprint of its ornate clubhouse was too small to accommodate contemporary attractions, like a new Olympic-sized swimming pool and an indoor hockey rink. While it still had a robust membership, VSC should have sold its clubhouse and built a new facility. Although it would have been prohibitively expensive to erect a building in the same neighborhood for its exclusive use, it could have entered into a joint venture with a developer to build a multiuse building including condominiums, hotel rooms, businesses, and a new sports club for itself featuring luxurious state-of-the-art facilities. Sadly, it is too late for VSC.

Concluding Thoughts

Membership associations and cooperatives are akin to businesses in the sense of having a fiduciary duty to uniquely identifiable individual persons, but they are akin to government in the way they are controlled through direct election of officers and participation in group decisions. To balance their budgets, membership organizations can increase membership dues, which function like a tax. However, they must be careful to balance the cost they impose on their members against the benefits provided.

Whereas the operations of ordinary nonprofits are guided by abstract values, the operations of membership associations and cooperatives are guided by common interests of their members. The interests may be economic or noneconomic. Economic interests are primary for cooperatives, business leagues, and labor, agricultural, and horticultural organizations, although they frequently promote noneconomic values as well. Noneconomic values are primary for literary, scientific, and professional societies, civic leagues and social welfare organizations, and social and recreational clubs, although their members may share common economic interests.

Appendix: ASAE/ CAL Metrics of Financial Capacity for Membership Associations

ASAE/CAL and this book have a similar perspective on the concept of financial capacity and sustainability without using precisely the same formulas. The following metrics are found in the ASAE/CAL *Operating Ratio Report* (2008). In the following formulas, *total fund balance* and *total fixed assets* are analogous to *net assets* and *land, buildings, and equipment (LB&E)*, respectively. Actually, the *Operating Ratio Report* does not specify the denominator of the fraction for formula B; total revenue is used here because it is more commonly used than expenses. The value for the median organization represented by ASAE/CAL members is also given.

$A \equiv$ Total liabilities/Total fund balance $= 0.5$
$B \equiv$ (Total revenue $-$ Total expense)/Total revenue $= 6.0\%$
$C \equiv$ Total revenue/Total assets $= 1$
$D \equiv$ (Total assets $-$ Total fixed assets)/Total assets $= 2.2$

Simple algebraic manipulation establishes the following transformation from the ASAE/CAL system to the system adopted in Chapter 6. The numerical values are calculated using the median values of the data items reported by all survey respondents (ASAE/CAL 2008, 27):

- Equity ratio $=$ Net assets/Total assets $= 1 - [A/(1 + A)] = 0.67$
- Return on assets (in %) $=$ Total surplus/Total assets $= B * C = 6.0\%$
- Months of spending $= 12 *$ (Net assets $-$ Equity in LB&E)/Expenses $= 12 * A * D/[C * (1 + A) * (1 - B)] = 9.4$
- Markup $= B/(1 - B) = 6.4\%$
- Status quo expense margin $= 3.4\% *$ Total assets/Expenses $= 3.6\%$

A few liberties were taken in the equation for months of spending. Because the median association had no long-term debt, equity in LB&E was replaced with LB&E alone. Likewise, interest and depreciation are only 1.5 percent of association expenses, so total expenses was used in the denominator.

CHAPTER 8

Endowed Service Providers
Serving the Next Generation, Too

Famous University and its host community have sparred for years. Many citizens and council members believe that the tax-exempt university should make voluntary payments in lieu of taxes (PILOTs) to the city. To support their position, they produce copies of the university's financial statements, which in some years show a total surplus nearly equal to revenue—a 100 percent "profit"! In reality, Famous University earns just a few percentage points above the minimum required for long-term sustainability. The disparity between popular belief and the reality of its financial condition suggests that an endowment complicates financial analysis. This chapter presents diagnostic tools for evaluating the financial condition of endowed service providers. Grantmakers are covered in Chapter 9.

This chapter characterizes an endowed organization as a service provider with a mutual fund subsidiary that supplies it with annual income according to a predetermined formula (Bowman 2002b). Several diagnostic tools are modified to accommodate the unique features of endowed organizations. This first section provides background on the history of endowments and the debate over their efficacy. The next section presents diagnostic tests of capacity and sustainability that parallel formulas from Chapter 6. The chapter closes with a summary of research on endowment building.

As defined in Chapter 3, an endowment is a portfolio of investments that provides an organization with a perpetual source of income. The point of having one is to permanently self-subsidize goods and services below their cost of production. An organization is *presumptively endowed* if it has at least as many dollars in securities and other investments as it has in annual total expenses. (The remainder of this chapter omits the adjective *presumptively* but it is implied.) Other nonprofits should use the formulas in Chapter 6. The book's companion web site, www.wiley.com/go/bowmanfinance, has spreadsheets that perform all calculations automatically.

Organizations with securities and other investments no larger than expenses should use formulas in Chapter 6. For simplicity, all diagnostic formulas applied to Famous University are calculated using data for a single year. In practice, diagnostics should be averaged over a three-year period to reduce volatility, as are Tables 8.1 through 8.3.

Introduction

Throughout history, disparate cultures have made use of endowments. In ancient Rome, Pliny the Younger "left a great sum of money for the support of 100 freedmen who had been his slaves, adding that after their deaths the income was to be used to provide an annual banquet for the people" (Panas 1984, 12). Monasteries owned one-third to one-half of all land in England at the time of their dissolution by Henry VIII (Fremont-Smith 1965, 17, citing Orton 1931). The Ottoman Empire committed as much as one-third of its vast lands to endowing projects for the benefit of the public (Goodwin 1999). In the American colonies, much of the capital needed by for-profit businesses came from endowments of charitable, educational, and religious institutions (McCarthy 2003; Hall 2006).

There are no data of the number of endowed nonprofits in the United States, but 10,000 public charities were endowed in 2003. Data on the sector used in this chapter are for a smaller set of 7,103 service providers that were endowed in at least three years between 1998 and 2003. (All are author's estimates.)

Table 8.1 shows the importance of endowed organizations to different fields of activity, excluding grantmaking—the subject of the next chapter. Although the majority of endowed organizations is dedicated to education, health care, or cultural activities, more than one in five of the following types are endowed: philanthropy and volunteerism, animal-related, medical research, education, science and technology research, social; science research, arts and culture, and environment. These percentages are biased upward because the sample excluded numerous small organizations (see Chapter 6) but the rank order is probably accurate.

Endowment is a financing tool that distinguishes the nonprofit and for-profit sectors. Profit-seeking businesses are not endowed unless required by law (e.g., cemeteries) or else legally organized as nonprofits (e.g., IKEA). Not even profit-seeking universities, hospitals, and theaters that compete with endowed nonprofit universities, hospitals, and theaters are endowed.

Contrary to common perception, endowed public charities own more wealth than do private foundations. Fremont-Smith (2002, 1) reports that

TABLE 8.1 Tax-Exempt Organizations in Fields of Activity Where Investments Provide More than 5 Percent Income, 2001–2003, Ranked by Percent and Number

% of Category		N	
29	Philanthropy and volunteerism (T)	1,433	Education (B)
27	Animal-related (D)	1,130	Health care (E)
26	Medical research (H)	927	Arts and culture (A)
24	Education (B)	888	Human services (P)
23	Science and technology research (U)	659	Housing (L)
23	Social science research (V)	254	Philanthropy and volunteerism (T)
21	Arts and culture (A)	247	Community improvement (S)
21	Environment (C)	229	Youth (O)
15	Health care (E)	187	Environment (C)
15	International and foreign affairs (Q)	169	Disease-related (G)
14	Housing (L)	140	Animal-related (D)
14	Youth (O)	124	Religious (X)
13	Public and society benefit (W)	110	Mental health and crisis prevention (F)
12	Disease-related (G)	106	Recreation (N)
12	Public safety and disaster relief (M)	103	Medical research (H)
11	Community improvement (S)	94	International and foreign affairs (Q)
11	Religious (X)	87	Science and technology research (U)
10	Recreation (N)	64	Public and society benefit (W)
8	Human services (P)	50	Employment (J)
7	Civil rights, social action, and advocacy (R)	48	Crime prevention and legal (I)
5	Agriculture, food, and nutrition (K)	32	Social science research (V)
4	Mental health and crisis prevention (F)	29	Civil rights, social action, and advocacy (R)
4	Crime prevention and legal (I)	27	Public safety and disaster relief (M)
4	Employment (J)	24	Agriculture, food, and nutrition (K)

Grantmakers and mutual benefit organizations are excluded. Data here is based on sample used in Chapters 6 and 8. NTEE code in parentheses.

financial holdings of endowed public charities, other than churches, grew from $777 billion in 1988 to $1.77 trillion in 1998. The growth of nonprofit financial holdings was 7.8 percent in real terms, including new contributions as well as investment earnings, which is greater than annual real growth of 4.8 percent in households' financial wealth and 3.5 percent in business holdings. However, endowed public charities still own only 10 percent of the market value of all stocks and bonds of U.S. corporations.[1]

From society's point of view, endowments promote intergenerational equity. As James Tobin, the 1981 Nobel laureate in economics, pointed out, "The trustees of an endowed institution are the guardians of the future against the claims of the present" (Tobin 1974, 427).

Individual gifts, bequests, corporate gifts, and foundation grants fluctuate year to year with greater volatility than gross domestic product, and endowments provide a more stable base for charitable spending (Irvin 2007). Endowments increase the chances of organizational survival, thereby enhancing society's institutional memory and storehouse of expertise.

Practitioners who see the value of their organization's endowment may be surprised to discover policy makers challenge its social value. "If one considers the tax benefits arising from exemptions and charitable deductions as current subsidies, it is a short step to conclude that taxpayers have an immediate right to a real return on that subsidy" (Fremont-Smith 2002, 2). A McKinsey team led by former Senator Bill Bradley alleged that nonprofits "hold about $270 billion in excess capital in their endowments," and urged that it be spent down over 25 years (Bradley, Jansen, and Silverman 2003, 99).

Scholars (Frey 2002; Brody 1997; Hansmann 1990) argue that endowments shortchange the current generation because the economy is likely to grow and per capita income is likely to increase, which implies that future generations should subsidize the current generation (assuming it were possible) and not the other way around as endowments do.

There are other criticisms: (1) "excessive" endowments cause distrust of the entire nonprofit sector, (2) the economic return on the government's investment is long-term,[2] (3) endowments foster mission perversion and they can outlive the usefulness of their intended purpose, and (4) endowments put decision making in the hands of social elites (Irvin 2007).

"Annual giving to the nonprofit sector does not necessarily benefit from a redistribution of wealth to the wealthy," because 1 percent of households own one-third of private wealth and "people do not necessarily respond to nonprofit organizational distress during recessions by increasing their giving" (Irvin 2007, 451). On the contrary, individual giving correlates with booms and busts of the economic cycle. Endowments increase organizations' chances of surviving an economic downturn. The only legitimate justification for endowments, Hansmann (1990) acknowledges, is long-term survival.

Endowment critics view nonprofits as producers of goods and services only for *current* consumption and downplay their contribution to society's investment in itself. As Table 8.1 shows, endowments are prevalent among organizations dedicated to research and preserving society's cultural patrimony. If nonprofits relied entirely on current gifts, basic research would become extremely vulnerable to recessions, wars, natural disasters, and the vicissitudes of public policy. With no endowments, such catastrophes would inevitably interrupt crucial research projects and extinguish cultural patrimony piecemeal. Future generations might grow financially richer but they would wax poorer in other ways.

Long-Term Objective: Maintaining Services

A service provider's endowment functions like a wholly owned mutual fund subsidiary. Provided that the annual income produced by an endowment is based on a sustainable spending formula, endowment assets can and should be set aside when analyzing an organization's finances (Bowman, Tuckman, and Young forthcoming). In other words, long-term analysis should ignore the "mutual fund subsidiary" and focus on the service provider. The formulas in this section are the same as corresponding equations in Chapter 6, except that endowment assets are subtracted from total assets and net assets.

Financial Capacity

The metric of long-term capacity for an endowed service provider is the familiar equity ratio stripped of endowment assets:

$$ERe = (\text{Total net assets} - \text{Endowment assets})/(\text{Total assets} - \text{Endowment assets})$$

or equivalently, in terms of line numbers on the pre-2008 IRS Form 990:

$$ERe = (73B - 54aB - 54bB - 56B)/(59B - 54aB - 54bB - 56B)$$

Endowments tend to have negligible liabilities, so the formula assumes all liabilities are concentrated in the first term.[3] When endowment assets exceed total *net* assets, the numerator of ERe is negative.

The benchmarking method used to produce Tables 8.2 and 8.3 is explained in Chapter 6. According to Table 8.2, half of all endowed nonprofits have an ERe between 0.30 and 0.95 with a median of 0.77. Comparing Tables 8.2 and 8.3 with the corresponding tables of Chapter 6 shows endowed organizations to be similar to ordinary nonprofits in their long-term capacity—except that the percentage of solvent endowed organizations is surprisingly smaller.

TABLE 8.2 Capacity and Sustainability Percentiles for Endowed Nonprofits

Endowed: $N = 7,103^*$	Percentiles				
	25th	50th (Median)	75th	% > 0	% > SQ
Equity ratio	0.30	0.77	0.95	82	n.a.
Return on assets (%)	−11.6	−0.4	8.9	48	36
Months of spending	4.0	8.1	17.6	100	n.a.
Markup (%)	2.7	19.1	51.1	79	67
Liquidity (months)	1.0	4.3	12.5	84	n.a.
Change in liquidity (months)	−1.8	0	1.9	49	49

*Does not include grantmakers.
n.a. = Not applicable.

This oddity is probably an artificial result of the calculation's assumption that investments of securities and other assets (alternative investments) are in the endowment and none are in operating reserves. As Chapter 3 showed, one-quarter of Famous University's investments were not in its endowment. Therefore, it is reasonable to believe that all long-term statistics on Tables 8.2 and 8.3 are biased downward.

TABLE 8.3 Capacity Percentiles for Endowed Nonprofits by Field of Activity, Averages of 2001–2003 (Interquartile Range in *Italics*)

Field of Activity (NTEE)*	N	Solvent%†	ERe	MSe	Liquidity
Arts and culture (A)	927	94	0.90	8.0	5.2
			0.27	*10.0*	*11.2*
Education (B)	1,420	90	0.69	8.6	4.4
			0.51	*13.2*	*10.7*
Health care (E)	1,102	77	0.69	11.8	4.8
			0.91	*25.0*	*16.9*
Housing (L)	663	55	0.10	3.8	1.7
			1.12	*8.7*	*8.5*
Human services (P)	838	78	0.76	5.8	2.6
			0.86	*9.2*	*7.1*
	4,950				

Note: The interquartile range is the difference between the 75th and 25th percentiles.
*NTEE: National Taxonomy of Exempt Entities. NTEE group excluded where $N < 500$.
†Solvent % = Percent of organizations where total assets − securities and other assets > total liabilities.

The new IRS Form 990 requires information about assets in an endowment, providing actual data for future calculations. However, the closeness of the numbers between Chapters 6 and 8 suggests that the working assumption that all investments are in the endowment is a reasonable approximation. (See also Bowman, Tuckman, and Young, forthcoming.)

Financial Sustainability

The return on assets should be calculated in a manner consistent with ERe. The numerator of the following expression replaces investment revenue with allowed spending from endowment pursuant to a formula, and the denominator removes endowment assets from total assets:

$$\text{ROAe} = 100\% \cdot \text{Operating surplus}/(\text{Total assets} - \text{Endowment assets})$$

or equivalently,

$$\text{ROAe} = 100\% \cdot [1e + 2 + 3 + 6c + 9c + 10c + 11 + 0.05 \\ \cdot (54aA + 54bA + 56A) - 17]/(59B - 54aB - 54bB - 55cB)$$

If investments are zero, the expression becomes identical to the corresponding expression for ordinary service providers, and ROAe = ROA. If the spending formula is unknown, use a pro forma 5 percent of investments in securities plus other investments from an organization's IRS Form 990 return. Once again, the status quo ROAe is the same as the long-run rate of inflation. An actual ROAe above this rate will increase capacity; an actual ROAe below this rate will decrease it.

Half of all endowed nonprofits have an ROAe between –11.8 percent and 8.9 percent, with a median of –0.4 percent. The median is close to the ROA for ordinary service providers (1.0 percent), but endowed service providers have a wider range of ROAs. These differences with ordinary service providers may likewise be attributable to the assumption about which assets are in the endowment. If true, we must conclude that the long-term financial performance of endowed service providers is similar to that of ordinary service providers. It seems that increased wealth does not necessarily produce increased profitability over the long term.

Short-Term Objective: Resilience

The formula for short-term financial capacity of endowed service providers is quite different from the corresponding formula for ordinary service providers because, within reasonable limits, above-normal amounts of endowment assets *can* be spent in emergencies. In terms of the metaphor of endowed service providers introduced in this chapter, the "mutual fund subsidiary" comes to the aid of its service provider parent organization temporarily.

Financial Capacity

As explained in Chapter 3, the Uniform Prudent Management of Institutional Funds Act (UPMIFA) establishes a rebuttable presumption in favor of a 7 percent spending rate in economic emergencies caused by external conditions. Assuming a normal sustainable spending rate of 5 percent, the new 7 percent emergency standard allows increased spending for short periods, even if the market value of an endowment falls below the historic dollar value of restricted gifts. In effect, UPMIFA allows an organization to borrow from itself with a concomitant obligation to restore its endowment to the level before the crisis in real terms.

The numerator of the short-term capacity formula is the sum of an organization's operating reserve (or cash and savings on a Form 990 return) plus 10 percent of marketable securities. The latter figure is the difference between a sustainable 5 percent spending rate and a 7 percent emergency rate multiplied by five years. The five-year time span is arbitrary, but UPMIFA clearly contemplates emergencies to be temporary followed by restoration of an endowment to its precrisis level plus an increment to allow for inflation during the interim.

In the following formula, X equals actual operating reserve on financial statements, and Y equals cash plus savings on a Form 990 return. Months of spending for endowed nonprofits (MSe) are:

$$\text{MSe} = 12\,\text{months}$$
$$\cdot\,(\text{X or Y} + 10\%\,\text{of Marketable securities})/\text{Spending on operations}$$

or equivalently,

$$\text{MSe} = 12\,\text{months} \cdot [45\text{B} + 46\text{B} + 0.10 \cdot (54\text{aB} + 54\text{bB})]/(17 - 42\text{A})$$

This formula assumes all cash and marketable securities are available to deal with a crisis, not just securities in the endowment. There is no published benchmark that specifically applies to endowed organizations, but it is reasonable to use the same standard as for ordinary service providers, namely MSe $\geq$ 3 months.

Overall, according to Table 8.2, half of endowed nonprofits have an MSe between 4.0 and 17.6 months, with a median of 8.1 months. These figures are considerably more robust than the corresponding figures for ordinary service providers, but this is expected because endowments as a rule hold considerable wealth.

Financial Sustainability

Short-term sustainability is the degree to which operations and a spending formula contribute to maintaining physical asset value.[4] The key variable in the numerator of the following formula is operating surplus, which excludes all investment-related revenue (interest, dividends, and realized and unrealized capital gains and losses) but includes net assets released from restrictions and spending from endowment pursuant to a spending formula.

The key short-term sustainability concept is annual cash surplus expressed as a percentage of spending on operations. This is analogous to markup in the business literature (notably in retailing), which is net earnings expressed as a percent of cost. The markup for endowed organizations (MUe) is:

MUe = 100% · (Operating surplus + Depreciation)/Spending on operations

where Operating surplus = Unrestricted operating revenue + Net assets released from restrictions for operations − Total return on investments + Allowed spending from endowment pursuant to formula − Total expenses.

If using IRS Form 990 data, Operating surplus = Noninvestment revenue plus 5 percent of endowment assets minus Change in restricted net assets. The 5 percent rate is pro forma. It approximates the maximum sustainable rate over the long term (DeMarche 1990; see Chapter 3). In terms of pre-2008 IRS Form 990 line numbers:

$$MUe = 100\% \cdot [1e + 2 + 3 + 6c + 9c + 10c + 11 + 0.05 \cdot (54aA + 54bA)$$
$$+ 56A − (68B − 68A) − (69B − 69A) − 17 + 42A]/(17 − 42A)$$

An organization is sustainable in the *short* term if markup is zero or greater and unsustainable if markup is negative. However, over the long term MUe must *also* equal or exceed SQ-MUe, which is given by:

MUe ≥ SQ-MUe
= 3.4% · (Total assets − Endowment assets)/Spending on operations

Half of all endowed nonprofits have a MUe between 2.7 percent and 51.1 percent, with a median of 19.1 percent (Table 8.2). These rates are substantially larger than corresponding numbers for ordinary service providers, especially at the median and 75th percentiles. The difference is probably attributable to many unrestricted gifts to the endowment.

Current Objective: Paying Bills

Like any other organization, endowed organizations have bills to pay. Therefore, formulas for current financial capacity (liquidity) and current sustainability (change in liquidity) are exactly the *same* for endowed and ordinary service providers.

Half of endowed nonprofits have a number of months of liquidity between 1.0 and 12.5 with a median of 4.3, which is more robust than the corresponding figures for ordinary service providers, especially at the median and 75th percentiles. Over 84 percent have adequate liquidity, which is similar to ordinary nonprofits.

The change in liquidity for half of endowed nonprofits is between −1.8 and 1.9 months, with a median of zero. This is also very similar to ordinary service providers. These patterns suggest that most nonprofits handle liquidity similarly and they try to optimize around a liquidity level that is adequate for staying current on their bills.

Application: Famous University

University financial statements account for tuition revenue on a net basis—that is, institutional aid (scholarships) is deducted from nominal tuition—but the IRS Form 990 reports tuition on a gross basis and institutional aid as an expense (see Chapter 3). The following statistics are calculated from data on Famous University's financial statements for 2007.

Equity ratio, endowed*	0.65	Standard ≥ 0.50
Return on assets, endowed	4.8%	Status quo = 3.4%
Months of spending, endowed	4.4	Standard ≥ 3.0
Markup, endowed	8.4%	Status quo = 5.3%
Liquidity (months)	1.3	Standard ≥ 1.0
Change in liquidity (months)	(0.1)	Status quo ≥ 0

*Uses actual investments in endowment from Table 3.3. Other data are from Tables 2.1 through 2.3.

Famous University's capacity across all time frames is superior. According to Table 3.3, investments in endowment are three-quarters of total investments. Using this figure, ERe is 0.65. This robust figure is expected because Famous University is one of the best-endowed universities in the United States. The school's short-term capacity is a healthy 4.4 months of spending. Likewise, liquidity is equivalent to 1.3 months.

The school's long- and short-term sustainability metrics are calculated using operating surplus from Table 2.2. Gifts and grants for buildings and equipment must be added to obtain the numerator of ROAe. Famous University does not include net assets released from restrictions in operating revenue, so this must be added to operating surplus to obtain the numerator of MUe (see Chapter 4).

In the long term, Famous University is sustainable. ROAe is 4.8 percent, compared to a SQ-ROAe of 3.4 percent. Its markup (budget surplus) is 8.4 percent, compared to a SQ-MUe of 5.3 percent, indicating that budget surpluses are sufficient to sustain it over the long term. The university is financially robust—its MUe is 3 percentage points above the status quo rate. However, its markup is 8.4 percent, not 100 percent as some local critics allege. Liquidity deteriorated slightly during the year, but liquidity was ample so a small negative change is no cause for concern.

The working assumption used in benchmarking is that all investments are in the endowment, which produces an ERe of 0.36, supporting the conclusion that the ERe figures on Table 8.2 are biased downward.

Building an Endowment[5]

Building an endowment using only cash flow from annual operating surpluses is both difficult and time consuming. Endowments require major gifts. There is no generally accepted definition of major gift but a rule of thumb might be 50 to 100 times the median gift received in routine annual solicitations. Prospecting for and cultivating major donors requires a substantial investment of time and money long before receiving the first major gift.

Ronald Ehrenberg's experience as Vice President for Finance at an Ivy League university is illustrative. During a five-year $1.5 billion capital campaign, his university spent 8 cents per dollar raised. However, "many academic units felt poorer, rather than richer, in the short run [because] university development is funded through a "tax" on the units.

While the units were paying 8 cents for each dollar raised, those dollars that went into the endowment yielded them only 4 cents of income per dollar raised in the initial year" (Ehrenberg 2000, 47). The "tax" to pay the cost of the capital campaign came from each unit's general operating budget but the new money funded new initiatives. In the meantime, existing activities were squeezed.

Many gifts were actually pledges, which further reduced the academic units' returns from fund-raising in the short run. Some projects turned out to be inadequately funded, such as an endowed chair without adequate funds for associated space and staff support. In these cases, the affected academic unit had to make up the difference out of its general operating budget (Ehrenberg 2000).

Brody (1997, 938) wonders why anyone would give money to institutions with multibillion-dollar endowments. However, "People do not give because there is a need. . . . [D]onors run away from 'needs.' They hide from institutions that are not financially stable" (Panas 1984, 35). "Donors like the idea of perpetuity" (Ostrower 1995, 4).

"[Endowment] definitely is a kind of institutional solidification. . . . What it means long-term is enormous. It's got to make funders more confident" (Lee 2004, B7).[6] Big donors think of their gifts as investments (Schumacher 2003) and a well-endowed organization, with its obvious track record as a financial steward, is better able to protect their investment.

The social dimension to major gifts cannot be ignored. James Gamble, grandson of the founder of Procter & Gamble, "says that he feels there is a great deal of giving by association. People enjoy being part of the club. People enjoy being associated with prominent men and women who are giving to the same cause" (Panas 1984, 51).

"Organizations are not merely conduits for philanthropy or intermediaries between individual donors and beneficiaries, but are themselves the focal point of donors' interests and concerns" (Ostrower 1995, 141). Even when donors have no connection to an institution, their regard for it often dominates their interest in the project.

As Arthur Rubloff, the late Chicago real estate developer, explained his multimillion-dollar gifts to the University of Chicago and Northwestern University: "I had no particular interest in either project—I gave because of my regard for both institutions" (Panas 1984, 81).

Because of the broad support enjoyed by cultural and educational institutions, giving to them will evoke admiration extending well beyond their circle of friends and acquaintances. The common values associated with culture and education "contribute to defining a distinctive and shared culture of philanthropy among the elite" (Ostrower 1995, 139).

In the 1960s, the future looked bleak for the 143-year-old Brooklyn Academy of Music (abbreviated BAM; Bowman 2007). There was much talk of closing the doors and converting the property into tennis courts. The situation worsened in the 1980s when crack cocaine made inroads into the surrounding community. BAM's response was to stimulate interest by creating something new. The academy launched the Next Wave Festival, which it has produced every year since. After the festival proved it had staying power, BAM inaugurated an endowment in 1992. After years of struggling to survive, BAM was reborn thanks to a $6.8 million facelift and major gifts that increased its endowment from $18 million to $50 million.

The Brooklyn Academy of Music demonstrated wise sequencing. Donors are wary of a dying institution. A life-saving gift creates what insurance companies call moral hazard, meaning the gift reduces an institution's incentive to change its ways. If a large gift does not rescue the institution, the money is wasted. Donors prefer to give to viable and relevant institutions. Furthermore, BAM is not cutting back on fund-raising. Its newly enhanced endowment "buys some breathing space for long-range planning amid the hectic pace of [annual] fund-raising" (Lee 2004).[7] BAM did not make the same mistake as the organization in the opening vignette of Chapter 3.

Concluding Thoughts

This chapter characterized an endowed organization as a service provider with a mutual fund subsidiary that supplies it with annual income according to a predetermined formula. It presented several diagnostic tools modified to strip away the mutual fund to expose the finances of the service provider.

Endowment plays a dual role as part of a nonprofit's capital structure and as a revenue generator. An endowment provides a perpetual source of generally unrestricted income. An endowment severs the connection between cost and income, which expands the possibilities open to values-centered management. An endowment enables an organization to contribute to society's investment in itself by providing services below their actual cost indefinitely.

The median long-term financial performance of endowed service providers, as measured by return on assets, appears to be similar to the performance of ordinary service providers. In other words, managers of endowed organizations behave so that an organization's wealth per se does not necessarily and uniformly lead to increased profitability in the long term.

Endowed service providers tend to be more liquid than ordinary service providers, but both appear to have a target level of liquidity that they strive to maintain.

The greatest difference between endowed and ordinary service providers is in the short term. Endowed organizations have more resources to fall back on in an emergency and their operating surpluses appear to be uniformly greater.

CHAPTER 9

Grantmaking Organizations
Serving Service Providers

In the public's mind, *foundation* is a term identified with grantmaking. However, technically it describes an organization's tax status, not its function. Because this chapter emphasizes function over form, it refers to non-profits with program grants comprising at least one-third of their program expenses as *grantmakers*.[1] Organizations *not* classified as foundations by the Internal Revenue Code (IRC), but having grantmaking as a primary purpose, are variously known as *public organizations, public foundations*, and *grantmaking public charities* (Collins 2008). This chapter utilizes these terms interchangeably with a particular usage determined by the source cited.

Grantmaking finance models are amazingly varied. This chapter illustrates the point with data on three real corporate grantmakers. (Primary colors are used as substitute names here.) Red is a private foundation with a modest endowment. Blue has no endowment and it qualifies as a public organization by the "30 percent public support" test. Yellow is heavily endowed, qualifying as a public organization by the "10 percent public support plus facts and circumstances test." (Chapter 5 describes these tests.) Yellow is the only grantmaker that provides direct service to the public in addition to making grants.

This chapter begins by sorting out differences between public organizations and private foundations. It differentiates between types of grantmakers, focusing on endowed grantmakers because the issues of capacity and sustainability are particularly relevant for this category. An applications section examines the finances of Red, Blue, and Yellow and explores the question of why people give money to a corporate foundation when they would not give directly to the corporation itself. An appendix shows how

metrics of creditworthiness developed by Standard & Poor's are algebraic
transformations of the metrics of capacity developed in Chapters 6 and 8.

Foundation Types

The IRC divides 501(c)(3) organizations into public organizations and private
foundations based on their funding sources. However, the grantmaking
community divides grantmakers by sponsorship: independent, corporate,

TABLE 9.1 Foundation Number and Characteristics by Type, 2007

	All ($ in Mn)	Percent of Total	Largest* ($ in Bn)	Percent of Total
Independent				
Number	63,059	89%	273	64%
Giving	$ 25,199	69%	$ 11,470	58%
Assets	$455,570	83%	$225,964	82%
Gifts received	$ 17,365	55%	$ 2,854	23%
Corporate				
Number	2,607	4%	74	17%
Giving	$ 3,995	11%	$ 2,372	12%
Assets	$ 17,795	3%	$ 6,942	3%
Gifts received	$ 4,008	13%	$ 2,156	18%
Community				
Number	707	1%	60	14%
Giving	$ 3,217	9%	$ 2,391	12%
Assets	$ 44,583	8%	$ 30,489	11%
Gifts received	$ 5,586	18%	$ 3,953	32%
Operating				
Number	4,722	7%	21	5%
Giving	$ 3,990	11%	$ 3,520	18%
Assets	$ 32,602	6%	$ 12,838	5%
Gifts received	$ 4,504	14%	$ 3,315	27%
Total				
Number	71,095	100%	428	100%
Giving	$ 36,401	100%	$ 19,753	100%
Assets	$550,550	100%	$276,233	100%
Gifts received	$ 31,463	100%	$ 12,278	100%

*Foundations that make more than $10 million in total grants annually.

Source: Foundation Center (2007, x–xi).

and community (see Table 9.1). Only the latter group predominantly consists of public organizations as defined by the IRC.

Regardless of how these grantmaking organizations are classified, they have "come to be counted on as a critical, and often first, funding source for new and innovative nonprofit sector projects." Further, their "giving continues to grow in size and is expected to explode as the baby-boom generation ages and declines" (Deep and Frumkin 2001, 2). Public acceptance and legitimacy of these organizations assume spending policies that address human needs and social change, promote pluralism, and are cost-effective in targeting resources (Prewitt 2006, 359).

Financing Models

The threshold question is whether a foundation is to be perpetual or to have a limited life. The answer depends on the founding donor's philosophy, and it is fraught with operational implications. At an analytical level, the concept of sustainability only makes sense when applied to perpetual endowments.

Assuming that a founder's plans call for a grantmaker to have perpetual existence, should it be an endowed or a conduit organization? This section looks at issues for founders making such a choice. A perpetual conduit obviously requires a perpetual donor, which requires a corporate or community sponsor.

Perpetual or Limited Life?

Several studies have found that 8 to 10 percent of foundations have plans to spend all assets within a fixed time period (Ostrower 2009). These *limited-life,* or sunsetting, foundations typically have less than $10 million in assets and a living donor. Foundations supporting human services and the arts are more likely to plan for a limited life (ibid.).

An early proponent of sunsetting grantmaking foundations was Julius Rosenwald, a Sears Roebuck founder, who declared, "By adopting a policy of using the fund within this generation we may avoid those tendencies toward bureaucracy and a formal or perfunctory attitude toward the work which almost always develops in organizations which prolong their existence indefinitely" (quoted in Bradley, Jansen, and Silverman 2003, 99).

Other critics of perpetual foundations point out that their goals and objectives tend to drift away from those of founding donors (e.g., the Ford Foundation) (Thelin and Trollinger 2009). Among foundations whose founders are deceased, 91 percent of spokesmen for limited-life foundations say adherence to the founding donor's wishes is "very important" compared to 65 percent of spokesmen for perpetual foundations (Ostrower 2009, 5).

The choice between limited or perpetual life is a donor's prerogative. "It is true that foundations may do things in the future that the donor would not like, but the donor takes that risk in specifying that a foundation will exist a long time"[2] (SSIR 2004, 58). Experts stress that "the decision about foundation lifespan should be made at the outset and stated explicitly in the foundation's organizing documents [and] . . . should be a matter of strategy for achieving desired philanthropic outcomes" (Thelin and Trollinger 2009, 38).

According to Deep and Frumkin (2001), additional arguments in favor of limited life foundations include:

1. concentrating resources on a problem may actually solve it and, in any case, will prevent it from getting worse (e.g., finding a cure for a disease or acquiring wilderness land);
2. the benefits that a given generation of taxpayers realizes from grant-making should roughly equal the loss of tax revenue from the founding gift;
3. future generations will be wealthier and able to finance grantmaking without assistance from earlier and relatively poorer generations; and
4. spending down an endowment improves a foundation's legitimacy in the eyes of the public and elected representatives.

However, proponents of perpetual foundations argue (Deep and Frumkin 2001):

1. problems are likely to become worse so resources must be conserved to address them in the future, and good stewardship demands husbanding resources in perpetuity;
2. spending down an endowment is prodigal;
3. future social needs are hard to predict, and new problems will certainly emerge; and
4. there are limits to the amount of money that any grantee can effectively utilize, and a rapid spend-down may exceed these limits and waste the funds.

The arguments in favor of *community* foundations, all of which have perpetual life, are somewhat different. Despite their common designation as foundations, community foundations are typically 501(c)(3) public organizations with a mission to support charitable work within a particular geographic area (community) that accept donations of all sizes from multiple donors. These foundations, unlike those established by great estates, are constantly raising money. As Peter Hero, president of Community Foundation of Silicon Valley said:

> *With community foundations, there is not only the opportunity but the obligation to aggregate wealth that's being created at the time it's being created because it may not be there forever. The first community foundation was created in Cleveland in 1914. Cleveland in 1914 was Silicon Valley in 2001, with the steel, coal, and oil industries creating enormous growth. By 1950, however, Cleveland had been passed by and its economy was deteriorating. It was the community foundation, which by then had aggregated close to a billion dollars, that led Cleveland's downtown revitalization and helped bring the city back.* (SSIR 2004, 57)

Sears founder Rosenwald worried that grantees would become too dependent on grants and ossify. On the other side of the coin, nonprofits in small niches have difficulty raising money, and grants are their lifeblood. A headline in the *New York Times* summed it up: "As Foundations Close, Anxiety for Charities." The story reported that "Concerns run highest among lightly financed charities that rely on just a few major donors. When the Paul Rapoport Foundation said in July that it would give away all of its $8 million endowment by 2014, the recipient charities—which serve gay, lesbian, and transgender people of color in the New York area—were deeply concerned" (Johnston 2009).

Conduit or Endowed?

The dominant financing model identifies a grantmaker as a conduit or an endowed organization. A *conduit* (or *pass-through*) is a grantmaker that acts as agent for a living donor or a corporation, distributing funds to multiple recipients without accumulating large amounts of assets and holding them for long periods of time. By contrast, endowed grantmakers rely heavily, often primarily, on an investment portfolio to generate a perpetual stream of income.

Grantmakers tend to be endowed or conduits but many corporate foundations are hybrids. A *corporate foundation* is a grantmaking organization sponsored by a taxable for-profit business corporation that serves as its primary funding source. A corporate foundation is legally separate from its sponsor (for tax purposes) but it is not always independent. Corporate representatives may be board members and the corporation may provide staff to its foundation from the corporate payroll.

Corporate foundations "[m]ay maintain small endowment and pay out most of the contributions received annually in grants, or may maintain endowment to cover contributions in years when corporate profits are down" (Johnston 2009, 48; see Yellow in the financial data table later in the chapter). In 2003 there were 2,549 corporate foundations owning $15.4 billion in assets and distributing $3.5 billion.

Direct giving by corporations, however, was nearly three times higher—$10.0 billion.[3] "[C]orporate direct giving programs have no IRS classification and are not subject to public disclosure requirements" (Collins 2008, 5). This book does not examine direct grantmaking by corporations. Since many grantmakers finance their largesse by a combination of endowment income and current donations from their sponsors, there is a need for a practical definition that enables researchers and policymakers to classify grantmakers as either conduits or endowed.

There are competing definitions of conduits. "A foundation functions as a conduit when it makes qualifying distributions equal to 100 percent of all contributions received in the year involved, whether money or property" (Hopkins 2008, 4). However, researchers at the Urban Institute define a conduit foundation as one that makes grants equal to or exceeding 20 percent of its assets (Boris, Renz, Barve, Hager, and Hobor 2006, 15). By this criterion, 22 percent of foundations are conduits.

This chapter applies two tests jointly. *A grantmaker is presumptively endowed if it simultaneously passes this book's endowment test (securities and other investments exceed expenses)* and *fails the Urban Institute's conduit test.* The proportion of private foundations that are presumptively endowed by this standard is 52 percent.

Conversely, *a grantmaker is presumptively conduit if it either passes the conduit test* or *it fails the endowment test.* The proportion of private foundations that are presumptively conduits is 48 percent—approximately double the estimate by Boris et al.[4] The difference in estimates indicates a substantial group of foundations that strongly exhibit characteristics of both types.

For reasons spelled out in the next section, the concepts of capacity and sustainability do not apply to grantmakers without an endowment. The following section parallels previous chapters by offering metrics for measuring financial performance. These metrics are compared with those used by Standard & Poor's (S&P), a credit rating agency.

Capacity and Sustainability

The Foundation Center (2004, 47–48), recognized 66,398 private foundations and public organizations in 2003. Foundations "vary substantially not only by size but also in ways they accomplish their work, the geographic scope of their giving, and the kinds of programs they undertake. These differences have a pronounced effect on charitable expenditures" (Boris et al. 2006, 3).

Eighty-seven percent of foundations make grants, compared to only 18.4 percent of public organizations. However, some foundations give very little. Foundations whose *primary* purpose is grantmaking comprise 81 percent of private foundations and 9.7 percent of public organizations (by the one-third rule; author's calculation). The IRC determines whether a grantmaker is a private foundation or a public organization.

It would be unreasonable to apply the concepts of financial capacity and sustainability to conduits, because current grantmaking is closely tied to current contributions. The capacity and sustainability of conduits are the same as the capacity and sustainability of their principal donor or donors—which is proprietary information.

Operating foundations function more like service providers than like grantmakers. It is pointless to analyze the capacity and sustainability of limited-life and conduit grantmakers, so this section focuses on grantmakers organized as endowed, nonoperating private foundations or as endowed public organizations. Indeed, many authors argue that perpetual endowment is the hallmark of a modern grantmaker (Thelin and Trollinger 2009; Prewitt 2006; de Borms 2005; Foundation Center 2004).

Grantmaking Capacity

Over 95 percent of grantmakers have a minor amount of liabilities (Commonfund 2009, 52).[5] "Foundations are prohibited [by federal law] from issuing tax-exempt debt for noncapital purpose or for arbitrage. Thus, allowable tax-exempt debt is frequently quite modest relative to an organization's asset base" (Standard & Poor's 2001; arbitrage is described in the Glossary).

For grantmakers with appreciable liabilities and operating foundations, the metrics of Chapter 6 are appropriate, and they are closely related to capacity concepts used by the credit rating agency, Standard & Poor's (S&P). Table 9.2 presents calculations translating S&P's minimum values for 2001 into the corresponding capacity metrics used in this book.

The equity ratio of endowed private foundations are not comparable to the equity ratios of endowed service providers because equity ratios for endowed service providers are calculated without their endowment assets whereas endowed private foundations are essentially free-standing endowments. Since most private foundations are nonoperating and are barred from issuing long-term debt except for capital construction, they have substantial long-term capacity thanks to low debt.

The recommended operating reserve for ordinary service providers is three months of spending (MS), which is well below the minimum for a BBB rating. The median of 1.2 months for that population is even lower. Unfortunately, necessary data are not available to enable calculation of a median for private foundations but a low actual figure for service providers compared to grantmakers is to be expected.

TABLE 9.2 Minimum Values of Key Financial Ratios per Standard & Poor's, 2001

	AAA	AA	A	BBB
Long-Term Capacity (Ordinary and Endowed)				
Expendable resources-to-debt	10.0	5.0	2.0	1.0
Equity ratio (in %)	90.9	83.3	66.7	50.0
Expendable resources-to-operations	10.0	6.0	2.0	0.5
Equity ratio (in %)	90.9	85.7	66.7	33.3
For comparison: Median equity ratios				
Actual population	99.9			
Endowed providers		77.0		
Short-Term Capacity (Ordinary)				
Unrestricted resources-to-debt	10.0	5.0	2.0	1.0
Months of spending	120.0	72.0	24.0	6.0
Unrestricted resources-to-operations	10.0	6.0	2.0	0.5
Months of spending	120.0	72.0	24.0	6.0
For comparison: Median months of spending				
Actual population	n.a.	n.a.	n.a.	n.a.
Ordinary providers			2.7	
Short-Term Capacity (Endowed)				
Cash and investments-to-debt	10.0	5.0	2.0	1.0
Months of spending	10.0	6.0	2.0	0.5
Cash and investments-to-operations	10.0	6.0	2.0	0.5
Months of spending	10.0	6.0	2.0	0.5
For comparison: Median months of spending				
Actual population	20.2			
Endowed providers	8.1			

If, as S&P avers, "grantmaking foundations have more budgetary flexibility than foundations that run their own programs," it is also true that they have more flexibility than ordinary service providers that do not make grants. Flexibility is reflected in lower operating reserves, which months of spending (MSe) represents.

The recommended operating reserve for endowed service providers is similarly three months of spending. The median for that population is 8.1 months, which is in the AAA category, and the median for private foundations is nearly 20.2 months (also AAA). The large securities portfolios found among all endowed organizations improve short-term capacity.

Like all organizations, grantmakers must have adequate liquidity, but their needs are different (Commonfund 2009). Grantmaking usually occurs according to an easily anticipated schedule. Professionally managed grant-makers arrange to liquidate investments on a predetermined schedule and maintain a line of credit as backup for emergencies. They can endure weeks and months with very little liquidity and yet have ample liquidity when they need it. Unfortunately, S&P does not include liquidity among its capacity metrics.

According to Standard & Poor's (2001), "The overall credit quality of the foundation sector is quite high, with 14 or 70% of these [rated] entities rated in the 'AAA' or 'AA' category. As of 2001, the credit outlook for this sector is fairly solid, with all publicly rated foundations carrying a 'stable' outlook." A reasonable interpretation of this statement is that credit quality is analogous to capacity, and outlook is analogous to sustainability.

Grantmaking Sustainability

Similar to endowed service providers, endowed grantmakers are sustainable if a payout rate plus the long-term rate of inflation is no greater than the average long-term return on a portfolio (DeMarche 1999). The federally mandated minimum annual payout for all foundations is based on assets. It has little impact on 48 percent of foundations that are conduits. That is the point. It is designed to prevent foundations from becoming "warehouses of wealth" (Toepler 2004), and conduits raise fewer public policy concerns.

Federal law requires a minimum annual payout of approximately 5 percent of qualified assets,[6] which was 2.65 percentage points less than average investment returns between 1971 and 1996 (Deep and Frumkin 2001). The difference approximates the long-term rate of inflation. American foundations distribute, on average, 5.5 percent and even during the recent market collapse payouts averaged 5.8 percent (Commonfund 2009).

"Distribute" is not the same as "give away." Qualifying distributions include most operating expenses as well as set-asides and charitable investments. Actual grants exceed 5 percent of assets for no more than two in three foundations (author's calculation). Program-related investments (PRIs; see Chapter 3) qualify as distributions provided the investments of "significantly further the foundation's exempt activities. They must be investments that would not have been made except for their relationship to the exempt purposes" (U.S. Department of the Treasury 2009c).

For the 10,000 largest foundations, ranked by giving, the sum of charitable operating and administrative expenses represents 6 percent for the largest corporate foundations, 7 percent of qualifying distributions for most private foundations, and 8 percent for the largest community foundations (Boris et al. 2006; see Table 9.1). The higher figure for community foundations probably reflects their constant fund-raising efforts, which distinguish them from other foundations.

Occasionally proposed legislation would require a higher minimum payout and/or excluding administrative expenses from the qualifying distribution.[7] A Commonfund benchmark survey reported that the investment return (net of management fees) objective for most of its survey respondents is the consumer price index plus a target distribution rate ranging from 4 to 6 percent (Commonfund 2009, 30). A higher minimum payout would likely result in inflation eroding the purchasing power of endowment portfolios or capital losses diminishing them as foundations chase higher returns by making riskier investments (Toepler 2004).

Donors want their names "attached to something that would provide value to society in perpetuity" (SSIR 2004, 58). If foundations had mandatory payout rates that were unsustainable while operating charities (ordinary service providers) did not, there would be "a half dozen to a dozen categories of operating charities that would be appealing and very easy for donors to endow"—thereby depriving foundations (59).

As Toepler (2004) observes, reform proposals often have unintended consequences. Currently, a private foundation must pay a 2 percent tax on investment income, which is reduced to 1 percent if it meets certain distribution requirements.[8] This has the perverse effect of discouraging deviations from long-term averages, as the following example describes:

> *Suppose that for the current year only, the managers are considering increasing the payout rate [from 5%] to 5.01% . . . this increase in the payout rate will still allow the foundation to pay only one percent excise tax in the current year but will increase the threshold that it has to meet in future years' payouts. If the foundation continues to pay out only five percent in subsequent years, it will fail to meet this threshold, thereby doubling its excise tax rate to two percent of NII [net investment income]* in each and every year *in the future* (Deep and Frumkin 2001, 26; emphasis in the original).

The effect of this requirement is mixed. Some foundation managers "make their spending decisions in a manner so as not to be saddled with the higher excise [tax] rate in the foreseeable future. The only way to do this is to increase the payout rate only when foundation managers are certain they will be able to sustain the higher payout rate forever" (Deep and Frumkin 2001, 27). Other foundations ignore it in their spending decisions.

"Payout regulation is efficient and appropriate as long as it ensures that future grant distributions exceed whatever deductions the donor was allowed to take in the first place," with future grants being discounted to the present (Toepler 2004, 736; the Glossary explains present value). By this standard, the current requirement is satisfactory.

Illustrations

Table 9.3 presents data from IRS Forms 990 and 990-PF for three real grant-makers sponsored by corporations having the corporate sponsor's name in their titles. Two of them are public organizations because at least 30 percent of their income comes from the general public, which raises an interesting question: Since no one *gives* money to corporations, why do they give money to corporate foundations? Although they may support a corporate foundation's projects, they might worry that public donations would give the sponsoring corporation an incentive to reduce its financial support (a "crowding out" effect). These foundations have discovered clever solutions to this problem.

How do the corporate-sponsored foundations obtain public support? Yellow joins with small local charities to co-sponsor fund-raising events. The local charities do the work of organizing the event, Yellow provides administrative support and helps with marketing, and they share the proceeds. Blue runs frequent lotteries. These techniques leave unmistakable signatures on the data.

The sponsor of Red gave it money only once in the past five years. The sponsors of Yellow and Blue give them in-kind contributions annually. The numbers for Red in Table 9.3 are five-year averages; for Yellow and Blue they are one-year figures. The table omits investment-related income and substitutes a pro forma payout from endowment (investments) in calculating operating revenue.

The metrics in the last three lines of Table 9.4 are calculated according to Chapters 6 and 8 formulas. Blue's low equity ratio is due to income from games of chance being considered deferred revenue (a liability) until the organization awards prizes.

As expected, the endowed organization has a very large short-term capacity when the formula for ordinary service providers is used. Short-term capacity as measured by the formula appropriate to endowed service providers is ample but not ridiculously high.

Conversely, Blue, a conduit, has larger short-term capacity when measured by the formula appropriate for endowed service providers. Using the appropriate formula in each case gives results in the 12 to 24 range, which likely to earn an AAA rating from S&P for all three, other things being equal.

Concluding Thoughts

As with other nonprofits, mission is paramount for perpetual grant-makers. All experience a constant tension between accomplishing their mission and paying the bills. In 2007 the Aspen Institute convened five

TABLE 9.3 Financial Data on Selected Corporate Grantmakers

	Red[*]	Yellow	Blue
Total contributions	$ 3,058,524	$ 25,315,909	$ 514,786
Note: Noncash receipts		*2,008,588*	*234,418*
Program service revenue		9,975	
Gross receipts from events		6,480,080	321,672
Gross sales of inventory			234,918
Other revenue	919,820	81,550	819,118
Operating revenue[†]	**$ 6,947,410**	**$ 86,960,519**	**$ 883,005**
Grants distributed	3,749,811	81,328,066	3,093,424
Depreciation		121,217	
Taxes	46,451		
Prizes			309,437
Other expenses	186,215	7,276,696	134,614
Total expenses	$ 3,936,027	$ 88,604,762	$ 3,537,475
Operating surplus BITDA	**$ 3,011,383**	**$ (1,644,243)**	**$(2,654,470)**
Current assets	$ 2,297,271	$ 13,456,174	$ 8,044,251
Investments (securities) BOY	37,474,965	224,606,650	
Investments (securities) EOY	37,708,719	284,741,459	
Investments (other) BOY	21,906,356	1,119,074,958	
Investments (other) EOY	18,665,575	862,572,195	
LBE, net EOY		797,168	
Other assets		538,448	
Total assets BOY	62,229,794	1,173,606,130	6,474,224
Total assets EOY	**58,671,566**	**1,161,566,996**	**8,044,251**
Accounts payable	811,568	800,430	24,123
Grants payable		29,767,338	2,922,830
Deferred revenue			1,703,198
Mortgages	90,448		
Temporarily restricted net assets BOY			
Temporarily restricted net assets EOY			1,007,489
Permanently restricted net assets BOY			
Permanently restricted net assets EOY		2,003,776	
Net assets EOY	**$57,859,998**	**$1,130,999,228**	**$ 3,394,100**

[*]Five-year average.

[†]Revenue other than investment-related + pro forma payout − change in restricted net assets.

TABLE 9.4 Three Examples of Corporate Grantmakers

	Red*	Yellow	Blue
Type	PF + endowed	PC + endowed	PC + conduit
Programs[†]	0	Museum 11%	0
Sources of income[†]	Corporation 78%	Events 7%	Raffles 43%
		In-kind 2%	Events 17%
			Sales 12%
			In-kind 12%
Equity ratio	0.99	0.97	0.42
Months spending, ordinary	176	153	12
Months spending, endowed	24	17	20

*Based on five-year average data.
[†]Expressed as % of operating revenue.

forums with leaders of perpetual foundations in three major cities to explore how they balance their duty to increase assets and advance their mission without compromising either (Billitteri 2007). There was consensus that foundations must be reflective and have a written giving strategy and spending policy, and must review it periodically. Both strategy and spending policy should be robust with respect to market conditions. Moreover, foundations should have board members who "speak for the program side" of their work and should maintain a dialogue with founders or founder heirs.

Appendix: S&P Metrics of Financial Capacity for Grantmakers

Standard & Poor's (S&P), the well-known credit rating agency, uses six "key ratios" to evaluate an organization's credit—that is, its ability to repay debt. S&P assigns ratings from AAA (the most creditworthy) to BBB and even lower. The minimum values for the six ratios were given on Table 9.2.

1. SP1 ≡ Unrestricted and temporarily restricted net assets minus equity in land, buildings, and equipment (LBE) to debt.
2. SP2 ≡ Unrestricted and temporarily restricted net assets minus equity in LBE to operating expenses.
3. SP3 ≡ Unrestricted net assets minus equity in LBE to debt.
4. SP4 ≡ Unrestricted net assets minus equity in LBE to operating expenses.

5. SP5 ≡ Cash and investments to debt.
6. SP6 ≡ Cash and investments to operating expenses.

The even-numbered metrics can be derived from the odd-numbered metrics by multiplying by the ratio of operating expenses to debt, so only four metrics are independent: either the odd- or even-numbered ones, in addition to the ratio of debt to operating expenses. Comparing the minimums for the odd- and even-numbered ratios, the acceptable range for the ratio of operating expenses to debt is from 0.83 (AA) to 2.0 (BBB).

S&P metrics are simple transformations of the three capacity metrics presented in Chapters 6 and 8, assuming an acceptable ratio of operating expenses to debt (represented by Z) is 1.0. The following are the minimum acceptable values for this book's capacity metrics expressed in terms of S&P's metrics.

- *Long-term capacity:* $SP2 = SP1/Z$, which, given $Z = 1$, implies $ER = 100\% \cdot SP1/(SP1 + 1)$
- *Short-term capacity (ordinary):* $SP3 = SP4 \cdot Z$, which, given $Z = 1$, implies $MS = 12 \cdot SP4$
- *Short-term capacity (endowed):* $SP5 = SP6 \cdot Z$, which, given $Z = 1$, implies $MSe = 12 \cdot SP6$

S&P, of course, is primarily interested in creditworthiness, so it uses metrics that are related to ER, not ERe, which is stripped of endowment assets. There is insufficient information to derive ERe from the S&P metrics.

CHAPTER 10

Beyond Sustainability
Managing Revenue to Maximize Growth

On the Upper West Side of Manhattan, across Central Park from the Metropolitan Museum of Art (the Met), stands the New-York Historical Society (the Society). It was founded in 1804 as both a museum *and* a library 66 years before the Met and 91 years before the *nonprofit* New York Public Library (NYPL).[1] The combined expenses of these much younger institutions are now 30 times greater than the Society's. This chapter shows how the composition of its revenue sources contributed to this outcome.

The New-York Historical Society is over 200 years old, so sustainablity is not an issue, but it ceded its preeminent role among New York's museums and libraries to younger rivals. Sustainability is a necessary condition for long-term success but it is not sufficient. At issue is how an organization should manage its revenue composition to go beyond sustainability to maximize growth potential.

The chapter begins with a comparison of the finances of the three nonprofits in this vignette, as revealed in IRS Form 990 reports, which are publicly available through GuideStar (2010). It concludes with a discussion of the issues related to competition between tax-exempt and taxable entities, which the taxable entities complain is unfair.

Revenue Sources

Table 10.1 shows broad categories of revenue for major segments of the nonprofit sector. Private payments for selling goods and services to households and businesses provide over half. Government grants and payments

TABLE 10.1 Nonprofit Revenue Sources, 2005

	Total Revenue (bn $)	Distribution %				
		Private Gifts	Private Payments	Public Sources	Invest' Income	Other
Arts, culture, and humanities	23	**42.4**	29.1	12.5	9.2	6.7
Education	190	12.6	**56.0**	12.1	17.0	2.3
Higher education	152	10.8	**56.9**	11.1	19.1	2.1
Other education	38	19.8	**52.5**	16.0	8.7	3.0
Environment and animals	11	**48.0**	23.8	12.2	7.4	8.9
Health care	673	2.4	**56.4**	36.5	2.9	1.8
Hospitals	519	1.5	**54.1**	39.8	2.8	1.8
Other health care	154	5.6	**64.0**	25.5	3.3	1.5
Human services	143	15.8	**41.2**	36.3	2.7	4.0
International	20	**71.5**	5.6	19.8	1.9	0.6
Other reporting charities	41	22.3	**34.5**	31.4	8.9	2.9
Total	1,100	9.2	**51.7**	31.1	5.7	2.3

Note: Boldface indicates the dominant revenue source for each segment of the nonprofit sector.
Source: Wing, Pollak, and Blackwood (2008), appendix to chap. 4, p. 134.

for the services are next, comprising 31 percent. Private gifts, at 9.2 percent, are far behind in importance; however, this section shows that philanthropy has far greater impact than this number suggests. This section also explores issues related to commercial revenue.

Philanthropy

Philanthropy appears to be of minor importance. However, the figure in Table 10.1 is based on a very narrow definition of private giving, namely total money gifts from individuals divided by the total revenue of all non-profits (weighted average). Using a broader definition of philanthropic reve-nue as the sum of direct public support (gifts and grants), including noncash contributions, indirect support (United Way, Combined Federal Campaign, etc.), and net income from special events,[2] philanthropic revenue is 11.5 percent.[3]

However, even this understates philanthropy's impact. A better understanding is gained by calculating the ratio of philanthropic revenue to total revenue for every nonprofit and then averaging (un-weighted average). The average ratio is a more substantial 28 percent. (These calculations exclude endowed organizations because they are not typical of the sector.) The difference between 11.5 and 28 percent is due to smaller nonprofits having the same impact on the average as a large organization and gifts being a more significant part of the revenues of small nonprofits.

A second way to judge the importance of philanthropic revenue to ordinary nonprofits is to measure the proportion of them having more than 1 percent of total revenue. By this standard, 71 percent of ordinary nonprofits have more than minimal amounts of philanthropic revenue.

A third way to judge its importance is by the proportion of nonprofits that would have had a deficit *except for* philanthropic revenue. By this standard, philanthropic revenue prevented two of every five nonprofits from slipping into the red.[4]

Taking these results in their entirety, it appears that private philanthropy is very important to ordinary nonprofits as a group. However, as Chapter 1 pointed out, it is difficult to raise capital through private philanthropy, and capital constraints often limit nonprofits' growth potential; but there are exceptions.

In a study seeking commonalities among the largest 100 nonprofits[5] plus 144 nonprofits that grew to at least $50 million in revenues since their inception in 1970 or later, researchers identified 10 funding models (Foster, Kim, and Christiansen 2009). Three models relied heavily on philanthropic revenue:

1. A small number of large donors, who believe that certain problems can be solved once and for all by a "huge influx of money," support nonprofits that target these problems. The classic example is the March of Dimes. Other examples: Conservation International and Stanley Medical Research Institute.
2. Many small donations combine to provide huge resources to nonprofits that target popular causes. Corporate sponsorships of these organizations tap into the mass appeal. Examples: Make-a-Wish Foundation and Susan G. Komen for the Cure.
3. Some highly specialized organizations rely heavily on gifts in kind. Businesses are their primary donors, and the goods would otherwise go to waste if not gifted to nonprofits. Examples: Greater Boston Food Bank and AmeriCares Foundation.

Despite exceptions, Chapter 1's point about most nonprofits facing capital constraints remains generally valid.

Commercial Revenue

Many scholars are concerned that commercial operations may divert the attentions of nonprofit managers away from helping their beneficiaries (Weisbrod 2004). It also raises the policy question of whether especially commercial nonprofits, such as hospitals, continue to deserve their tax exemption. Nonprofits seeking further earned income should realize they are stepping into this debate. However, they should also realize every source of funds has side effects, not always desirable (Froelich 1999, 261).

Industries where increasing commercialism is most dramatic (like health care) are those where technology and institutional changes have made product pricing more feasible and where "tax and subsidy advantages to, and constraints upon, nonprofits have been lifted since the early 1980s" (James 1998, 279).

Museums, social service organizations, zoos, and public broadcasting have exhibited financing patterns that are more consistent with the conventional hypothesis that nonprofits become more commercial and "*cross-subsidize* when they are driven to do so by a reduction in public or private donations" (James 279). (Cross-subsidy occurs when net earnings from one part of an organization subsidize below-cost production in another part of an organization.)

Higher levels of commercial revenue do not significantly improve an organization's mission achievement and service and/or program delivery, nor do they appear to affect the relationship between an organization and donors (Guo 2006, 135). Although some segments of the nonprofit sector seem to be increasingly reliant on commercial income, it is not true of the sector as a whole (Kerlin and Pollak 2010).

Goal displacement is more likely to occur in nonprofits that find new revenue in unrelated businesses *or* net earnings of taxable subsidiaries. Note: the term *unrelated* applies only to revenue earned by a tax-exempt nonprofit, not to net earnings of a taxable subsidiary of a tax-exempt nonprofit.

One in five tax-exempt nonprofits operates at least one unrelated taxable activity. Average annual revenues of these activities are $1.5 million (Yetman and Yetman 2009, 495). Taking the sector as a whole, taxable revenues earned by taxable subsidiaries are at least as large as the taxable revenues earned by unrelated businesses.

Reasons to establish a taxable subsidiary include shielding the parent organization from business risks associated with a commercial venture and protecting the parent's tax-exempt status. The Mozilla Foundation, owner of rights to Firefox, a popular Web browser, formed a corporate subsidiary in 2005 to promote wider adoption, documentation, and browser standards.

In 2008 it formed another taxable subsidiary to promote Thunderbird, its e-mail product. Mozilla Foundation will continue technical development of its open-source products with a worldwide army of volunteer programmers. In 2009, Foundation expenses were $2.5 million and assets were $27.5 million.

Establishing a taxable subsidiary requires competent legal advice.[6] The following six general principles, however, may help preliminary planning (Plunkett and Christianson 2004):

1. The exempt parent may serve as the sole shareholder.
2. The parent's board may appoint one or more persons to serve on the subsidiary's board. Each board should keep separate minutes.
3. The CEO of the parent many be the CEO of the subsidiary, but the subsidiary's day-to-day affairs should be managed by a different person.
4. The parent may capitalize the subsidiary, but there should be a written agreement specifying the assets. The transferred assets must be free of donor restrictions. After the transfer, the parent's balance sheet should show an asset reflecting an equivalent ownership share in the subsidiary.
5. Sharing of space and staff should occur only pursuant to a written agreement, and the subsidiary must pay fair market value.
6. Financial operations, bank accounts, internal controls, and tax identification numbers must be separate.

Theories of Revenue Composition

All dollars are not equal. Every revenue source has specific characteristics. The most important characteristics are predictability and autonomy.[7] In most cases, gift revenue is particularly unpredictable (Pratt 2004; Froelich 1999). Gift restrictions and contract requirements limit an organization's autonomy and can cause recipients to change their goals primarily to please their donors (*goal displacement*).

Table 10.2 covers the most common sources of revenue. Few nonprofits have all of them.[8] Predictability and autonomy are likely to depend on specific circumstances. To illustrate: Foundation grants, which are at the bottom of both lists, are predictable, at least for a finite period, and may allow considerable autonomy if they are unrestricted or paying for activity that the recipient would have undertaken regardless.

There is no shortage of theories of revenue management. The best known is resource dependency theory, which posits that "the activities of nonprofit organizations are influenced by their outside funders . . . the nonprofit organization and its funders reach agreement [often implicitly] on a set of goals and, in turn, negotiate a stable source of revenues to accomplish

TABLE 10.2 Characteristics of Common Revenue Sources

	Predictability	Autonomy
Endowment income	High	High
Government contracts*	High	Moderate
Earned income (third-party payers)	High	Low
Federated gifts and grants	High	Low
Individual contributions (small/many)	Moderate	High
Membership dues	Moderate	High
Earned income (individual payers)*	Moderate	High
Individual contributions (large/few)*	Low	Low
Foundation grants	Low	Low

Adapted from Pratt (2004) and *Froelich (1999).

those goals" (Kearns 2007, 299). This section focuses on two theories: portfolio theory and normative theory.

From portfolio theory comes the idea that revenue diversification can reduce financial vulnerability to recession and other external economic shocks (Chang and Tuckman 1991, 1994; Tuckman and Chang 1991; Kingma 1993).[9] It may seem counterintuitive, but a combination of two highly volatile revenue sources are more predictable than either one separately—provided they are uncorrelated (see Chapter 3).

As Table 10.3 shows,[10] some ordinary service providers rely almost exclusively on philanthropy, whereas others rely on it hardly at all.

TABLE 10.3 Revenue Composition of Ordinary Nonprofits, 1998–2004

	PSR ≤ 1% of total revenue	PSR > 1% of total revenue
Gifts ≤ 1% of total revenue	$N = 7.8$ K (2.9%) Mean gift = 0% Mean PSR = 0% Mean gov. = 79%	$N = 72.4$ K (26.7%) Mean gift = 0% Mean PSR = 82% Mean gov. = 14%
Gifts > 1% of total revenue	$N = 48.6$ K (17.9%) Mean gift = 61% Mean PSR = 0% Mean gov. = 35%	$N = 142.1$ K (52.4%) Mean gift = 30% Mean PSR = 51% Mean gov. = 16%

Note: PSR = program service revenue; gov. = government support.

Data source: NCCS digitized data.

Approximately 18 percent use a funding model heavily dependent on philanthropy and not at all on commercial revenue, but 30 percent virtually ignore it. One-half of all ordinary service providers use a model that mixes non-trivial amounts of both. Only about 3 percent use neither and, as might be expected, their average ratio of government support to total revenue is 79 percent.

Dependence on philanthropy varies considerably by type of activity (NTEE group), as Table 10.4 shows. The most dependent ordinary

TABLE 10.4 Importance of Philanthropy and Earned Income by Field of Activity, 1998–2004

Activity	NTEE	N(1,000)	% with Gifts	Average % Gifts	% with PSR	Average % PSR
All		270.9	70	27	79	49
Advocacy	R	2.1	92	56	49	16
Animal-related	D	2.2	**98**	54	86	35
Arts	A	21.0	95	43	89	40
Community	S	12.2	74	30	68	31
Disaster prep.	M	1.2	66	24	65	43
Education	B	26.9	79	24	83	58
Employment	J	7.2	58	12	82	57
Environment	C	39.6	88	48	71	30
Food	K	2.1	85	41	68	29
Health care	E	39.0	45	<u>12</u>	**90**	74
Housing	L	26.3	<u>37</u>	<u>12</u>	88	**61**
Human services	P	61.2	75	21	80	47
International	Q	3.0	88	55	51	26
Legal	I	6.9	81	32	53	23
Medical research	H	1.8	85	50	57	30
Mental health	F	15.8	63	13	84	49
Philanthropy	T	6.8	94	**79**	<u>28</u>	<u>11</u>
Public benefit	W	2.5	72	41	74	41
Recreation	N	5.5	84	36	86	53
Religion	X	5.7	87	55	72	36
Science	U	1.7	62	21	81	54
Social science	V	0.6	81	40	76	40
Voluntary health	G	7.1	88	46	62	29
Youth	O	7.9	97	55	73	29

Note: Boldface is highest number in a column; underline is the lowest.

Data source: NCCS digitized data.

service providers are in the categories of arts, animal-related, youth, advocacy, and philanthropy. The average nonprofit in this group receives over 90 percent of its revenue from philanthropy. Housing and health care are the least dependent, with only 12 percent of their revenue from this source.

Nonprofit health care providers are particularly dependent on earned income (90 percent). Arts and housing are close behind (89 and 88 percent, respectively). Nonprofits that are the least dependent on earned income are the philanthropy category (11 percent). Advocacy is not far behind (16 percent). No other category comes close. The largest nonprofits in the fields of youth services and environment rely on a single funding source.

It seems that many large nonprofits experiment with multiple funding sources in the early stages of development and become large by embracing one particular type (Foster, Dixon, and Hochstetler 2003). Out of 200,000 nonprofits that have obtained exempt status recognition since 1970, only 144 now have at least $50 million in annual revenue. Most of them raised the bulk of their money from a single type of funding source and "they created professional organizations that were tailored to the needs of their primary funding sources" (Foster and Fine 2007, 46).

Normative Theory

The key to growth is finding the right revenue mix, which may in fact be a single source. "Sources of income should correspond with the nature of benefits conferred on, or of interest to, the providers of those resources" (Young 2007, 341).

Each type of income is appropriate to a different provider/recipient combination. An income portfolio reflects the mix of benefits it provides in addition to responding to "basic organizational challenges." Normative theory is a sophisticated variant of resource dependency rooted in public finance, a branch of economics. This section sketches the elements of this theory, beginning with a few economic definitions.

Economists define three pure types of goods and services: private, collective, and relational. The category to which any actual good or service belongs is determined by rivalry and excludability. A *rival* good means that two or more people cannot consume the same good at the same time without interfering with each other.[11] An *excludable* good is one that producers can prevent nonpaying individuals from consuming.

Pure private goods and services are both rival and excludable. Markets are the primary producers of private goods, although nothing prevents governments and nonprofits from producing them. To remain viable, for-profit firms must sell private goods at or above cost of production. Nonprofits may sell private goods below cost if they have alternative income sources.

Pure collective goods are neither rival nor excludable. Because producers of collective goods cannot prevent nonpayers from consuming them, they tend to be financed with taxes or voluntary donations. Markets rarely produce collective goods, because people called free riders would consume them without voluntarily providing adequate compensation. Nonprofits, however, are able to produce collective goods because they have alternative sources of income, such as gifts, grants, membership dues, and endowment income.

Relational goods are pure collective goods produced in personal networks that can be enjoyed only by participating in a social process.[12] Nonprofits, especially membership associations, are the predominant producers of relational goods. One can find examples of markets and governments producing such goods, but such cases are rare because they are at a competitive disadvantage.[13]

Building on these definitions, one can analyze the revenue composition of a nonprofit in terms of who receives benefits (Young 2007):

- *Private benefits* accrue specifically to individual consumers or clients, who recognize them and are willing to pay for the goods and services that cause them. The nonprofit sets a market price that covers costs of production. If mission dictates a price that does not cover costs, it seeks cross-subsidy or endowment income. (Example: the Met's admission fees and gift shop net income.)
- *Group benefits* are collective goods that benefit a subgroup of society and are valued by donors interested in helping that subgroup. Values-centered management influences the choice of group and defines the benefits conferred. These types of goods and services are most likely to find support from specific groups of donors and organization partners. Endowment income and some targeted government funding programs are possibilities. (Examples: the Met's appeal to art lovers and the NYPL's appeal to researchers.)
- *Public benefits* are collective goods that accrue to a sufficiently large segment of the general public such that government financing is politically supported. Unlike the preceding situation, no particular group is favored. Widespread benefits attract government funding. (Example: the New York Public Library's service to the community.)
- *Trade benefits* are private goods acquired by institutions or groups that supply resources to nonprofits. These benefits correspond with the specific missions or interests of those suppliers. Volunteers and organizational partners are ideal sources of support.

Young and Wilsker (2008, 6) argue that the degree of "publicness" of a nonprofit's services influences the degree of revenue diversification: "Nonprofits that offer a mix of public and private goods may be expected to combine contributions and earned income to reflect the relative degrees of 'publicness' and 'privateness' of their services, and generally become more diversified than those offering strictly public or strictly private type goods or services."

Application

The New-York Historical Society is a museum *and* a library. Although both divisions of the Society are dedicated to preservation of artifacts, the revenue-raising potential of each is very different. Most museums are private whereas most libraries are publicly owned and operated, which suggests that it is difficult to support a library on either earned income or private philanthropy.

Museums can generate substantial revenue from admissions fees and gift shop revenue. Libraries would probably wither if they tried to charge admission fees, and they rarely have gift shops (bookstores). Both institutions may have dues-paying members, but these so-called members do not have the privilege of electing the board of directors so their role is more akin to donors.

The data reflect these differences: Total expenses of the Met and the NYPL are approximately equal but the museum's program service revenue is eight times larger, its membership income is 10 times larger, and its net income from sale of inventory is 45 times larger. However, government support for the NYPL is over six times that for the Met.

Table 10.5 compares the New-York Historical Society's revenue mix with a combination of the Met and NYPL. The Society is almost entirely

TABLE 10.5 Composition of Revenue Comparison

	Historical Society	Met and NYPL
Current support for budget	71%	18%
Government contributions	8%	36%
Program service revenue	8%	10%
Membership dues and assessments	3%	5%
Endowment support (estimated)	9%	31%
Total	100%	100%

Source: Author. Data from IRS Form 990 reports for 2007.

dependent on gifts. Its competitors derive approximately one-third of their combined revenues from government support and another third from endowment income. The Society's philanthropic support is under stress, paying for activities that competing institutions finance with different sources of income.[14]

During most of its existence, the Society had no government support. Even today it is only 8 percent of reported expenses, so we infer that the Society's museum is cross-subsidizing its library. In reaction to successive budget crises, the Society historically cut the budgets of both the museum and library to be fair to each one (Guthrie 1996). Although the Society's inner workings are private, it is highly plausible that this evenhanded policy reduced the museum's subsidy to the library, thus aggravating the overall budget problem.

Assuming that the library has negligible program service revenue, it therefore has first claim on unrestricted gifts, which likely leaves the museum inadequately funded. Without government support, the library division of the Society has never achieved its growth potential. With the museum division cross-subsidizing the library division, the museum has been deprived of resources it needed to achieve its own growth potential.

Normative theory explains the growth trajectories of the organizations in the opening vignette of this chapter. The Met and the NYPL tailored their revenue structures to the groups they served. The Society relied too heavily for too long on philanthropy. Normative theory suggests the Society defined its constituency too narrowly for its own good over the long term and confirmed by observation (Guthrie 1996).

This broad-brush examination is an example of peer-group analysis (Pratt 2006)[15] that answers the question: Which sources of revenue are compatible with the kinds of goods and services we produce? An organization can identify possibilities for revenue development by comparing how much of its revenue is derived from each source and comparing the percentages with comparable information from other organizations with a similar mission and service delivery method. This information is given by IRS Form 990 reports, which are publicly available through GuideStar (2010).

Unfair Competition

Nonprofit organizations cannot sell stock to raise capital, so federal law assists them to overcome this constraint by exempting them from the corporate income tax (Hansmann 1981). However, this benefit stokes anxiety about the possibility of unfair competition, even in situations like the YMCA, which was well established before for-profit health clubs appeared (Weisbrod 2004).

The issue is a complex one (Weisbrod 1998). To begin, "unfair" competition has multiple meanings and manifestations. It might refer to (1) nonprofits charging prices below market or (2) nonprofits siphoning trade from for-profit firms by their mere existence although they charge the same prices.

An analysis of claims of unfairness must set aside competition in industries where tax-exempt nonprofits are engaging in unrelated business activity, because such income is taxed. The real issue is whether nonprofits are unfairly competing in areas where they have an exempt purpose interest—like the YMCA.

The point of charging below-market prices is to increase access by people who cannot afford to pay market prices. If the for-profit firms were meeting the demand, nonprofits would have no interest in competing. Besides, the complaints are a response to the YMCA's broadening its base and moving into higher-income neighborhoods. If its new members are able and willing to pay market rate, the YMCA would be foolish not to charge it.

If tax exemption gives nonprofits a competitive advantage in the second sense (their mere existence), nonprofits that rely on commercial revenue should have a higher share of commercial revenue in high-tax states. This is observed: location in one of the 10 states with the highest commercial property tax rates raises the commercial revenue share of nonprofits by three percentage points, and where corporate income tax rates are especially high, the commercial revenue share of nonprofits is four percentage points higher (Cordes and Weisbrod 1998).

Rose-Ackerman argues that unrelated business income tax (UBIT) "creates more unfairness than it can possibly prevent" (1982, 1038). Steinberg (1991, 361) concludes that "tax and regulatory differentials are necessary (in many cases) if NPs are to play a distinctively different role in the economy" but we do not know enough about the impact of taxes and regulations on performance to design the ideal structure. However, he adds, the burden of proof should fall neither on each nonprofit to justify its exemption nor on the sector as a whole.

Concluding Thoughts

Arguably it is harder to manage a nonprofit organization than a for-profit business because nonprofits have many potential sources of revenue whereas a for-profit business has only the income earned from selling its products. Each nonprofit revenue source has a unique combination of predictability and autonomy, along with its own cost of development. Furthermore, different funding sources have different objectives for the work their resources will be financing. All of these things must be carefully blended to maximize growth potential.

CHAPTER 11

The Nonprofit Difference
Doing Good Well

According to news accounts, a certain foundation provides networking opportunities for young professionals but it raises most of its $5 million annual budget from sumptuous events open to the general public.[1] To outsiders it appears that persons closely associated with it are primarily interested in having a good time. If this were all, it would be an oddity, possibly with a questionable tax status, but there is more.

The CEO resigned after an independent review of 15 years of the foundation's financial records could not account for hundreds of thousands of dollars each year. Annual deficits are the norm and its liabilities currently exceed its assets. It probably stays afloat by mortgaging its luxurious clubhouse, because it owes $2 million on a building it purchased 25 years earlier for less than $1 million.

Whichever way it manages its finances, it appears to be accomplishing some purpose in grand fashion. However, as Chapter 1 pointed out, every organization has a fiduciary duty to act in the best interests of a group of persons, and being unable to account for funds is a failure of fiduciary duty at the most basic level. Repeated deficits jeopardize its existence, and whatever work it does will cease—the ultimate breach of fiduciary duty.[2]

This chapter is a summing up of the lessons of this book, accompanied by some new material on the duties and responsibilities of a board and board members. It emphasizes the differences between nonprofits and for-profits.

Control Environment

A board of directors is the custodian of an organization's values, the designer of its strategy, and its general fiduciary. Boards are implicated in every systemic failure, as the opening vignette suggests. This section documents the duties of board members with an emphasis on conflicts of interest.

Governance

The board is a critical component of what accountants call the *control environment*, which "reflects top management's awareness and commitment to the importance of controls throughout the organization, and encompasses management integrity, ethical values, and operating philosophy. . . . [It] sets a tone of integrity which influences the ethical and control consciousness of employees" (Callaghan 2007). Auditors assess the control environment as a standard part of the audit process.

In a nonprofit the board is the protector of the interests of people an organization serves and the steward of assets entrusted to it for use on their behalf.[3]

Though state laws vary, directors of nonprofit corporations have three fiduciary duties in most states (Fremont-Smith 2004):

1. *Duty of care* to be diligent in their oversight of the organization, including its finances and investments.
2. *Duty of loyalty* to act in the interest of the organization rather than to benefit any personal, business, or private interest.
3. *Duty of obedience* to keep the organization in compliance with applicable laws and internal policies, and true to its mission.

If an organization is harmed by a good-faith error of judgment rather than a breach of duty, then the directors and officers are not liable under the Business Judgment Rule. Most directors are volunteers who serve out of a sense of civic duty, so courts are reluctant to impose financial liabilities when suits are brought for breach of duty (Fishman 2003).

The Sarbanes-Oxley Act makes it illegal for any organization, including nonprofits, to punish a whistle-blower in any manner. All organizations must have a formal process to deal with complaints and prevent retaliation. It behooves officers and directors to take all complaints seriously. They have an obligation to investigate all allegations and to resolve problems or justify inaction (BoardSource and Independent Sector 2006, 9).

The Sarbanes-Oxley Act also imposes a duty on all organizations to have a written document retention and periodic destruction policy. "If an official investigation is underway or even suspected, nonprofit management must stop any document purging in order to avoid criminal obstruction charges" (BoardSource and Independent Sector 2006, 10).

The revised IRS Form 990 (Part VI, Section B) asks whether a nonprofit has a written whistle-blower protection policy and written document retention and destruction policy.

Other provisions of the Sarbanes-Oxley Act, although applicable only to publicly traded companies, nevertheless serve as a template for nonprofit practice (BoardSource and Independent Sector 2006). One in particular is worth noting:

"It is strongly recommended that nonprofit organizations not provide personal loans to directors or executives. If such loans are provided, they should be formally approved by the board. The process for providing the loan should be documented and the value and terms of the loan should be disclosed" (BoardSource and Independent Sector 2006, 10).

Many states prohibit related-party transactions, such as personal loans, use of organizational assets by directors, and sale or lease of assets to a director on favorable terms. However, enforcement appears lax: 221 organizations reported loan debts to officers or directors of $10,000 or more despite being located in a jurisdiction with laws prohibiting or limiting such loans (Lipman and Williams 2004).

BoardSource and the Independent Sector provide this good general advice: "Nonprofits must start by protecting themselves. They must eliminate careless and irresponsible accounting practices and benefit from an internal audit that brings to light weak spots and installs processes that are not vulnerable to fraud and abuse. Written policies that are vigorously enforced by executive staff and the board send a message that misconduct is not tolerated. These policies should cover any unethical behavior within the organization—including sexual harassment" (BoardSource and Independent Sector 2006, 9).

Conflict of Interest

The duty of loyalty demands that officers and directors avoid conflicts of interest, which are arguably the most common ethical problems in nonprofits. There are no IRS regulations on conflict of interest, but the new Form 990 asks whether an organization has a policy, whether its directors and officers are "required to disclose annually interests that could give rise to conflicts," and whether it monitors and enforces compliance.

The IRS publishes a sample policy as Appendix A to the instructions for Form 1023—Application for Recognition of Exemption Under Section 501(c) (3) of the Internal Revenue Code (U.S. Department of the Treasury 2006). The following discussion is based on this document.

A conflict of interest exists when a decision maker's public duty requires action that, in fact or appearance, diminishes his beneficial interest in the outcome or conversely when her beneficial interest in an outcome, in fact or appearance, may compromise her public duty. Notice: (1) the appearance of a conflict has equal status with actual conflict, and (2) this definition covers both financial and nonfinancial conflicts, such as nepotism and arranging for an organization to give preferential treatment to oneself, family, or friends.

Every organization should have a conflict of interest policy. Once a year, every officer and director should sign a statement attesting to having received a written copy and having read it, and that he or she understands it and agrees to abide by it.[4] The IRS's definition of a conflict of interest is more limited than the one just given, and begins with a definition of financial interest (U.S. Department of the Treasury 2006, 25):

> *A financial interest exists when a person has, directly or indirectly, through business, investment, or family, an ownership or investment interest in any entity with which the Organization has a transaction or arrangement, or a compensation arrangement with the Organization or with any entity or individual with which the Organization has a transaction or arrangement, or a potential ownership or investment interest in, or compensation arrangement with, any entity or individual with which the Organization is negotiating a transaction or arrangement.*

Not every financial interest represents a conflict. A conflict of interest exists only after the board or one of its committees, after investigating and discussing in the absence of the interested person, determines by a majority vote of its disinterested members that a financial interest rises to the level of a conflict.

If a conflict exists, the board may nevertheless approve the transaction upon further investigation to determine whether better terms are available from a disinterested party and, if not, that the transaction or arrangement is in the organization's "best interest, for its own benefit, and whether it is fair and reasonable" (U.S. Department of the Treasury 2006, 26).

The minutes of the governing board and relevant committees should contain the particulars of the matter and record "the names of the persons who were present for discussions and votes relating to the transaction or arrangement, the content of the discussion, including any alternatives to the proposed transaction or arrangement, and a record of any votes taken in connection with the proceedings" (U.S. Department of the Treasury 2006, 26).

Finally, a conflict of interest is not the same as *divided loyalties*, which occur when two or more public duties make conflicting demands on a decision maker, which might happen when a person sits on the boards of two or more competitors. This situation raises different ethical questions. The best way to avoid divided loyalties is for board candidates to make full disclosure of their other board memberships.

Being Businesslike

Nonprofits should be businesslike, but not necessarily be run like a business. This is not a contradiction. To be run like a business is to mimic for-profit businesses, including their goals. An online search of definitions for *businesslike* turned up: methodical, systematic, purposeful, earnest, practical, unemotional, careful, diligent, enterprising, industrious, hardworking, thorough, and more. For-profit businesses do not have a monopoly on these admirable characteristics.

The call for nonprofits to be more businesslike is hardly new. During the eighteenth century so-called joint stock philanthropies spearheaded a reform movement. They did not have stockholders in a legal sense. They earned the name by being managed like commercial enterprises with a chief executive and a board of directors. Like businesses that raise capital from the general public instead of relying on a few partners to bankroll a project, joint stock philanthropies solicited the general public for donations rather than relying on the generosity of a single individual or family (Elliott 1995). Charities still follow this model.

Nonprofit financial management has six chief concerns: procedures, liquidity, resilience, sustainability, growth, and strategy. A new chief financial officer stepping into a messy situation might tackle the financial problems in approximately the following sequence with some overlap. None of the synonyms require a businesslike organization to use any particular tool associated with business. As this book has shown, certain business tools and concepts need to be redefined before they are useful to nonprofits.

Procedures

The most important aspect of any organization's finances is the control environment. Nonprofits need to pay attention to ethics and proper procedures for handling money to prevent theft (internal controls). The procedures are very similar for both for-profits and nonprofits and there are many books on the subject, so these matters are not developed in detail here. Two differences with for-profits worth noting are theft and CEOs on boards.

Financial crimes are more common in the nonprofit sector than in business or government (Ethics Resource Center 2007). This is plausible because many nonprofits have untrained persons responsible for handling money. Anecdotal evidence suggests that the nonprofit working environment places a high value on the virtue of trust, and perpetrators typically are persons far above suspicion: they are dedicated and loyal, and never take a day off. Two easy and important steps for discouraging theft are: (1) separation of functions, with more than one person being responsible for completing a transaction, and (2) require two continuous weeks of vacation for financial managers.[5]

It is common for a CEO of a for-profit corporation to sit on his or her own board, but in the business world a board represents the interests of stockholders, and CEOs are usually stockholders. It is far less common for nonprofit CEOs to sit on their boards, because nonprofit boards represent the interests of people they have a duty to serve. Their interests are often uncertain and must be intuited. A dialogue between managers, who are in day-to-day contact with the clientele, and their boards, which are drawn from the larger community, is a useful discovery tool, which is enhanced by maintaining separate and distinct roles.

A chief responsibility of a board is to hire a CEO, to set goals and evaluate his or her performance, and to fire when necessary. It is also responsible for verifying enforcement of applicable laws, like the whistle-blower protections and document retention requirements of the federal law known as Sarbanes-Oxley. Boards tend to be clubby, so these oversight functions are compromised when the CEO sits on the board, even if the CEO is not on an oversight committee and abstains from voting on oversight matters (*recusal*).

Liquidity

The first operating imperative is to pay bills as they come due. A financial manager's biggest nightmare is running out of cash. Nearly all ordinary nonprofits understand this intuitively. Almost 90 percent have positive liquidity and a majority has a comfortable amount, defined as the equivalent of one month of nonprofit working capital or more.

Nonprofits and for-profits measure liquidity by the extent to which cash and near-cash assets (current assets) exceed liabilities coming due within one year (current liabilities)—generally known as working capital. However, business finance texts include marketable securities as near-cash assets, whereas nonprofits have reasons for holding marketable securities that do not apply to for-profits (see the discussion of operating reserve in the next subsection), so nonprofits should exclude them from working capital. Furthermore, without donated income, for-profits do not have assets with donor restrictions. Nonprofits should exclude them from working capital, too.

Although deficits frequently produce cash shortages, surpluses do not necessarily result in larger cash balances. Helping Hand had adequate surpluses but was chronically short of cash. The statement of cash flows is an indispensable tool for gaining understanding about causes of cash shortages. If Helping Hand had used this tool it would have seen that aggressive capital spending was the cause of its cash difficulties.

If deficits in unrestricted funds are causing a liquidity problem, they must be eliminated first, as the anonymous nonprofit learned too late in Chapter 2. The key to doing this is balancing the budget—and actually using it to control spending. Chapter 4 showed the connection between Helping Hand's budgetary balance (or imbalance) and surpluses (or deficits) on its financial statements, which is more complicated for nonprofits than for-profit businesses.

Resilience

When annual surpluses and adequate liquidity become routine, the next task is to build an adequate operating reserve to have a margin for error and a cushion in case of sudden economic adversity.

For-profits generally do not have operating reserves. When economic adversity strikes, they cut costs, for example, by laying off workers. Nonprofits that experience economic adversity try to avoid laying off workers and cutting services, so they need an operating reserve.

To build a reserve, a series of extraordinary annual surpluses is necessary. However, once an organization obtains an adequate reserve, its surpluses can retreat to a lower level needed for stasis until it must replenish the reserve following a deficit year.

The question is: How large should a reserve be? The Nonprofit Operating Reserves Initiative Workgroup (NORI), an ad hoc group sponsored by the National Center for Charitable Statistics, Center on Nonprofits and Philanthropy at the Urban Institute, and United Way Worldwide, has endorsed a figure equivalent to three months of spending on operations (NORI 2008).

Ordinary nonprofits intuitively understand the utility of having a reserve. The proportion having positive reserves is nearly as large as the proportion with positive liquidity, and approximately half follow the NORI recommendation.

However, every organization should evaluate the NORI recommendation in light of its own circumstances. It should evaluate the likelihood that it will need sudden access to cash on a short-term basis and evaluate how much it is likely to need. Arts organizations may need more (if they have an off-season) and research organizations may need less (if their sole source of funds is an endowment).

The assets identified as being available in an emergency do not need to be as liquid as cash and cash equivalents, but they do need to be convertible into cash within the span of a few months at the most.

Sustainability

The *sustainability principle* focuses on the long run. A nonprofit's annual surpluses must be large enough to sustain financial capacity in all time frames indefinitely and to make additional investments for growth.

The nonprofit rule for long-run sustainability is that return on assets (ROA) must be at least as large as the long-run rate of inflation. This is a critical difference between nonprofits and for-profit businesses.

For-profit businesses tend to focus on return on investment (ROI) instead of ROA. However, as Chapter 6 pointed out, ROI favors riskier, debt-financed financial activity, thereby increasing bankruptcy risk. Shareholders of a for-profit business that increases its borrowing can manage the additional risk individually by buying or selling its stock—depending on their appetite for risk.

Nonprofits have no stockholders, so the people they serve bear all increased risk from borrowing, and they have neither a voice in selecting managers nor the tools to manage unwanted risks. When a for-profit firm considers undertaking a new project, it can focus on return and ignore risk without violating its fiduciary responsibility. By contrast, nonprofits have to be especially careful to evaluate the organization's risk exposure in any new venture. Its fiduciary responsibility requires no less.

The single most important formula that is not commonly found in nonprofit finance texts is one that emphasizes perpetual stewardship. Given that the long-term rate of inflation is 3.4 percent, the minimum annual budget surplus needed to maintain assets at their replacement cost is: Budget surplus (in percent) = 3.4 percent times Total Assets and divided by Spending on Operations. This is a sufficient condition for delivering service at the same volume and quality indefinitely.

The data show that nonprofits tend to focus on the short term at the expense of the long term. As mentioned earlier, half or more have adequate liquidity and operating reserves, but not quite 40 percent of ordinary nonprofits are sustainable in the long run. This finding is consistent with anecdotal observations of nonprofits struggling to serve their clientele and being loath to turn anyone away. However, this short-term compassion has a long-term downside for the health of the organization. Failure to maintain assets at their replacement cost necessitates periodic capital campaigns to renew the existing capital stock.

Growth

Once an organization is sustainable, it has a base on which to grow. Managing growth is harder for nonprofits than for for-profits because nonprofits have access to many types of revenue whereas for-profits just have earned income from selling goods and services.

Having more revenue options is both good and bad. More options mean access to more dollars but more options multiply the number of strategic decisions required about which sources of revenue to pursue. A diversified revenue portfolio provides some protection from the downside risk of any one of them drying up, but each source of revenue presents different management issues, which expands the skill set nonprofit managers need.

Alternative income (gifts, grants, dues, and investment income from endowments) turns the logic of production on its head. In for-profit firms, output determines revenue but alternative income determines output. Alternative income weakens the link between costs and production. This is good because it allows nonprofit clients to receive more services at lower prices than the market would charge, but it renders management more difficult and nonprofit finance less intuitive.

Nonprofits cannot sell stock to raise capital so they must have large operating surpluses or stage capital campaigns, which have long lead times and are expensive. For many nonprofits this restricts their growth prospects.

Each type of income is appropriate to a different provider/recipient combination. The key is having sources of income consistent with the nature of benefits conferred on, or of interest to, the providers of resources. In some cases this may lead to reliance on a single source; in other cases it may require a multiplicity of revenue sources. Long-run growth is the thorniest problem a nonprofit organization faces.

Approximately 18 percent of ordinary service providers use a funding model heavily dependent on philanthropy, while 30 percent virtually ignore it, relying primarily on earned income. One-half use a model that mixes both philanthropy and earned income. Only about 3 percent have neither kind of income, relying almost entirely on government.

Values

Nonprofits *are* different. They are in the *business* of promoting values and there is evidence that they *act* differently from profit-seeking firms—even in industries with the greatest dependence on commercial income.

Nonprofit organizations must become more sophisticated at "defining, producing, and documenting the unique and value-oriented outcomes that only mission-driven work can deliver" (Frumkin and Clark 2000, 158). This represents an effort to serve people in the best possible way—the fiduciary responsibility of nonprofits—and it gives nonprofits a competitive edge over for-profit rivals.

An organization's values are integral to its long-range strategy for delivering service, which in turn determines the amount of long-term financial capacity needed. Values may not change but the environment does, which may change how values are expressed. Updating the kinds of services provided and the service delivery model should be done periodically, but this is a board responsibility, which brings us back to where the chapter began.

Concluding Thoughts

The usual question following a long presentation is: What is the takeaway? The single word that best summarizes this book's message is *stewardship*. Nonprofit organizations have a duty to act in the best interests of persons who, unlike corporate stockholders, cannot hedge against the negative consequences of bad business decisions. Nonprofit managers are held to higher standards of excellence and ethics—as it should be. The nonprofit legal structure insulates inept managers from market discipline, so boards must be doubly vigilant.

This chapter's opening vignette featured an extreme case of an organization without a vigilant board—possibly because, as insiders, board members received special benefits related to the organization's lavish functions. Although not a conflict of interest in a financial sense, it is a conflict nonetheless that degrades the discharge of fiduciary duty.

The organization has been able to keep going because it maintained liquidity but only by eroding its long-tern capacity through mortgaging its key asset. Unless it changes course, it will soon be insolvent due to inadequate capital. The single most important formula in this book emphasizes perpetual stewardship: budget surplus in percent equals 3.4 percent (the long-term inflation rate) times total assets not in endowment, divided by spending on operations. This formula tells managers the minimum budget surplus they need to maintain an organization's assets at their replacement cost—a necessary condition for delivering service at the same volume and quality indefinitely. By this test, the errant organization fails miserably.

Notes

Chapter 1

1. Although IKEA's origins are Swedish, it is incorporated as INGKA, a Dutch *stichting* (foundation) (*Economist* 2006). For-profit companies organized as nonprofits are called *for-profits in disguise.*

2. The primary financial objective in a sample of chief financial officers of faith-based nonprofits was to break even (36 percent), maximize net revenue (7 percent), and make a small surplus (7 percent). Other responses were stated in terms of costs, cash flow, and risk (Zietlow, Hankin, and Seidner 2007, 13).

3. Financial capacity is similar to the concept of organizational slack (Bourgeois 1981, Bourgeois and Singh 1983). Another name is *financial position*; financial sustainability is also known as *financial performance.*

4. This definition actually first appeared in the Tariff Act of 1913 to describe those organizations that were exempt from the new federal income tax (O'Neill 2002, quoting Hopkins 1998, 32).

5. Peter Pruzan (1998) wrote of *values-based* management, envisioning it as the antithesis of control. He described his approach as migrating "[f]rom a focus on efficiency and control to a values-based perspective on management, corporate identity and success. And from a focus on legal compliance and financial performance to a focus on corporate social and ethical responsibility and accountability." But this book assumes that management implies purposeful control. Consequently, it uses the term *values-centered* management to avoid confusion with Pruzan's term. This also avoids confusion with "value- [singular] based management" in the traditional management literature, which refers to maximizing net cash flow.

6. In most cases, individual patrons will receive a share of remaining assets upon dissolution. A patron may or may not be a member. See Chapter 7.

7. Upon dissolution of a U.S. charitable tax-exempt nonprofit, its remaining net assets must be transferred to another charitable nonprofit (see Glossary for definition of nonprofit organization). Membership associations do not issue stock, but members typically share remaining net assets upon dissolution.

8. For a summary of alternative theories drawing on disciplines other than economics see Anheier (2005) and O'Neill (2002).

9. Most of this section, including Table 1.1, is from Bowman (2011b), copyright Berkeley Electronic Press, used with permission.

10. This protection is known as *limited liability*. Thus, the personal assets of officers and directors are secure from the organization's creditors.

11. For centuries, bequests were managed in the Anglo-American tradition through a legal construct known as a *trust*. Modifying the purpose of a trust requires judicial action whereas modifying the purpose of a nonprofit corporation requires only a majority vote of the board and filing an amendment to its corporate charter—another advantage of the corporate option.

12. Writers often refer to obligations to stakeholders (Freeman 2010). A fiduciary is analogous to a dominant, or senior, stakeholder whose interests take priority over other stakeholders in the event of conflict among their interests (Bowman 2010c). The analysis in this book is superficially similar to principal-agent analysis, but, unlike for-profit principal-agent relationships, many nonprofit principals have no way to express their interests or to choose leaders (Brody 1996). Exceptions are membership associations and conduit grantmakers.

13. The author is familiar with two examples of for-profit firms receiving donations to stay afloat: *Paste* magazine (Georgia) in 2009 and Heartland Cafe (Illinois) in 2010. Both are unique small businesses.

14. An independent organization with an independent board provides such assurance. New York City sponsors dozens of nonprofit corporations—mostly for community development and cultural affairs. Nonprofit organizations themselves may spin off functions to new organizations to insulate the parent organization from risks of various kinds.

15. See Bowman (1999). Reorganization freezes collection actions, prevents utility shutoffs, and ultimately reduces outstanding liabilities. Being a debtor in possession means that the organization continues to conduct its own affairs, instead of being governed by a creditors' committee, which is common in for-profit reorganizations.

16. *Riley v. National Federation of the Blind of North Carolina, Inc.*, 487 U.S. 781 (1988); *Maryland v. Joseph H. Munson Co.*, 467 U.S. 947 (1984); *Village of Schaumberg v. Citizens for a Better Environment*, 444 U.S. 620 (1980).

17. Museums and other service providers may offer memberships involving special privileges, but these persons are not true members because they exercise no control.

Chapter 2

1. The accounting profession describes a not-for-profit organization as "An entity that possesses the following characteristics that distinguish it from a business enterprise: (a) absence of ownership interests like those of business enterprises, (b) operating purposes other than to provide goods or services at a profit, and (c) contributions of significant amounts of resources from resource providers who do not expect commensurate or proportionate pecuniary return" (FASB 1980, paras. 4–6; criteria reordered by author). Although (a) and (b) conform to the UN definition, (c) is best understood not as definitional but as identifying the type of organizations to which certain accounting principles apply. If an organization obtains no "resources from resource providers who do not expect commensurate or proportionate pecuniary return," the rules for recognizing the types of income that are peculiar to not-for-profits are hardly relevant.

2. Author's estimate based on 2003 reports filed on Form 990 with the Internal Revenue Service. Expenses of the median not-for-profit that uses cash accounting are $65,000 compared to over a half-million dollars for the median not-for-profit using accrual accounting. However, comparisons are imprecise because they use different accounting rules.

3. IRS Form 990, Part IX-1 (2008) or Box F (earlier years), indicates which system an organization uses. Persons doing comparative financial studies should limit comparisons to organizations using accrual accounting following SFAS 116 and SFAS 117.

4. Other statements specific to not-for-profits are: SFAS 93, *Recognition of Depreciation by Not-for-Profit Organizations* (FASB 1987b); SFAS 124, *Accounting for Certain Investments Held by Not-for-Profits* (FASB 1995); SFAS 136, *Transfers of Assets to a Not-for-Profit Organization or Charitable Trust That Raises or Holds Contributions for Others* (FASB 1999); and SFAS 164, *Not-for-Profit Entities: Mergers and Acquisitions* (FASB 2009).

5. PP&E is the accounting term corresponding to LB&E.

6. The donor must explicitly specify the intended purpose of the gift in writing, and the recipient must agree to the terms.

7. Lacking donors, for-profit businesses have no restrictions on their assets.

8. According to SFAS 93 (FASB 1987b, as amended, para. 6), "depreciation need not be recognized on individual works of art or historical treasures

whose economic benefit or service potential is used up so slowly that their estimated useful lives are extraordinarily long. A work of art or historical treasure shall be deemed to have that characteristic only if verifiable evidence exists demonstrating that (a) the asset individually has cultural, aesthetic, or historical value that is worth preserving perpetually and (b) the holder has the technological and financial ability to protect and preserve essentially undiminished the service potential of the asset and is doing that."

9. Several categories are combined for simplicity. Expense detail in particular is omitted because expenses are unrestricted, by definition, and there is little difference in the way not-for-profits and for-profit businesses report them. In this case expense detail is just a list of functions: instruction, research, and so on.

10. *Measurable* means that a transaction can be assigned an unambiguous dollar value. *Earned* implies a legal obligation to be paid. On financial statements, gifts and grants are called public support and treated as if they were revenue. For simplicity, the term *revenue* in this book in cludes public support.

11. GAAP recognizes expenses when they are incurred in order to generate revenue or in the accounting period when a cost is used up or has expired. Some for-profit firms may gain tax advantages by using other, more computationally complicated, methods of depreciation. Because not-for-profits do not (usually) pay income taxes, they tend to adopt the simplest method, which is straight-line depreciation.

12. This item reflects reclassification of net assets from temporarily restricted to unrestricted. It appears twice on the statement of activities: as a negative item under change in restricted net assets and as a positive item of the same magnitude under change in unrestricted net assets. It therefore has no impact on a change in total net assets. Of course, there should be no reclassifications of permanently restricted net assets.

13. Assets = Liabilities + Net assets implies that Δ Assets = Δ Liabilities + Δ Net assets, which implies Δ Cash + Δ Other assets = Δ Liabilities + Δ Net assets, from which the equation in the text follows.

Chapter 3

1. A Ponzi scheme is where a person uses money from recent participants to pay earlier participants. The word *participant* is used in preference to *investor* because the scheme is not a legitimate investment. Of course, the participants think of themselves as investors.

2. There is an old journalism maxim: If your mother says she loves you, check it out. This level of skepticism applies to investing.

3. Strictly speaking, an investment involves acquisition of an asset. Derivatives are not assets but contracts that provide for one party to make specified payments to another party (counterparty) where the payment amount depends on the market value of assets.

4. A working cash fund consists of actual cash and cash equivalents. It is not to be confused with working capital (current assets minus current liabilities). A credit card is an example of an external revolving loan fund.

5. Standard deviation is the square root of the average sum of squared deviations from the mean. It is also called the root mean square.

6. Di Teresa and Frengel (2002). Fees are usually expressed in basis points. One basis point is 1 percent of 1 percent, so these fees are 70 and 143 basis points, respectively.

7. This section draws heavily from an article by Bowman (2009) in the *Chronicle of Philanthropy*, used with permission.

8. The precedent setting is *Harvard College v. Amory,* 9 Pick. (26 Mass.) 446, 461 (1830).

9. It superseds the 30-year-old Uniform Management of Institutional Funds Act (UMIFA). A copy of the uniform act and a list of states are on the Uniform Law Commission web site at www.nccusl.org/Update; accessed April 3, 2009.

10. The quote is by Susan Gary (2007), one of the drafters. Charities with endowments of less than $2 million must notify the state attorney general 60 days in advance of a spending withdrawal that is expected to reduce the value of investments below the historic dollar value of restricted gifts. It does not require approval by the attorney general. Rather, its purpose is to give the attorney general an opportunity to comment and counsel the charity. Nonprofits with small ($25,000 or less) and old (20+ years) endowments may liquidate them without the costly and time-consuming process of obtaining court approval.

11. In such cases only disinterested board members may approve related-party transactions and the transactions must be arm's-length or produce a net benefit for the organization. Nonprofits must also disclose related-party transactions to the board and/or the public.

12. An unknown fraction of cash is in endowment, but for analytical purposes, the simplest working assumption is that all cash is outside of endowment and all investments are in endowment.

13. If securities plus other investments > expenses, then 5 percent of the left-hand side of the inequality (the pro forma spending rate) > 5 percent of the right-hand side.

14. The 990 form gives information about noncash gifts but not about their expensing. This formula assumes that noncash gifts are expensed in the same year.

15. This section extensively quotes Bowman, Keating, and Hagar (2007), copyright by AltaMira Press and used with permission; it was primarily written by Keating.
16. These numbers actually apply to a broader class of investments linked to mission but they are emblematic of the growing popularity of PRI.

Chapter 4

1. A growing organization also should revisit its policies and procedures for safeguarding its assets and to deter and detect fraud and theft (known as *internal controls*), but this topic is beyond the scope of this book. It is briefly revisited in Chapter 11.
2. Encumbrance budgeting requires having someone responsible for receiving goods other than the person who placed an order. The receiver's job is to verify that a purchase order had been properly issued. If a valid purchase order is not on file, the receiver refuses to accept shipment or returns the goods unopened for credit.
3. We say such items are *expensed.*
4. There are other ways to allocate indirect costs; see Finkler (2005) and Anthony and Young (2003).
5. Conversely, program expansion usually involves increasing employee FTEs.
6. Some nonprofits incorrectly budget on a net basis, showing only one line in the organization's operating budget for net income from special events.

Chapter 5

1. Much of the activity carried on in its name is through local affiliates, further protecting the tax status of the foundation.
2. This classic article presents a comprehensive digest of a complex topic at a greater level of detail.
3. Calculation based on a sample of 26 cities.
4. This number is derived from Table 1.1 based on categories specified in the preceding paragraphs of this section.
5. IRC 29 sections 521(b), 1381(a)(1), and 1382(c).
6. Known as the Girard case (the name of the testator), it is officially *François Fenelon Vidal et al. v. The Mayor, Aldermen, and Citizens of Philadelphia.* Vidal was Girard's niece who sued to defeat the will and claim the estate.
7. The third, fourth, and sixth proscriptions are designed to erect barriers between tax-exempt entities and the business and government

sectors—the reason for the nonprofit sector being referred to as the independent sector. The fifth proscription is the basis on which the judiciary prohibits racial discrimination by federally tax-exempt entities. As the opening vignette of the Sierra Club illustrates, the sixth test forces tax-exempt advocacy nonprofits to restructure; see the section on lobbying and political action.

8. Institutions specifically identified in Section 170(b)(1)(A) of the IRC also avoid classification as private foundations. These include churches and denominational associations; schools with a regular faculty; hospitals or medical research institutions that provide medical care, offer education, or perform research; and governmental units of the United States. It is not sufficient that an organization calls itself a church or school; it must actually function as one. However, as 501(c)(3) organizations, they are still required to meet the organization and operations tests described earlier.

9. Prior to 1976 the mandated payout was the greater of investment income or 6 percent of assets. Between 1976 and 1981 it was the greater of investment income or 5 percent of assets. After 1981 5 percent of assets alone was sufficient.

10. Many of these rules came into being with the 1969 Tax Act.

11. Although fund managers are not legally required to accept the donor's advice, most do (Jones 2004).

12. Some nonprofit organizations "receive contributions that are institutional (rather than individual), but are not organized as private foundations. These funders include charitable trusts, tribal councils, public grantmaking charities (which appear in the Public-Society Benefit subsector), and professional associations or membership groups" (Center on Philanthropy 2004, 76).

13. The second corporation was chartered by Connecticut for commercial purposes in 1732.

14. The last state to allow churches to incorporate was Virginia in 2003.

15. Contributions to organizations exempt under Sections 501(c)(8), (10), (13), and (19) of the Internal Revenue Code are deductible only to the extent they are applied to a charitable purpose.

16. There is also a 509(a)(4) category for product safety testing that is too specialized to demand attention here.

17. There are two types of 501(a)(3) organizations. However since this chapter is concerned more with private foundations than public charities, the distinction is not discussed further. See Bryce (2000, 77-80).

18. Bryce (2000, 96), citing a study conducted for the IRS by Paul Arnsberger.

19. Internal Revenue Service—Circular 230 Disclosure: As provided for in Treasury regulations, any advice (but none is intended) relating to federal taxes in this section is not intended or written to be used, and

cannot be used, for the purpose of (1) avoiding penalties under the Internal Revenue Code or (2) promoting, marketing, or recommending to another party any plan or arrangement addressed herein.

20. In general, passive income (rent, interest, royalties) is not considered UBI except when the payment is based on a percentage of the payer's income or net income, or if the income is from debt-financed property and falls outside one of the specific exceptions. These details are outside the scope of this section.

21. See note 19.

22. For the complete story, see King and Roth (2006).

23. The law was the Taxpayer Bill of Rights of 1996. The rulemaking process, which requires preliminary regulations, hearings, and a public comment period, is lengthy. For the text of the law, see Tax Almanac (2005).

24. The disclaimer in note 19 applies to this section as well. Except as otherwise noted, the source of information in this section is the Federal Election Commission (FEC 2011).

25. The sample was not random. Large nonprofits are overrepresented.

Chapter 6

1. This figure is exceeded by only 10 percent of tax-exempt public charities. Author's calculation based on 2003 National Center for Charitable Statistics digitized data ($N \approx 254,000$).

2. The author has been personally acquainted with this organization for 30 years.

3. In the equations that follow, unless otherwise stated, all balance sheet data are end-of-year. In the following equations a dot indicates multiplication and a slash indicates division.

4. Line numbers refer to the pre-2008 IRS Form 990, which is used in preference to the current version because the IRS numbered lines consecutively throughout on the old form. Translation to the current form is straightforward.

5. The business literature defines ROA as net income divided by total assets, but for-profit businesses do not have restricted assets. When applying the concept to nonprofits, one must decide how to treat restricted assets. This formulation assumes that in the long run restricted assets are as good as unrestricted. Technically, beginning-of-year (BOY) asset values, or an average of both, is arguably better practice than end-of-year (EOY) values, but some financial statements report only EOY asset values. If analysts adopt an EOY convention, they will get the same answer whether they use financial statements or IRS data, which reports both

BOY and EOY asset values. The formula in the text is an approximation. Letting C = capacity, X = numerator of capacity, and Y = denominator, and small letters represent change in the corresponding variable, the rules of calculus imply $c = (x\,Y - X\,y)/Y^2$; but an organization's scale (assets or spending) usually changes slowly over time, so y is approximately zero. In this case, the formula reduces to $c = x/Y$.

6. The data are from consumer price index (CPI) data by Inflation Data (2006). The author's calculation for the period 1913–2007 yielded 3.42 percent. DeMarche (1990) calculated 3.2 percent for the period 1926–1989 and rounded up to 4 percent for his study of sustainability of endowments. However, nonprofits may not experience inflation as households do: "College- and university-specific inflation, as represented by the Higher Education Price Index (HEPI), is typically higher than CPI. On average since HEPI's inception in 1962, it has averaged about 0.9 percentage points higher than CPI annually (Cambridge Associates 2008, 4). *Finance Fundamentals for Nonprofits* uses a historic 3.4 percent figure but it does not adjust for differences between the prices of consumer goods and prices that nonprofits pay for their inputs.

7. *Unrestricted financial assets* = Total assets – Restricted assets – Property, plant, and equipment. *Unsecured debt* = Total liabilities – Secured debt. (After 2008 also subtract escrowed liabilities.) *Spending on operations* = Total expenses – Depreciation. Note that assets financed with borrowed funds do not contribute to short-term capacity; if all PP&E is financed with debt, PP&E and secured debt cancel. *Depreciation* is an expense associated with capital consumption, but it does not use cash as other expenses do, so it does not constitute spending.

8. It is financially vulnerable in the Tuckman-Chang sense.

9. In retailing, "markup" is the difference between revenue and cost (expenses) expressed as a percentage of cost per unit sold.

10. Spending restricted gifts for purposes at variance with donor restrictions does not release assets from restrictions. Instead, it diminishes unrestricted surplus or increases unrestricted deficit.

11. This is an approximation to the rate of change in PP&E equity that ignores the repayment of mortgage principal, which is not readily available from Form 990 data. Depreciation is a negative change in the book value of PP&E, but there is a minus sign in front of PP&E equity in the MS equation. The two negatives cancel, leaving depreciation with a positive sign.

12. Charity Navigator (www.charitynavigator.org) uses this formula without the adjustments just described.

13. Organizations were excluded having a nonzero total for the sum of paid-in capital, capital stock, and retained earnings.

Chapter 7

1. Membership Association for the Deaf is a pseudonym.
2. Recent research has identified another type: *accountability* clubs exercise quasi-governmental regulatory powers in a particular field of activity (Gugerty and Prakash 2010). This is an important, but small, group. There are no more than a few hundred of these (Bowman 2010c).
3. Club theory is very general. Researchers use it to explore congestion pricing in transportation systems—for example, where system users correspond to members.
4. Tschirhart (2006) considers the case of coerced membership—such as trade unions in closed-shop states and certain religious congregations.
5. Cornes and Sandler (1986, 188) do not include governance among their key characteristics, because there are rare instances in which the shared good is provided competitively by numerous replicable clubs, and the same resource allocation is achieved without member ownership.
6. Economists would say they are payment for excludable collective goods.
7. "There is usually substantial overlap between the 'members' and the 'patrons' of a cooperative. A cooperative, however, may do business with members on a nonpatronage basis, and it may conduct business on a patronage basis with nonmembers" (Frederick 2005, 15).
8. Formerly the American Society of Association Executives.

Chapter 8

1. Author's calculation from data available at World Federation of Exchanges (2008).
2. Irvin (2007) calculates that the government is repaid for the charitable deduction in 10 years but it will take 141 years before the value of public benefits from a gift to the endowment will equal the value of a gift spent on immediate needs.
3. Charitable life annuities and some other planned giving instruments have attached liabilities. If audited financial statements are the source of data for this calculation, an analyst may encounter designated net assets. These are unrestricted net assets that a board is earmarking for some future purpose. In these formulas, treat them as all other unrestricted net assets.
4. This is an approximation because some gifts provide for the permanent upkeep of physical facilities.
5. Portions of this section first appeared in Bowman, Keating, and Hagar (2007), copyright by AltaMira Press and used with permission.

6. Lee (2004), quoting Kate D. Levin, New York City cultural affairs commissioner. Material in the remainder of this section first appeared in Bowman 2007, copyright by AltaMira Press and used with permission.
7. Lee (2004), quoting Karen Brooks Hopkins, president of BAM.

Chapter 9

1. The number of public grantmakers is not sensitive to the choice of threshold. At the one-third level there are 24,800 public grantmakers. Increasing the threshold to three-fourths increases the number of grantmakers by only 1,400.
2. Attributed to Paul Brest, president and CEO of the William and Flora Hewlett Foundation in Menlo Park, California.
3. Based on a Center on Philanthropy (2004) estimate.
4. This implies that 25 percent of foundations are not endowed *and* distribute less than 20 percent of their assets annually.
5. Only 5 percent have liabilities that exceed 1 percent of assets and only 2 percent have liabilities exceeding 50 percent.
6. The minimum annual payout is not 5 percent of total assets. First, "included assets are reduced by any acquisition indebtedness with respect to them and a cash reserve for operations presumed to equal 1.5 percent of total includable assets" (Hopkins 2008, 72). Second, annual payout is based on the foundation's payout over the average of 12 months "with any cumulative payout carry-forward being applied to the current year. In addition, certain 'set-asides' of funds for future use count toward the payout requirement for the year" (Collins 2008, 3).
7. Payout policies in Europe are less stringent. Toepler (2004) compared actual Ford Foundation payouts to simulated payouts following German rules. "Over the four-year period, Ford would have had to spend little more than one-third (36%) in Germany of what it was required to spend in the United States" (ibid., 734). He proposes a middle ground to Deep and Frumkin's policy recommendation, namely "[e]nforcing minimum payouts until 'tax investments' are recouped and freeing foundations from these regulations thereafter" (ibid., 737).
8. The requirements are either of the following: "(a) The foundation makes qualifying distributions during the tax year equal to the sum of assets of the foundation multiplied by the average percentage payout of the foundation NII [net investment income] for the tax year. The base period is understood as five years previous to the current tax year. If under any of these previous five years the foundation paid one percent of tax, this tax will have to be deducted from the

qualifying distributions of that year in order to calculate the average payout ratio"; or "(b) The foundation was not liable for Chapter 42 excise tax for any of the base periods" (Deep and Frumkin 2001, 24).

Chapter 10

1. The NYPL was formed by the merger of the private Astor and Lenox libraries and received the bulk of Samuel Tilden's estate at the outset. The Astor's founding date is obscure, but its founder died in 1848. The Lenox was founded in 1871. (The New-York Historical Society's name is indeed hyphenated.)
2. Using the NCCS digitized data files of 501(c)(3) tax-exempt nonprofits for 1998 to 2004 ($N \approx 254,000$).
3. Using the panel data to calculate philanthropic support as in the table, the author obtained the same figure as in the table. In other words, differences between the numbers in the table and numbers in the text are due almost entirely to sample screens and definitional differences.
4. Counting philanthropic revenue, 25 percent in the panel have a negative change in total net assets, but after subtracting philanthropic revenue, 64 percent would have had a deficit. The difference is 39 percent, or nearly two in five.
5. The study used the *Nonprofit Times* list for 2006 to identify the largest nonprofits.
6. Internal Revenue Service—Circular 230 Disclosure: As provided for in Treasury regulations, any advice (but none is intended) relating to federal taxes in this section is not intended or written to be used, and cannot be used, for the purpose of (1) avoiding penalties under the Internal Revenue Code or (2) promoting, marketing, or recommending to another party any plan or arrangement addressed herein.
7. These are Pratt's (2004) terms. The academic literature generally frames the issues as volatility (the opposite of predictability) and goal displacement (an alternative to autonomy). Academic findings are translated into Pratt's more familiar terms for consistency.
8. Pratt (2004) did not include endowment income and did not split individual donations into large and small. In general, the table reflects his subjective assessments of reliability and autonomy; but where Froelich (1999) found contradictory empirical studies, her results were substituted.
9. Revenue diversification is measured by a Herfindahl-Hischman index. To calculate it, divide every revenue source by total revenue, square all ratios, and add. The total will lie between 1.0, where there is only one

revenue source, and $1/N$, where N is the number of revenue sources. Lower numbers indicate greater diversification.

10. Gifts = the sum of direct and indirect support reported on IRS Form 990; PSR = program service revenue. Total revenue is "excess" reported on line 17 of pre-2008 IRS Form 990. It includes realized capital gains but excludes unrealized capital gains, so it is closer to cash-basis surplus than accrual-basis surplus. Data were screened to make sure that total revenue was positive and all percentages fell between 0 and 1, inclusive.

11. Also, the marginal cost of production is zero.

12. This definition paraphrases Ben-Ner and Gui (2003, 14). Relational goods are not as widely recognized by the economics literature as private and collective goods. Relational goods are similar to club goods, discussed in Chapter 7.

13. Neighborhood taverns are examples of private producers that create relational goods, and public senior citizen centers are an example of governments doing the same.

14. A simplistic calculation involving the ratio of gifts to total revenue, holding the number of the Society's gift dollars constant, shows that it could be four times larger today if it could suddenly match the ratio of gifts to total revenue for the Met and NYPL combined. If it had had more non-gift income from the beginning it would be even larger.

15. Pratt calls it cohort analysis, but *cohort* has a temporal dimension. *Peer* merely implies similarity.

Chapter 11

1. It is not primarily a grantmaking foundation. Its scholarship grants amount to 3 percent of its expenses. Events described here occurred several years ago, but the financial data are from recent Form 990 filings. Its clubhouse is located in a gentrifying neighborhood and is presumably worth much more that the mortgage balance.

2. The classic business definition of a fiduciary is narrower, emphasizing asset ownership and making financial decisions on another party's behalf (Investor Words 2011).

3. The Policy Governance® model, developed by John and Miriam Carver, focuses on ends and leaves means to hired managers. "Policy Governance boards demand accomplishment of purpose, and only limit the staff's available means to those which do not violate the board's pre-stated standards of prudence and ethics" (Carver and Carver 2010). However, a board's fiduciary duties include supervision of certain means. This comment should not be construed as a criticism of the

model but as a reminder to boards that have adopted the model to be careful about discharging their fiduciary duties. For Carver's position on fiduciary responsibility, see Carver (1996).

4. The IRS recommends that statements of 501(c)(3) organizations contain a clause that the person understands that the organization is charitable and must adhere to its exempt purpose to maintain its exempt status.

5. This is why movie theaters have different people sell tickets and take them when they could simply admit customers upon payment. If it is impossible to have two people handle cash, have some other way to verify collection. Separation of functions means that one person should not be responsible for all aspects of money control. At a minimum have a different person—perhaps a volunteer—balance the checkbook.

Glossary

accounts payable Obligations that an organization has to other parties to pay them within a year for services they have rendered to it.

accounts receivable Obligations that other parties have to an organization to pay it within a year for services it has rendered to them.

accrual accounting An accounting method that recognizes (records) a revenue transaction when it is measurable and earned (or gifted) and an expense when it is measurable and incurred—not necessarily when cash changes hands. Pledges are recognized as revenue when they are made, not when they are fulfilled (paid). Spending on capital is not an expense in the year it occurs. Rather, its cost is distributed in annual increments over its useful life in the form of a depreciation expense. See *cash accounting* and *depreciation.*

advance Cash received before being earned. See *deferred revenue.*

alternative income (for nonprofits) Income other than program service revenue; it includes gifts, grants, dues, and investment income from endowments.

alternative investments Investments other than stocks and bonds, such as private equity, real estate, venture capital, commodities, derivatives, and hedge funds.

arbitrage A situation in which an investor profits from buying an asset at a low price in one market and selling it for a higher price in a different market. It includes borrowing money at tax-exempt rates (which historically have been lower than taxable rates) and lending it at higher rates to taxable entities.

archetype A category of nonprofit defined by the nature of its fiduciary duty. See *fiduciary.*

asset Something an organization owns having either (1) market value or (2) income-producing value, as measured in dollars.

asset allocation The mix of asset types (stocks, bonds, alternative investments) in a portfolio.

bond An instrument of indebtedness representing an agreement between a borrower (issuer) and a lender (investor) spelling out the terms of a loan: maturity, interest, and so on.

book value The value of an asset or net assets recorded on a statement of financial position. Land is recorded at original cost. Property and plant are recorded at original cost minus accumulated depreciation. Marketable securities are recorded at their market value.

bottom line The difference between inflows and outflows of resources. In the nonprofit sector it can take several forms: total revenue minus expenses (*total surplus*), unrestricted revenue minus expenses (*unrestricted surplus*), and operating revenue minus operating expenses (*operating surplus*). In the for-profit sector, it is variously called net earnings, net income, and profit.

bright line Describes an unambiguous and precise test that separates permissible activity from impermissible activity.

budget A document showing how an organization plans to pay for its spending in a given year (operating budget) or how it plans to finance capital projects in a given year (capital budget). After adoption by the governing body, it becomes the basis for financial control. See *operating budget* and *capital budget*.

capacity (financial) For a nonprofit, it consists of the resources necessary to seize opportunities and respond to threats on any time scale without compromising the volume or quality of its current services.

capital The money, property, and other valuable assets that collectively represent the wealth of an individual or organization (Investor Words 2011).

capital budget A budget that provides for acquisition of land, buildings, and equipment, including major upgrades to lengthen their useful lives. Items in a capital budget (1) are expensive, (2) have long useful lives, and therefore (3) are purchased less frequently than annually. They may also include the services of investment bankers on bond transactions. See *LB&E* and *budget*.

capital gain The increase in market value of securities or other assets over a specified period of time. See *realized capital gain (or loss)* and *unrealized capital gain (or loss)*.

capital project A project that involves acquiring or making improvements to land, buildings, and/or equipment. See *LB&E*.

cash Currency and deposits or other accounts with financial institutions that may be deposited or withdrawn without restriction or penalty.

cash accounting An accounting method that records all transactions only when they increase or decrease an organization's cash balance.

cash equivalents Short-term and highly liquid investments that convert readily to cash and carry little risk of change in value at maturity due to interest rate changes.

cash flow Cash coming into an organization minus cash going out. Alternatively, end-of-period cash minus beginning-of-period cash. Cash in this case may include cash equivalents.

charitable Includes relief of the poor, the distressed, or the underprivileged; advancement of religion; advancement of education or science; erecting or maintaining public buildings, monuments, or works; lessening the burdens of government; lessening neighborhood tensions; eliminating prejudice and discrimination; defending human and civil rights secured by law; and combating community deterioration and juvenile delinquency (U.S. Department of the Treasury 2010a).

chart of accounts A codebook that classifies transactions by type (and by administrative unit in large organizations). Accounts are normally divided into five groups: assets, liabilities, equity, revenue, and expenses.

club A voluntary group deriving mutual benefit from members sharing one or more of the following: production costs, the members' characteristics, or a good characterized by excludable benefits (Cornes and Sandler 1986, 159). Synonym in this context: *membership association.*

collective good Something desirable that is consumed jointly by groups of individuals. Collective goods are neither *rival* nor *excludable.*

common law A body of law based on custom and general principles, embodied in judicial decisions, which serve as precedent or is applied to situations not covered by statute (Findlaw 2011).

community foundation A Section 501(c)(3) public organization with a mission to benefit charitable work in a particular geographic area, which accepts donations of all sizes from multiple persons. See *Section 501(c)(3).*

comptroller (also, controller) An organization's chief accountant. This officer is responsible for proper recording of all financial transactions. In small organizations this function may be performed by a finance director with other duties. However, see *separation of functions.*

conduit (or pass-through) grantmaker An agent acting on behalf of a living donor or a corporation, distributing funds to multiple recipients without accumulating large amounts of assets and holding them for long periods of time. In this book, a grantmaker is presumptively conduit if it either (a) makes grants equal to or exceeding 20 percent of its assets, or (b) is not presumptively endowed.

contribution A transfer of cash or other assets to an organization, or a settlement or cancellation of its liabilities, in a voluntary nonreciprocal transfer by a person or independent organization. Synonyms: *gift, donation.*

cooperative An enterprise in which individuals voluntarily organize to provide themselves and others with goods and services via democratic control and for mutually shared benefit. Members generally contribute to, and control via a democratic process, the cooperative's capital (Reference for Business 2011). See *social economy*.

corporate foundation A grantmaking organization sponsored by a taxable, for-profit business corporation that serves as a major, but not necessarily primary, funding source. Legally it is usually a *private foundation,* but some are *public organizations.*

corporation A legal entity possessing an identity independent of any natural persons with an indefinite life and a centralized management empowered to act in the corporation's name, subject to laws regarding fiduciary responsibility. It is able to own property in its own name, to sue, and to be sued. Liability for its debts is limited to its own capital (i.e., its directors' and officers' personal assets are not at risk).

CPI Refers to the consumer price index, which is used to measure inflation.

cross-subsidize Refers to a service provider using a surplus derived from one product or service to finance production of another product or service below its actual cost.

current assets Among for-profits, it is the sum of cash and cash equivalents, accounts receivable, inventory, marketable securities, prepaid expenses, and other assets that could be converted into cash in less than one year (Investor Words 2011). See *nonprofit current assets.*

current liabilities Debts of an organization due within a year, such as accounts payable and accrued wages and taxes.

deferred revenue An offsetting liability for cash received in advance of being earned. Upon being earned, the liability is reduced and the cash is recognized as revenue—hence the name.

depreciation The cost of using up the future economic benefits or service potentials of long-lived tangible assets in a given year (FASB 1987b, para. 3). It is an expense that does not use cash. Land and cultural artifacts do not depreciate. See *expense.*

diversification Refers to a combination of different assets (or revenue sources). It is a technique for minimizing risk for a given return or maximizing return for a given risk. Proper application requires that the returns on the assets (or the revenues) be uncorrelated. See *asset allocation.*

dividend A payment declared by a taxable company's board of directors and given to its stockholders from the company's net earnings (Investor Words 2011).

due diligence A process of discovering all material facts before undertaking an action.

encumbrance The amount that is deducted from a budget account at the moment a comptroller authorizes an employee to place an order for goods by issuing a purchase order. This procedure ensures that budget accounts will not be overdrawn accidentally due to the time lag between ordering goods and receiving a bill for them. See *comptroller.*

endowed organization See *presumptively endowed.*

endowment As used in this book, it is a portfolio of investments managed so as to produce a perpetual source of income for current operations to self-subsidize production of goods and services below cost. See *presumptively endowed.*

equity (1) Equals total assets minus total liabilities; however, (2) equities (plural) refers to shares of stock. Context should make clear which definition applies.

equity in PP&E The value of property, plant, and equipment (PP&E) minus mortgage balances and other debt for which PP&E is collateral.

equity ratio (ER) The fraction of an organization's assets that it owns free and clear of liabilities. It equals total net assets divided by total assets. ERe refers to the equity ratio of endowed service providers, which excludes assets in endowment.

excludable benefit or good Something desirable that its producer can prevent nonpaying individuals from consuming. See *collective good.*

exempt purpose The activity of a nonprofit organization that qualifies it for tax exemption. The exempt purpose must be the primary activity of an organization and not merely ancillary.

expense In accrual accounting, expense decreases net assets. It is recognized when measurable and incurred. See *spending on operations.*

family foundation A private foundation not sponsored by a corporation, whose funds are derived from members of a single family. See *private foundation* and *corporate foundation.*

FASB The Financial Accounting Standards Board, the source of generally accepted accounting principles. See *GAAP.*

fiduciary An entity "who obligates himself or herself to act on behalf of another . . . and assumes a duty to act in good faith and with care, candor, and loyalty in fulfilling the obligation" (Findlaw 2011).

financial statement A report describing the finances of an organization. GAAP requires financial statements to be prepared on an accrual basis and to report assets, liabilities, revenues, expenses, and cash flows. A complete set of statements minimally consists of individual statements of financial position, activities, and cash flows together with explanatory notes. The statement for a health and welfare organization also includes a statement of functional expenses.

financially vulnerable organization An organization that is likely to cut back its service offerings immediately when it experiences a financial shock like a sudden reduction in asset values or revenue.

flow A change in the quantity of an asset over time. Example: cash flow.

Form 990 Refers to a form on which many tax-exempt entities report annually to the IRS. The short form for small organizations is 990-EZ and the form for private foundations is 990-PF. See *informational return.*

foundation Commonly refers to a grantmaking organization but legally it is any 501(c)(3) organization that is not a public organization. See *community foundation, private foundation, corporate foundation, operating foundation*, and *family foundation*.

FTEs Full-time equivalent employees.

GAAP Generally accepted accounting principles in the United States.

gifts in kind Donated goods and services. See *noncash*.

governance The framework of rules and practices by which a board of directors ensures accountability, fairness, and transparency in an organization's relationship with all of its stakeholders (Investor Words 2011).

grantmaker Organization with a mission of providing financial support to nonprofit organizations. This book uses a working definition of an organization that devotes at least one-third of its program expenses to grants. See *conduit (or pass-through) grantmaker*.

gross domestic product (GDP) The value of a country's output of goods and services, excluding net income from abroad, valued at market prices.

indefinite groups Groups of persons who cannot be identified by name— only by common characteristics such as income, age, culture, and interests.

indirect costs Costs that a single organization incurs in support of more than one program; they include cost of the organization as a whole.

informational return An annual report filed with the Internal Revenue Service by tax-exempt organizations on Form 990, Form 990-EZ (for small organizations), or Form 990-PF (for private foundations).

insolvency A condition of extreme financial weakness. The three kinds are (1) balance sheet insolvency (insolvency in liquidation), which occurs when total liabilities are greater than total assets; (2) cash flow (operational) insolvency, which occurs when an organization is chronically unable to generate adequate surpluses; and (3) capital adequacy insolvency.

instrumental club A membership association that provides useful services in the form of shared member benefits.

IRC The Internal Revenue Code.

IRS The Internal Revenue Service; attorneys refer to it as the Service.

LB&E Land, buildings, and equipment, a term appearing on IRS Form 990. See *PP&E*.

liabilities The value of all obligations an organization owes to other parties requiring transfer of assets or provision of services in the future (Investor Words 2011).

limited life, or sunsetting, foundation A foundation that plans to spend all assets within a fixed time period.

line items Specific sources of income and specific objects of spending in a budget.

line of credit A standing authorization to borrow up to a predetermined limit, subject to a minimum regular repayment schedule. Credit cards function like a line of credit.

liquidation When an organization ceases operations, sells all assets, and discharges its obligations to creditors to the maximum extent possible. Remaining cash is distributed to owners (if for-profit) or members (if an association), or transferred to another 501(c)(3) organization.

liquidity Consists of cash or financial resources without donor restrictions, which can be efficiently converted into cash quickly.

market value The highest estimated price for an item that a willing buyer would pay to a willing seller in an open and competitive market (Investor Words 2011).

marketable securities Stocks or bonds that are readily bought and sold. Marketable stocks are exchange-listed.

markup (MU) An organization's annual surplus expressed as a percentage of spending on operations. For ordinary service providers it is the change in months of spending divided by spending on operations. It is a proxy for budget surplus. MUe refers to markup of endowed service providers.

membership association An organization that has a duty to act in the best interests of a specific group of persons who are usually able to participate in election of the group's leaders. This book's working definition of a membership association is an organization with dues income at least one-third of total revenue.

months of spending (MS) The number of months an organization could survive after losing all current income and maintaining its spending on operations at a constant level. MSe refers to months of spending for endowed service providers.

natural category An accounting term similar to budget line items.

NCCS The National Center for Charitable Statistics.

net assets Total assets minus total liabilities. See *unrestricted net assets*.

net assets released from restrictions Prior-period gifts and grants that are legally available for spending in the current year in fulfillment of the initial restrictions; they also include prior-period pledges fulfilled (paid) in the current period.

noncash Refers to donated goods and services, and expenses that do not use cash. See *gifts in kind* and *depreciation*.

nondistribution constraint A legal prohibition on distributing net earnings of an organization to private parties; it is an essential characteristic of nonprofits.

nonprofit current assets Cash and cash equivalents, accounts receivable, inventory, and prepaid expenses.

nonprofit organization An organization that does not exist primarily to generate profits, either directly or indirectly, and is not primarily guided by commercial goals and considerations. It may accumulate surplus in a given year, but any such surplus must be plowed back into the basic mission of the agency and not distributed to the organization's owners, members, founders, or governing board (United Nations 2003, 18). See *nondistribution constraint* and *not-for-profit*.

nonprofit working capital Nonprofit current assets minus both current liabilities and temporarily restricted net assets. See *nonprofit current assets*.

NORI The Nonprofit Operating Reserves Initiative, a joint project of the Urban Institute and United Way Worldwide.

not-for-profit The accountants' preferred term for *nonprofit*.

NTEE The National Taxonomy of Exempt Entities.

operating budget A plan for spending on services and goods with a useful life of one year or less and financing it with current income. It is an organization's primary tool of financial control.

operating expenses Total expenses minus taxes, if any. See *spending on operations*.

operating foundation A foundation that conducts some programs of its own and/or provides direct services.

operating reserve Consists of funds set aside to cover unexpected budget shortfalls, to provide seed money for projects that will eventually become self-supporting, to save for purchase of equipment, and so forth. There are three categories: board-designated, undesignated, and available. Only the first kind is explicitly indicated on a financial statement.

operating revenue (nonprofit) Revenue for operations (not from operations, as in a for-profit). The sum of program service revenue, current unrestricted public support, net assets released from restrictions, and funds withdrawn from an endowment pursuant to a spending formula. Technically, the last two items are not revenue because they do not increase net assets, but they provide resources for current operations.

operating surplus Operating revenue minus operating expenses.

ordinary service provider A nonprofit organization with a duty to act in the best interest of one or more *indefinite* groups of persons or a subsidiary of another nonprofit organization, and having no endowment.

ownership (of an asset) Consists of three rights: right to benefit, right to control, and right to sell the other rights separately or jointly.

PAC A political action committee.

payout requirement (rate) The minimum amount of a private foundation's assets that the Tax Reform Act of 1969 requires it to spend each year. See *spending formula*.

permanent restrictions Expressions of a donor's wishes, to which a non-profit consents, for the use of his or her gift for as long as the recipient exists.

perpetual foundations Organizations whose founders intend them to function indefinitely; hence they are endowed.

philanthropic income Income that is manifested most simply by cash contributions to nonprofit organizations, but an alternate and broader definition includes noncash contributions; indirect support (United Way, Combined Federal Campaign, etc.); and net income from special events.

planning horizon A time period selected for purposes of planning and analysis.

pledge A promise to give assets in the future; it is recorded on financial statements as temporarily restricted revenue.

portfolio A collection of assets that are managed jointly. A revenue portfolio contains a multiplicity of revenue sources.

PP&E Refers to property, plant, and equipment, which is equivalent to land, buildings, and equipment (LB&E) on IRS Form 990.

present value The result of a calculation that converts the value of cash that is expected to be received T years in the future into a corresponding amount today, given the best available interest rate over the interval. Alternatively, present value (PV) is the amount we must invest today to obtain the given future value (FV). The relationship between present value and future value is: $PV = FV/(1 + r)^T$. In this formula, the interest rate, r, is called a discount rate and the calculation is called *discounting*. If we are making payments instead of receiving them, FV is negative.

presumptively endowed When the value of an organization's securities and other investments exceeds its total expenses.

private foundation One of two categories of 501(c)(3) organizations. The other is public organization. An applicant for 501(c)(3) recognition must pass a series of tests, mostly related to sources of support, to be classified as a public organization; failure on any one test defaults the applicant into the private foundation category.

private goods and services Goods and services that are rival and excludable. See *rival good* and *excludable benefit or good*.

pro forma A financial model based on certain specified assumptions or hypothetical conditions, frequently representing the most likely or most common situations.

program-related investing (PRI) Investing that supports charitable activities that involve the potential return of capital within an established time frame. PRI includes financing methods such as loans, loan guarantees, linked deposits, and even equity investments in charitable organizations or in commercial ventures for charitable purposes (U.S. Department of the Treasury 2010c).

Prudent Investor Rule A legal requirement that nonprofits manage the totality of their assets in the same manner a prudent person would manage his or her assets under similar circumstances.

public charities Organizations defined by a list of exempt purposes given in Section 501(c)(3) of the Internal Revenue Code: charitable, religious, educational, scientific, literary, testing for public safety, fostering national or international amateur sports competition, and preventing cruelty to children or animals.

public organization A 501(c)(3) nonprofit that passes one or more tests regarding its sources of income. The tests are described in Chapter 5.

public support Gifts and/or grants. See *contribution.*

qualifying distributions (by foundations) These include most operating expenses, set-asides, charitable investments, and grants.

real Refers to an adjustment having been made for inflation (except when referring to *real* estate).

realized capital gain (or loss) Gain (or loss) that occurs when cash received from the sale of an asset exceeds (or falls short of) its purchase price.

recognize (1) In accounting: to recognize a transaction is to enter it into the financial records. (2) In taxation: technically the IRS does not award tax exemption to an organization; the IRS recognizes it as tax-exempt. The law awards exemption; the IRS merely applies the law. Context should make clear which definition applies.

reporting organizations Federally tax-exempt nonprofits that file an informational return with the Internal Revenue Service.

restricted assets Gifts that donors make for a specific purpose. Donor restrictions may be permanent or temporary.

return on assets (ROA) The change in total net assets divided by total assets. ROAe is the return on assets of endowed service providers.

rival good A good that two or more people cannot consume at the same time without interfering with each other.

S&P The credit rating agency Standard & Poor's.

Section 501(c)(3) The section of the Internal Revenue Code providing for tax exemption of organizations with broad public purposes, of which charity is a residual category. Gifts to these organizations are tax deductible to donors.

secured debt Debt guaranteed by a designated portion of an organization's assets. If the organization cannot repay the debt, the lender is entitled to claim those assets and sell them to recover the balance owed.

securities Stocks and bonds.

separation of functions (or duties) A requirement that more than one person be responsible for completing a transaction. An example is a requirement for having two signatures on a check. Its purpose is to reduce the chances of fraud and ensure integrity of internal policies.

SFAS Statement of Financial Accounting Standards.

social economy The sector of an economy that produces goods and services by means of nonprofits and membership associations (including cooperatives). See *cooperative.*

socially responsible investing (SRI) An investment process that considers social and environmental consequences, both positive and negative.

solvency The ability of an organization to remain in business (that is, to be a *going concern*) while continuously satisfying all ongoing financial obligations in a timely manner. Compare *insolvency.*

spending A deliberately ambiguous term that refers to expenses in accrual-basis accounting, expenditures in cash-basis accounting, or encumbrances in encumbrance budgeting—depending on the context.

spending formula A board-adopted rule of an endowed service provider that regulates annual withdrawals from endowment. See *payout requirement (rate).*

spending on operations Total expenses minus taxes (if any) and depreciation. It approximates actual spending on the items one normally finds in an operating budget.

statement of activities The portion of a financial statement that summarizes revenue and expense transactions occurring over a given time period—usually one year. GAAP requires it to be included in a complete financial statement. See *financial statement.*

statement of cash flows The portion of a financial statement that reconciles changes in cash and cash equivalents with changes in all other items on a statement of financial position. GAAP requires it to be included in a complete financial statement. See *financial statement* and *cash flow.*

statement of financial position The portion of a financial statement that is an inventory of all assets and liabilities taken at a particular moment, usually at the end of a fiscal year. It is commonly referred to as the balance sheet. GAAP requires it to be included in a complete financial statement. See *financial statement.*

statement of functional expenses The portion of a financial statement that decomposes expenses on a matrix: (1) functional expenses, which are classified on the IRS 990 form as administrative, fund-raising, and program expenses, and (2) natural categories, analogous to budget line items. GAAP requires it to be included in a complete financial statement only for health and welfare organizations. See *financial statement.*

status quo markup (SQ-MU) The *markup* consistent with a long-term return on assets equal to the long-run rate of inflation. See *markup.*

status quo return on assets (SQ-ROA) Return on assets that is equal to the long-term rate of inflation, which this book calculates to be 3.4 percent.

stock (1) A transferable instrument of ownership of an organization, which, unlike a bond, never matures and the issuer may or may not pay stockholders a share of profit in a given year. (2) Anything measurable at a point in time, as contrasted to a flow, which must be measured over a time interval. Context should make clear which definition applies. See *flow*.

subsidy A means of financing production of a good or service below its actual cost. Sources of subsidy for nonprofits include philanthropy, endowment income, and surpluses from other goods and services. See *cross-subsidize*.

sustainability (financial) When the change in financial capacity over the long term is sufficient to maintain assets at their replacement cost and to maintain reserves at a level commensurate with anticipated economic risks.

sustainability principle The sustainability principle posits that the long run is reached through successive short runs requiring consistency between the short run (as measured by annual surpluses) and the long run (as measured by asset growth).

sustainable organization An organization that is able to produce indefinitely the same volume of goods and services of the same quality with the same service delivery model.

temporary restrictions Expressions of a donor's wishes for the use of his or her gift to which a recipient organization consents. The restrictions expire after a donor-specified period of time (time-restricted) or after the donor-specified purpose has been achieved (purpose-restricted). All pledges are reported as temporarily restricted until fulfilled (paid).

total return Total return (on an investment) equals current income from investments (dividends and interest) plus *capital gains* or losses.

total surplus In accrual accounting, it is total revenue minus expenses; also end-of-year net assets minus beginning-of-year net assets, also called change in total net assets.

true endowment Permanently restricted net assets.

unrealized capital gain (or loss) Gain (or loss) that occurs when the market value of an asset exceeds (or falls short of) a benchmark price (its purchase price or its price at the end of the prior accounting period) during a given period of time. Also called *paper* gain (or loss).

unrestricted assets Assets that a nonprofit may use for any purpose.

unrestricted net assets Unrestricted assets minus associated liabilities.

unrestricted surplus (1) Unrestricted revenue minus total expenses, (2) change in unrestricted net assets, (3) end-of-year unrestricted net assets minus beginning-of-year unrestricted net assets. These are equivalent.

UPMIFA The Uniform Prudent Management of Institutional Funds Act.

values-centered management A control regime in which social, cultural, and spiritual values join with economic necessity to define an organization's management objective.

working capital Current assets minus current liabilities. See *nonprofit working capital.*

working cash fund An internal revolving loan fund consisting of cash and cash equivalents that provides a high degree of liquidity.

References

AAII [American Association of Individual Investors]. 2011. "AAII Asset-Allocation Models." Accessed February 26. www.aaii.com/asset-allocation.

AICPA [American Institute of Certified Public Accountants]. 1996. *AICPA Audit and Accounting Guide: Not-for-Profit Organizations*. New York: AICPA.

Altman, Morris. 2009. "History and Theory of Cooperatives." In *International Encyclopedia of Civil Society*, ed. Helmut Anheier and Stefan Toepler. New York: Springer.

Anheier, Helmut. 2005. *Nonprofit Organizations: Theory, Management, Policy*. London: Routledge.

Anthony, Robert N., and David W. Young. 2003. *Management Control in Nonprofit Organizations*. 7th ed. Boston: McGraw-Hill/Irwin.

Anthony, Robert N., and David W. Young. 2005. "Financial Accounting and Financial Management." In *The Jossey-Bass Handbook of Nonprofit Management and Leadership*, 2nd ed., edited by Robert D. Herman, 466–512. San Francisco: Jossey-Bass.

ASAE/CAL [ASAE/Center for Association Leadership]. 2008. *The Operating Ratio Report*. 13th ed. Washington, DC: ASAE/CAL.

Avi-Yonah, Reuven S. 2005. "The Cyclical Transformations of the Corporate Form: A Historical Perspective on Corporate Social Responsibility." *Delaware Journal of Corporate Law* 30(3): 767–818.

Ben-Ner, Avner, and Benedetto Gui. 2003. "The Theory of Nonprofit Organisations Revisited." In *The Study of the Nonprofit Enterprise*, edited by Helmut K. Anheier and Avner Ben-Ner, 3–26. New York: Kluwer Academic/Plenum Publishers.

Billitteri, Thomas J. 2007. *Linking Payout to Mission: A National Dialogue with Foundation Leaders*. Washington, DC: Aspen Institute.

Black, Christopher. 2001. *Early Modern Italy: A Social History*. London: Routledge.

Blumenthal, Barbara. 2003. *Investing in Capacity Building: A Guide to High-Impact Approaches.* New York: Foundation Center.

BoardSource and Independent Sector. 2006. *The Sarbanes-Oxley Act and Implications for Nonprofit Organizations.* Washington, DC: BoardSource and Independent Sector.

Boris, Elizabeth, Lotren Renz, Asmita Barve, Mark A. Hager, and George Hobor. 2006. *Foundation Expenses and Compensation: How Operating Characteristics Influence Spending.* Washington, DC: Urban Institute, the Foundation Center, and Philanthropic Research.

Bourgeois, L. J. 1981. "On the Measurement of Organizational Slack." *Academy of Management Review* 6(1): 29–39.

Bourgeois, L. J., and J. V. Singh. 1983. "Organizational Slack and Political Behavior within Top Management Teams." *Academy of Management Proceedings*, 43–47.

Bowman, Woods. 1999. "Chapter 11 for Nonprofit Organizations." In *1999 Wiley Bankruptcy Law Update*, edited by Keith Shapiro and Nancy Peterman, 523–528. New York: John Wiley & Sons.

Bowman, Woods. 2002a. "The Institutional Property Tax Exemption Reconsidered." Research report for the Lincoln Institute of Land Policy, Cambridge, MA.

Bowman, Woods. 2002b. "The Uniqueness of Nonprofit Finance and the Decision to Borrow," *Nonprofit Management and Leadership* 12(3): 293–311.

Bowman, Woods. 2007. "Managing Endowment and Other Assets." In *Financing Nonprofits: Putting Theory into Practice*, edited by Dennis Young, 271–289. Lanham, MD: AltaMira Press of Rowman & Littlefield.

Bowman, Woods. 2009. "New Endowment Rules Signal Caution for Charities." *Chronicle of Philanthropy* 17 (September): 33.

Bowman, Woods. 2010. "Trends and Patterns in Nonprofit Accountability Clubs." In *Voluntary Regulation of NGOs and Nonprofits: An Accountability Club Framework*, edited by Mary Kay Gugerty and Aseem Prakash, 64–84. Cambridge, UK: Cambridge University Press.

Bowman, Woods. 2011a. "Competition between Nonprofits and For-Profits in Theory and Practice." Unpublished paper presented to the Association for the Study of the Grants Economy, January 8.

Bowman, Woods. 2011b. "The Contribution of Corporation Law to Civil Society." *Nonprofit Policy Forum*, 2(1). Online journal at www.bepress.com/npf/vol2/iss1/6.

Bowman, Woods. 2011c. "Financial Capacity and Sustainability of Ordinary Nonprofits." *Nonprofit Management and Leadership* 22(1).

Bowman, Woods, and Marion Fremont-Smith. 2006. "Nonprofits and State and Local Governments." In *Nonprofits and Government: Collaboration and Conflict*, edited by Elizabeth T. Boris and C. Eugene Steuerle, 181–217. Washington, DC: Urban Institute Press.

Bowman, Woods, Elizabeth Keating, and Mark A. Hagar. 2007. "Investment Income." In *Financing Nonprofits: Putting Theory into Practice*, edited by Dennis R. Young, 157–181. Lanham, MD: AltaMira Press of Rowman & Littlefield.

Bowman, Woods, Howard P. Tuckman, and Dennis R. Young. Forthcoming. "Methodological Issues in Nonprofit Finance Research: Surpluses and Endowments." *Nonprofit and Voluntary Sector Quarterly*.

Brody, Evelyn. 1996. "Agents without Principals: The Economic Convergence of the Nonprofit and For-Profit Organizational Forms." *New York Law School Law Review* 40(1 & 2): 457–536.

Brody, Evelyn. 1997. "Charitable Endowments and the Democratization of Dynasty." *Arizona Law Review* 39(3): 873–948.

Bradley, Bill, Paul Jansen, and Les Silverman. 2003. "The Non-Profit Sector's $100 Billion Opportunity." *Harvard Business Review* 81(5): 94–103.

Bryce, Herrington. 2000. *Financial and Strategic Management for Nonprofit Organizations*. 3rd ed. San Francisco: Jossey-Bass.

Callaghan, Joseph H. 2007. "Assessing the Control Environment Using a Balanced Scorecard Approach." Accessed March 4, 2011. www.nysscpa .org/cpajournal/2007/307/essentials/p58.htm.

Cambridge Associates. 2008. "Cambridge Associates' Letter to the Senate Finance Committee Regarding Their January 24, 2008, Inquiry to Large Colleges and Universities." Cambridge Associates LLC. Accessed February 8, 2011. www.universityofcalifornia.edu/news/cambridge ToSFC.pdf.

Capital Professional Services. Inflationdata.com. Capital Professional Services, LLC. Accessed June 25, 2009. www.inflationdata.com/Inflation/ Inflation_Rate/Long_Term_Inflation.asp.

Carver, John. 1996. *Three Steps to Fiduciary Responsibility*. San Francisco: Jossey-Bass.

Carver, John, and Miriam Carter. 2010. "The Policy Governance Model." Policy Governance. Accessed February 11, 2011. www.policygovernance .com/model.htm.

Center on Philanthropy at Indiana University. 2004. *Giving USA: The Annual Report on Philanthropy for the Year 2003*. Glenview, IL: Giving USA Foundation.

Ceres. 2007. *Ceres principles*. Ceres. Accessed February 26, 2011. www .ceres.org/Page.aspx?pid=416.

Chang, Cyril F., and Howard P. Tuckman. 1991. "Financial Vulnerability and Attrition as Measures of Nonprofit Performance." *Annals of Public and Cooperative Economics* 62(4): 655–673.

Chang, Cyril F., and Howard P. Tuckman. 1994. "Revenue Diversification among Nonprofits." *Voluntas* 5(3): 273–290.

Charity Navigator. 2011. "Working Capital." Charity Navigator. Accessed February 8. www.charitynavigator.org/index.cfm?bay=glossary.word&word=Working%20Capital%20Ratio&mid=4&cid=7&print=1.

Charles Schwab. 2011. "Select the Asset Allocation That Is Right for You and Stick with It." Accessed March 8. www.schwab.com/public/schwab/planning/financial_guidance/investing_principles/asset_allocation.html.

Collins, Sarah, ed. 2008. *Foundation Fundamentals.* 8th ed. New York: Foundation Center.

Commonfund. 2003. *Commonfund Benchmarks Study: Educational Endowment Report.* Wilton, CT: Commonfund.

Commonfund. 2009. *Commonfund Benchmarks Study: Foundation Report.* Boston: Commonfund Institute.

Cooch, Sarah, and Mark Kramer. 2007. *Compounding Impact: Mission Investing by U.S. Foundations.* San Francisco: FSG Social Impact Advisors.

Cordes, Joseph J., and Burton A. Weisbrod. 1998. "Differential Taxation of Nonprofits and Commercialization of Nonprofit Revenues." *Journal of Policy Analysis and Management* 17(2): 195–214.

Core, John E., Wayne R. Guay, and Rodrigo S. Verdi. 2004. "Agency Problems of Excess Endowment Holdings in Not-for-Profit Firms." *Journal of Accounting and Economics* 41(3): 307–333.

Cornes, Richard, and Todd Sandler. 1986. *The Theory of Externalities, Public Goods, and Club Goods.* Cambridge, UK: Cambridge University Press.

Cotter, Wendy. 1996. "The Collegia and Roman Law: State Restrictions on Voluntary Associations." In *Voluntary Associations in the Greco-Roman World*, edited by John S. Kloppenborg and Stephen G. Wilson, 59–73. London: Routledge.

De Borms, Tayart. 2005. *Foundations: Creating Impact in a Globalised World.* Chichester, UK: John Wiley & Sons.

Deep, Akash, and Peter Frumkin. 2001. *The Foundation Payout Puzzle.* Working paper No. 9. Cambridge, MA: Hauser Center for Nonprofit Organizations at the Kennedy School of Government of Harvard University.

Deller, Steven, Ann Hoyt, Brent Hueth, and Reka Sundaram-Stukel. 2009. *Research on the Economic Impact of Cooperatives.* Madison, WI: University of Wisconsin Center for Cooperatives.

DeMarche Associates, Inc. 1990. *Payout Policies and Investment Planning for Foundations: A Structure for Determining a Foundation's Asset Mix.* Washington, DC: Council on Foundations.

DeMarche Associates, Inc. 1999. *Spending Policies and Investment Planning for Foundations: A Structure for Determining a Foundation's Asset Mix.* 3rd ed. Washington, DC: Council on Foundations.

Economist. 2006. "Flat-Pack Accounting." *Economist,* May 13, 76.

Ehrenberg, Ronald G. 2000. *Tuition Rising: Why College Costs So Much.* Cambridge, MA: Harvard University Press.

Elliott, Dorice Williams. 1995. "Sarah Scott's Millenium Hall and Female Philanthropy." *Studies in English Literature: 1500–1900* 35(3): 535–553.

Ethics Resource Center. 2007. *National Nonprofit Ethics Survey: An Inside View of Nonprofit Sector Ethics.* Arlington, VA: Ethics Resource Center.

FASB [Financial Accounting Standards Board]. 1980. *Concepts Statement No. 4: Objectives of Financial Reporting by Nonbusiness Organizations, as Amended.* Norwalk, CT: FASB.

FASB [Financial Accounting Standards Board]. 1987a. *Statement of Financial Accounting Standards No. 93: Recognition of Depreciation by Not-for-Profit Organizations.* Norwalk, CT: FASB.

FASB [Financial Accounting Standards Board]. 1987b. *Statement of Financial Accounting Standards No. 95: Statement of Cash Flows, as Amended.* Norwalk, CT: FASB.

FASB [Financial Accounting Standards Board]. 1993a. *Statement of Financial Accounting Standards No. 116: Accounting for Contributions Received and Contributions Made.* Norwalk, CT: FASB.

FASB [Financial Accounting Standards Board]. 1993b. *Statement of Financial Accounting Standards No. 117: Financial Statements of Not-for-Profit Organizations, as Amended.* Norwalk, CT: FASB.

FASB [Financial Accounting Standards Board]. 1995. *Statement of Financial Accounting Standards No. 124: Accounting for Certain Investments Held by Not-for-Profits.* Norwalk, CT: FASB.

FASB [Financial Accounting Standards Board]. 1999. *Statement of Financial Accounting Standards No. 136: Transfers of Assets to a Not-for-Profit Organization or Charitable Trust That Raises or Holds Contributions for Others, as Amended.* Norwalk, CT: FASB.

FASB [Financial Accounting Standards Board]. 2009. *Statement of Financial Accounting Standards No. 164: Not-for-Profit Entities: Mergers and Acquisitions, as Amended.* Norwalk, CT: FASB.

FEC [Federal Election Commission]. 2011. "What Is a Political Action Committee?" FEC. Accessed March 1. www.fec.gov/ans/answers_pac.shtml.

Findlaw. 2011. "Fiduciary." Findlaw. accessed February 11. http://dictionary.findlaw.com/definition/fiduciary.html.

Finkler, Steven A. 2005. *Financial Management for Public, Health, and Not-for-Profit Organizations.* 2nd ed. Upper Saddle River, NJ: Prentice Hall.

Fisch, Edith L. 1964. "Restrictions on Charitable Giving." *New York Law Forum* 10: 307–332.

Fishman, James J. 2003. "Improving Charitable Accountability." *Pace Law Faculty Publications.* Paper 66. Accessed February 11, 2011. http://digitalcommons.pace.edu/lawfaculty/66.

Fisman, Raymond, and R. Glenn Hubbard. 2003. "The Role of Nonprofit Endowments." In *The Governance of Not-for-Profit Organizations,* edited by Edward L. Glaeser, 217–233. Chicago: University of Chicago Press.

Foster, William, Ben Dixon, and Matt Hochstetler. 2003. *Funding: Patterns and Guideposts in the Nonprofit Sector, a White Paper.* Boston: Bridgespan Group.

Foster, William, and Gail Fine. 2007. "How Nonprofits Get Really Big." *Stanford Social Innovation Review* 5(2): 46–55.

Foster, William, Peter Kim, and Barbara Christiansen. 2009. "Ten Nonprofit Funding Models." *Stanford Social Innovation Review,* 7(2): 32–39.

Foundation Center. 2004. *Foundation Growth and Giving Estimates.* New York: Foundation Center.

Foundation Center. 2007. *Guide to U.S. Foundations, Their Trustees, Officers, and Donors.* New York: Foundation Center.

Frederick, D. 2005. *Income Tax Treatment of Cooperatives: Background Cooperative Information Report 44 Part 1.* Washington, DC: U.S. Department of Agriculture.

Freeman, R. Edward. 2010. *Strategic Management: A Stakeholder Approach.* Cambridge, UK: Cambridge University Press.

Fremont-Smith, Marion. 1965. *Foundations and Government: State and Federal Law and Supervision.* New York: Russell Sage Foundation.

Fremont-Smith, Marion. 2002. *Emerging Issues in Philanthropy Seminar Series: Accumulation of Wealth by Nonprofits.* Washington, DC: Urban Institute and the Hauser Center.

Fremont-Smith, Marion. 2004. *Governing Nonprofit Organizations: Federal and State Law and Regulation.* Cambridge, MA: Belknap Press of Harvard University Press.

Frey, Donald. 2002. "University Endowment Returns Are Underspent." *Challenge* 45(4): 109–121.

Froelich, Karen A. 1999. "Diversification of Revenue Strategies: Evolving Resource Dependence in Nonprofit Organizations." *Nonprofit and Voluntary Sector Quarterly* 28(3): 246–268.

Froelich, Karen A., Terry W. Knoepfle, and Thomas H. Pollak. 2000. "Financial Measures in Nonprofit Organization Research: Comparing IRS 990 Return and Audited Financial Statement Data." *Nonprofit and Voluntary Sector Quarterly* 29(2): 232–254.

Frumkin, Peter, and Andre Clark. 2000. "When Mission, Markets, and Politics Collide: Values and Strategy in the Nonprofit Human Services." *Nonprofit and Voluntary Sector Quarterly* 29(1): 141–163.

Gamm, Gerald, and Robert Putnam. 1999. "The Growth of Voluntary Associations in America." *Journal of Interdisciplinary History* 29(4): 511–557.

Garner, Bryan A., ed. 2009. *Black's Law Dictionary*. 9th ed. St. Paul, MN: West.

Gary, Susan. 2007. "UPMIFA: Coming Soon to a Legislature Near You." *American Bar Association Property and Probate*, January–February. Accessed April 2, 2009. www.americanbar.org/publications/probate_ property_magazine_home.html.

Gentry, W. 2002. "Debt, Investment and Endowment Accumulation: The Case of Not-for-Profit Hospitals." *Journal of Health Economics* 21(5): 845–872.

Goodwin, Jason. 1999. *Lords of the Horizons: A History of the Ottoman Empire*. New York: Henry Holt.

Grønbjerg, Kirsten, Helen Liu, and Thomas Pollak. 2010. "Incorporated but Not IRS-Registered: Exploring the (Dark) Grey Fringes of the Nonprofit Universe." *Nonprofit and Voluntary Sector Quarterly* 39(5): 925–945.

Grønbjerg, Kirsten, and Steven Rathgeb Smith. 1999. "Nonprofit Organizations and Public Policies in the Delivery of Human Services." In *Philanthropy and the Nonprofit Sector in a Changing America*, edited by Charles T. Clotfelter and T. Ehrlich, 139–171. Bloomington: Indiana University Press.

Gross, Robert A. 2003. "Giving in America: From Charity to Philanthropy." In *Charity, Philanthropy, and Civility in American History*, edited by Lawrence J. Friedman and Mark D. McGarvie, 23–48. Cambridge, UK: Cambridge University Press.

Gugerty, Mary Kay, and Aseem Prakash. 2010. "Voluntary Regulation of NGOs and Nonprofits: An Introduction to the Club Framework." In *Voluntary Regulation of NGOs and Nonprofits: An Accountability Club Framework*, edited by Mary Kay Gugerty and Aseem Prakash, 3–38. Cambridge, UK: Cambridge University Press.

GuideStar. 2010. www2.guidestar.org.

Guo, Baorong. 2006. "Charity for Profit? Exploring Factors Associated with the Commercialization of Human Service Nonprofits." *Nonprofit and Voluntary Sector Quarterly* 35(1): 123–138.

Guthrie, Kevin M. 1996. *The New-York Historical Society: Lessons from One Nonprofit's Long Struggle for Survival*. San Francisco: Jossey-Bass.

Hall, Holly, Harvy Lipman, and Martha Voelz. 2000. "Charities' Zero-Sum Filing Game." *Chronicle of Philanthropy*, May 18, 1.

Hall, Peter Dobkin. 2006. "A Historical Overview of Philanthropy, Voluntary Associations, and Nonprofit Organizations in the United States, 1600–2000." In *The Nonprofit Sector: A Research Handbook*, edited by Walter W. Powell and Richard Steinberg, 32–65. New Haven, CT: Yale University Press.

Hammack, David C. 1998. *Making the Nonprofit Sector in the United States: A Reader*. Bloomington: University of Indiana Press.

Handy, Femida, Stephanie Seto, Amanda Wakaruk, Brianna Mersey, Ana Mejia, and Laura Copeland. 2010. "The Discerning Consumer: Is Nonprofit Status a Factor?" *Nonprofit and Voluntary Sector Quarterly* 39(5): 866–883.

Hansmann, Henry. 1980. "The Role of Nonprofit Enterprise." *Yale Law Journal* 89 (April): 835–901.

Hansmann, Henry. 1981. "The Rationale for Exempting Nonprofit Corporations from the Corporate Income Tax." *Yale Law Journal* 91(1): 45–100.

Hansmann, Henry. 1990. "Why Do Universities Have Endowments?" *Journal of Legal Studies* 19(1): 3–42.

Hansmann, Henry. 1996. *The Ownership of Enterprise.* Cambridge, MA: Belknap Press of Harvard University Press.

Heaton, J. B. 2007. "Solvency Tests." *Business Lawyer* 62(3): 983–1006.

Helft, Miguel. 2011. "Google Finds It Hard to Reinvent Philanthropy." *New York Times,* January 30.

Hemström, Carl. 2006. "Associations." In *International Encyclopedia of Comparative Law,* Volume XIII, Part 2, Chapter 8. Leiden and Boston: Mohr, Siebeck, Tubingen, and Martinus Nijhoff Publishers.

Hodgkinson, Virginia A., and Murray S. Weitzman. 2001. "Overview: The State of the Independent Sector." In *The Nature of the Nonprofit Sector,* edited by Steven J. Ott. Boulder, CO: Westview Press.

Hopkins, Bruce R. 1998. *The Law of Tax-Exempt Organizations.* 7th ed. New York: John Wiley & Sons.

Hopkins, Bruce R. 2006. *Tax Law of Associations.* Hoboken, NJ: John Wiley & Sons.

Hopkins, Bruce R. 2008. *Private Foundation Law Made Easy.* Hoboken, NJ: John Wiley & Sons.

Hunt, Edwin S. 1994. *The Medieval Super-Companies.* Cambridge, UK: Cambridge University Press.

Hurst, James W. 1970. *Legitimacy of the Business Corporation in the Law of the United States, 1780–1970.* Charlottesville: University of Virginia Press.

ICA [International Cooperative Alliance]. 2007. Accessed February 11, 2011. www.ica.coop/coop/principles.html.

Inflation Data. 2006. Accessed February 15, 2011. www.inflationdata.com/Inflation/Inflation_Rate/Long_Term_Inflation.asp.

Investor Words. 2011. Accessed February 10. www.investorwords.com.

Irvin, Renee. 2007. "Endowments: Stable Largesse or Distortion of the Polity?" *Public Administration Review* 67(3): 445–457.

Israelsen, Craig L. 2010. "Conscientious Investing." *OnWallStreet.* Accessed February 26, 2011. www.onwallstreet.com/fp_issues/40_11/conscientious-investing-2669411-1.html.

James, Estelle. 1987. "The Nonprofit Sector in Comparative Perspective." In *The Nonprofit Sector: A Research Handbook*, edited by Walter W. Powell, 397–415. New Haven, CT: Yale University Press.

James, Estelle. 1998. Commercialization among Nonprofits: Objectives, Opportunities, and Constraints. In *To Profit or Not to Profit: The Commercialization of the Nonprofit Sector*, edited by Burton A. Weisbrod, 271–285. Cambridge, UK and New York: Cambridge University Press.

Johnston, David Cay. 2009. "As Foundations Close, Anxiety for Charities." *New York Times*, November 12.

Jones, Grady (2004). Donor Advised Funds in Dwight F. Burlingame (ed.), *Philanthropy in America: A Comprehensive Historical Encyclopedia*. Santa Barbara, CA: ABC-CLIO, volume 1, p. 124.

Kearns, Kevin. 2007. "Income Portfolios." In *Financing Nonprofits: Putting Theory into Practice*, ed. Dennis R. Young, 291–314. Lanham, MD: Alta Mira Press of Rowman & Littlefield.

Kerlin, Janelle A., and Tom H. Pollak. 2010. "Nonprofit Commercial Revenue: A Replacement for Declining Government Grants and Private Contributions?" *American Review of Public Administration*. Not in print as of May 19, 2011; available online at http://arp.sagepub.com/content/early/2010/11/09/0275074010387293.full.pdf+html.

Khanna, Vikramaditya S. 2005. "The Economic History of the Corporate Form in Ancient India." *Social Science Research Network*. Accessed February 11, 2011. http://ssrn.com/abstract=796464.

King, Samuel P., and Randall W. Roth. 2006. *Broken Trust: Greed, Mismanagement & Political Manipulation at America's Largest Charitable Trust*. Honolulu: University of Hawaii Press.

Kingma, B. R. 1993. "Portfolio Theory and Nonprofit Financial Stability." *Nonprofit and Voluntary Sector Quarterly* 22(2): 105–119.

Kogelman, Stanley, and Thomas A. Dobler. 1999. *Sustainable Spending Policies for Endowments and Foundations*. New York: Goldman Sachs & Co.

Konrad, Peter, and Alys Novak. 2000. *Financial Management for Nonprofits: Keys to Success*. Denver, CO: Regis University School of Professional Studies.

KPMG and Prager, McCarthy and Sealy LLC. 1999. *Ratio Analysis in Higher Education: Measuring Past Performance to Chart Future Direction*. 4th ed. KPMG and Prager, McCarthy and Sealy LLC.

Lee, Felicia. 2004. "Endowment Doubles for Brooklyn Academy." *New York Times*, October 5, B1, B7.

Lerner, Josh, Antoinette Schoar, and Jialan Wang. 2008. "Secrets of the Academy: The Drivers of University Endowment Success." *Journal of Economic Perspectives* 22(3): 207–222.

Lipman, Harvey, and Grant Williams. 2004. "Assets on Loan." *Chronicle of Philanthropy*, February 5: 6.

Mason, David E. 1996. *"Leading and Managing the Expressive Dimension: Harnessing the Hidden Power Source of the Nonprofit Sector."* San Francisco: Jossey-Bass.

McCarthy, Kathleen D. 2003. *American Creed: Philanthropy and the Rise of Civil Society, 1700–1865.* Chicago: University of Chicago Press.

McGrew, Roderick C. 1985. "Hospital." In *Encyclopedia of Medical History, 134–142.* New York: McGraw-Hill.

McLaughlin, Thomas A. 2002. *Streetsmart Financial Basics for Nonprofit Managers.* 2nd ed. New York: John Wiley & Sons.

Micklethwait, John, and Adrian Wooldridge. 2003. *The Company: A Short History of a Revolutionary Idea.* New York: Modern Library.

NCBA [National Cooperative Business Association]. 2011. "Co-op Types." NCBA. accessed February 8. www.ncba.coop/ncba/about-co-ops/co-op-types.

Nonprofit Quarterly. 2005. "Story of the Membership Association of the Deaf." *Nonprofit Quarterly* 12(1): 28–32.

NORI [Nonprofit Operating Reserve Initiative Workgroup]. 2008. *Maintaining Nonprofit Operating Reserves: An Organizational Imperative for Nonprofit Financial Stability.* Washington, DC: NORI.

O'Neill, Michael. 1989. *The Third America.* San Francisco: Jossey-Bass.

O'Neill, Michael. 2002. *Nonprofit Nation.* 2nd ed. San Francisco: Jossey-Bass.

Orton, William A. 1931. "Endowments and Foundations." In *The Encyclopedia of the Social Sciences* 5:531. New York: Macmillan.

Ostrower, Francie. 1995. *Why the Wealthy Give: The Culture of Elite Philanthropy.* Princeton, NJ: Princeton University Press.

Ostrower, Francie. 2009. *Limited Life Foundations: Motivations and Strategies.* Washington, DC: Urban Institute Center on Nonprofits and Philanthropy.

Panas, Jerold. 1984. *Megagifts: Who Gives Them, Who Gets Them.* Chicago: Bonus Books.

Plunkett, J. Patrick, and Heidi Neff Christianson. 2004. "Quest for Cash: Exempt Organizations, Joint Ventures, Taxable Subsidiaries, and Unrelated Business Income." *William Mitchell Law Review* 31(1): 1–54.

Pratt, Jon. 2004. "Analyzing the Dynamics of Funding: Reliability and Autonomy." *Nonprofit Quarterly* 11(2): 8–13.

Pratt, Jon. 2006. "Financial Strategy Tools: Cohort Analysis." *Nonprofit Quarterly* 13(1): 80–84.

Prewitt, Kenneth. 2006. "Foundations." In *The Nonprofit Sector: A Research Handbook*, 2nd ed., edited by Walter W. Powell and Richard Steinberg, 355–377. New Haven, CT: Yale University Press.

Pruzan, Peter. 1998. "From Control to Values-Based Management and Accountability." *Journal of Business Ethics* 17(3): 1379–1394.

Ramsden, Dick. 2003. "Insights into the Yale Formula for Endowment Spending." *Commonfund News*, September 5.

Reference for Business. 2011. "Cooperatives." *Encyclopedia for Business*, 2nd ed. Accessed February 8. www.referenceforbusiness.com/encyclo pedia/Con-Cos/Cooperatives.html.

Robinson, Ellis M. M. 2003. *The Nonprofit Membership Toolkit.* San Francisco: Chardon Press of Jossey-Bass.

Rose-Ackerman, Susan. 1982. "Unfair Competition and Corporate Taxation." *Stanford Law Review* 34(5): 1017–1039.

Rose-Ackerman, Susan. 1997. "Altruism, Ideological Entrepreneurs and the Non-Profit Firm." *Voluntas* 8(2): 120–134.

Roy, William G. 1997. *Socializing Capital: The Rise of the Large Industrial Corporation in America.* Princeton, NJ: Princeton University Press.

Ruppel, Warren. 2007. *Not-for-Profit Accounting Made Easy.* 2nd ed. Hoboken, NJ: John Wiley & Sons.

Salamon, Lester M. 1987. "Partners in Public Service." In *The Nonprofit Sector: A Research Handbook,* edited by Walter W. Powell, 99–117. New Haven, CT: Yale University Press.

Salamon, Lester, Stephanie Geller, and S. Wojciech Sokolowski. 2011. *Taxing the Tax-Exempt Sector—A Growing Danger for Nonprofit Organizations.* Baltimore: Center for Civil Society at Johns Hopkins University. Accessed April 26, 2011. www.ccss.jhu.edu/pdfs/LP_Communiques/ LP_PILOTs_Communique.pdf.

Sansing, Richard. 1998. "The Unrelated Business Income Tax, Cost Allocation, and Productive Efficiency." *National Tax Journal* 51(2): 291–302.

Schlesinger, Mark, and Bradford H. Gray. 2006. "Nonprofit Organizations and Health Care: Some Paradoxes of Persistent Scrutiny." In *The Nonprofit Sector: A Research Handbook,* edited by Walter W. Powell and Richard Steinberg, 378–414. New Haven, CT: Yale University Press.

Schumacher, Edward C. 2003. *Building Your Endowment.* San Francisco: Jossey-Bass.

Simon, John, Harvey Dale, and Laura Chisolm. 2006. "The Federal Income Tax Treatment of Charitable Organizations." In *The Nonprofit Sector: A Research Handbook,* edited by Walter W. Powell and Richard Steinberg, 267–306. New Haven, CT: Yale University Press.

Skocpol, Theda. 2003. *Diminished Democracy: From Membership to Management in American Civic Life.* Norman: University of Oklahoma Press.

Smith, David Horton. 1973. *Voluntary Action Research.* Lexington, MA: Lexington Books.

Smith, David Horton. 2000. *Grassroots Associations*. Thousand Oaks, CA: Sage Publications.

Social Investment Forum. 2003. *The 2003 Report on Socially Responsible Investing Trends in the United States*. Washington, DC: Social Investment Forum.

SSIR [Stanford Social Innovation Review]. 2004. *Money Talk: Top Foundation Leaders Reveal How They Set Payout Rates, Executive Compensation, and Trustee Compensation*. Stanford, CA: SSIR.

Standard & Poor's. 2001. *Endowed Foundations: 2001 Ratings, Key Ratios, and Trends*. New York: Standard & Poor's.

Steinberg, Richard. 1991. "'Unfair' Competition by Nonprofits and Tax Policy." *National Tax Journal* 44(3): 351–363.

Steinberg, Richard. 2006. "Economic Theories of Nonprofit Organizations." In *The Nonprofit Sector: A Research Handbook*, edited by Walter W. Powell and Richard Steinberg, 117–139. New Haven, CT: Yale University Press.

Steinberg, Richard. 2007. "Membership Income Health." In *Financing Nonprofits: Putting Theory into Practice*, edited by Dennis Young, 121–155. Lanham, MD: AltaMira Press of Rowman & Littlefield.

Strom, Stephanie. 2007. "I.R.S. Finds Tax Errors in Reports of Nonprofits." *New York Times*, March 1.

Tax Almanac. 2005. *Treasury Regulations § 53.4958-(b)(1)(ii)*. Tax Almanac. Accessed February 11, 2011. www.taxalmanac.org/index.php/Treasury_Regulations,_Subchapter_D,_Sec._53.4958-4.

Teresa, Peter Di, and Elizabeth Frengle. 2002. "Demystifying the Mutual Fund, Part 2." Accessed April 19, 2011. www.kiplinger.com/basics/archives/2002/05/demystify2.html.

Thelin, John R., and Richard W. Trollinger. 2009. *Time Is of the Essence: Foundations and the Politics of Limited Life and Endowment Spend-Down*. Washington, DC: Aspen Institute.

Tobin, James. 1974. "What Is Permanent Endowment Income?" *American Economic Review* 64(2): 427–432.

Tocqueville, Alexis de. 2007. *Democracy in America*. New York: W.W. Norton and Company.

Toepler, Stefan. 2004. "Ending Payout as We Know It: A Conceptual and Comparative Perspective on the Payout Requirement for Foundations." *Nonprofit and Voluntary Sector Quarterly* 33 (December): 729–738.

Tschirhart, Mary. 2006. "Membership Associations." In *The Nonprofit Sector: A Research Handbook*, 2nd ed., edited by Walter W. Powell and Richard Steinberg, 523–541. New Haven, CT: Yale University Press.

Tuckman, Howard P., and Cyril F. Chang. 1991. "A Methodology for Measuring the Financial Vulnerability of Charitable Nonprofit Organizations." *Nonprofit and Voluntary Sector Quarterly* 20(4): 445–460.

Uniform Law Commission. 2010. "Prudent Management of Institutional Funds Act." *Uniform Law Commission.* Accessed February 24, 2011. www.upmifa.org/DesktopDefault.aspx.

United Nations. 2003. *Handbook on Non-Profit Institutions in the System of National Accounts.* New York: United Nations.

U.S. Department of the Treasury. Internal Revenue Service. 2001. "State Charitable Solicitation Statutes." Accessed February 11, 2011. www.irs .gov/pub/irs-tege/eotopici01.pdf.

U.S. Department of the Treasury. Internal Revenue Service. 2006. *Instructions for Form 1023.* Washington, DC: Government Printing Office.

U.S. Department of the Treasury. Internal Revenue Service. 2009. *Applying for 501(c)(3) Tax-Exempt Status.* Publication 4220. Washington, DC: Government Printing Office.

U.S. Department of the Treasury. Internal Revenue Service. 2010a. "Exempt Purposes—Internal Revenue Code Section 501(c)(3)." Accessed February 11, 2011. www.irs.gov/charities/charitable/article/0,,id=175418,00.html.

U.S. Department of the Treasury. Internal Revenue Service. 2010b. "Private Foundations." Accessed February 11, 2011. www.irs.gov/charities/ charitable/article/0,,id=96114,00.html.

U.S. Department of the Treasury. Internal Revenue Service. 2010c. "Program-Related Investments." Accessed February 11, 2011. www.irs .gov/charities/foundations/article/0,,id=137793,00.html.

U.S. Department of the Treasury. Internal Revenue Service. 2010d. "Section 509(a)(3) Supporting Organizations." Accessed February 11, 2011. www.irs.gov/charities/article/0,,id=137609,00.html.

U.S. Department of the Treasury. Internal Revenue Service. 2010e. *Tax on Unrelated Business Income of Exempt Organizations.* Publication 598. Washington, DC: Government Printing Office.

U.S. Department of the Treasury. Internal Revenue Service. 2011a. "Other Section 501(c) Organizations." Accessed February 11. www.irs.gov/ publications/p557/ch04.html.

U.S. Department of the Treasury. Internal Revenue Service. 2011b. "What Is the Ban on Political Campaign Activity?" Accessed March 1. www.irs .gov/charities/charitable/article/0,,id=179433,00.html.

Valentinov, Vladislav. 2008. "The Transaction Cost Theory of the Nonprofit Firm: Beyond Opportunism." *Nonprofit and Voluntary Sector Quarterly* 37(1): 5–18.

Vikramaditya, Khanna S. 2005. *The Economic History of the Corporate Form in Ancient India* (November 1). Available at SSRN: http://ssrn.com/ abstract=796464.

Weisbrod, Burton. 1975. "Toward a Theory of the Voluntary Sector in a Three-Sector Economy." In *Altruism, Morality and Economic Theory,* edited by Edmund S. Phelps, 171–195. New York: Russell Sage Foundation.

Weisbrod, Burton A. 1998. "The Nonprofit Mission and Its Financing: Growing Links between Nonprofits and the Rest of the Economy." In *To Profit or Not to Profit? The Commercial Transformation of the Nonprofit Sector*, edited by B. A. Weisbrod, 1–22. Cambridge, UK: Cambridge University Press.

Weisbrod, Burton A. 2004. "The Pitfalls of Profits." *Stanford Social Innovation Review* 2(1): 40–47.

Weisbrod, Burton A., Jeffrey P. Ballou, and E. D. Asch. 2008. *Mission and Money: Understanding the University*. Cambridge, UK: Cambridge University Press.

Wing, Kennard, Teresa Gordon, Mark A.Hager, Thomas H.Pollak, and Patrick Rooney. 2006. "Functional Expense Reporting for Nonprofits: The Accounting Profession's Next Scandal?" *Online CPA Journal, August*. Accessed September 19, 2009. www.nysscpa.org/cpajournal/2006/806/infocus/p14.htm.

Wing, Kennard, Thomas Pollak, and Amy Blackwood. 2008. *The Nonprofit Almanac*. Washington, DC: Urban Institute Press.

World Federation of Exchanges. 2008. "Statistics." World Federation of Exchanges. Accessed February 15, 2011. www.world-exchanges.org/statistics.

Yetman, Robert J. 2001a. "Nonprofit Taxable Activities, Production Complementarities, and Joint Cost Allocations." *National Tax Journal* 56(1): 243–258.

Yetman, Robert J. 2001b. "Tax-Motivated Expense Allocations by Nonprofit Organizations." *Accounting Review* 76(3): 297–311.

Yetman, Michelle H., and Robert J. Yetman. 2008. "Why Do Nonprofits Have Taxable Subsidiaries?" *National Tax Journal* 61(4, Part 1): 675–698.

Yetman, Michelle H., and Robert J. Yetman. 2009. "Determinants of Nonprofits' Taxable Activities." *Journal of Accounting and Public Policy* 28(6): 495–509.

Young, Dennis R. 1983. *If Not for Profit, for What?* Lexington, MA: D.C. Heath.

Young, Dennis R. 2007. "Toward a Normative Theory of Nonprofit Finance." In *Financing Nonprofits: Putting Theory into Practice*, edited by Dennis Young, 339–372. Lanham, MD: AltaMira Press of Rowman & Littlefield.

Young, Dennis R., and Amanda Wilsker. 2008. "Testing a Benefits Theory of Nonprofit Finance." Working Paper No. 08-04, Nonprofit Studies Program at the Andrew Young School of Policy Studies, Georgia State University.

Zietlow, John, Jo Ann Hankin, and Alan G. Seidner. 2007. *Financial Management for Nonprofit Organizations*. Hoboken, NJ: John Wiley & Sons.

About the Web Site

Please visit www.wiley.com/go/bowmanfinance to access the companion website that accompanies this book. Once there, you will find five Excel spreadsheets accessible via hyperlinks which you can download and use to automatically calculate and test the formulas presented in the book. All you have to do is input data from your IRS 990 forms. Here are the categories and titles for the five spreadsheets you will find at www.wiley.com/go/bowmanfinance:

- Diagnostic tests for ORDINARY organizations (expenses more than investments in securities)
  - 2007 and earlier IRS 990 long form.
  - 2008 and later IRS 990 long form.
- Diagnostic tests for ENDOWED organizations (investments in securities more than expenses)
  - 2007 and earlier IRS 990 long form.
  - 2008 and later IRS 990 long form.
- Size of capital campaign needed to maintain assets at replacement cost
  - For all organizations and all editions of the IRS 990 form.

Please note, however, that the calculations are valid only for organizations that use accrual accounting and Statement of Financial Accounting Standards 116 (regarding accounting for gifts). Only the 990 long form has sufficient data to obtain accurate answers. Cells left blank are treated as zeros.

About the Author

H. Woods Bowman, PhD, is an economist and Professor of Public Services Management at DePaul University in Chicago. Before joining the faculty he served as Chief Financial Officer of Cook County, Illinois, and earlier as an elected member of the Illinois House of Representatives, where he was chair of an appropriations committee. His nonprofit experience includes consulting, service on boards, and interim CEO of Goodwill Industries of Metropolitan Chicago, for which he received the 1998 Chairman's Award from Goodwill Industries International. He is the author of numerous papers that have appeared in peer-reviewed and practitioner journals, and as chapters in edited volumes and entries in edited encyclopedias. He writes the "Nonprofit Ethicist" column for the *Nonprofit Quarterly*.

Index